HMH

(into) Algebra™ 1

Journal and Practice Workbook

Contents

Journal and More Practice

© Houghton Mifflin Harcourt Publishing Company

© Houghton Mifflin Harcourt Publishing Company

© Houghton Mifflin Harcourt Publishing Company

© Houghton Mifflin Harcourt Publishing Company

© Houghton Mifflin Harcourt Publishing Company

UNIT 10 Data Analysis

Step It Out

Learn the Math

Mathematical closure means that an operation on two numbers from like sets will result in a value from the same set.

EXAMPLE 1   The value 7 is a rational number, and $\sqrt{7}$ is irrational. What happens when we multiply each of the following values?

A. $7 \times \sqrt{7} = 7\sqrt{7}$. Notice that even when simplified, the value still contains the irrational root $\sqrt{7}$, so the product is still irrational.

B. $7 \times 7 = 49$. The simplified value is a whole number, so the product of two rational values is also rational.

C. $\sqrt{7} \times \sqrt{7} = \sqrt{49} = 7$. It is important to notice that sometimes the product of two irrational numbers can be rational. This means that the irrational numbers are not closed under multiplication.

D. Notice that in Part A above, if the order of multiplication is reversed, we have $\sqrt{7} \times 7 = 7\sqrt{7}$. This is because multiplication, like addition, is commutative. The order of multiplication does not matter and results in the same product. This property does not apply to division or subtraction. In both of those operations, order does matter.

Do the Math A

Divide each number in the top row by each number in the left column to complete the table. Then answer the questions on closure.

$\div$	8	$\frac{1}{8}$	-3π	$\sqrt{7}$	0	$-\sqrt{13}$
8	☐	$\frac{1}{64}$	☐	☐	0	☐
$\frac{1}{8}$	☐	☐	☐	☐	☐	☐
-3π	☐	☐	☐	☐	☐	☐
$\sqrt{7}$	☐	☐	☐	☐	☐	☐
1	☐	☐	☐	☐	☐	☐
$-\sqrt{13}$	☐	☐	☐	☐	☐	☐

1. Will division of two rational numbers ever result in an irrational number?

2. Will division of two irrational numbers ever result in a rational number or a whole number?

3. Are the irrational numbers closed under division?

4. Are the rational numbers closed under division?

Do the Math B

Multiply each number in the top row by each number in the left column to complete the table. Then answer the questions on closure.

×	8	$\frac{1}{8}$	-3π	$\sqrt{7}$	0	$-\sqrt{13}$
8	☐	1	☐	☐	0	☐
$\frac{1}{8}$	☐	☐	☐	☐	☐	☐
-3π	☐	☐	☐	☐	☐	☐
$\sqrt{7}$	☐	☐	☐	☐	☐	☐
1	☐	☐	☐	☐	☐	☐
$-\sqrt{13}$	☐	☐	☐	☐	☐	☐

1. Will multiplication of two rational numbers ever result in an irrational number?

2. Will multiplication of two irrational numbers ever result in a rational number or a whole number?

3. Are the irrational numbers closed under multiplication?

4. Are the rational numbers closed under multiplication?

Name _____

LESSON 1.1
More Practice

ONLINE
Video Tutorials and
Interactive Examples

1. Which subset(s) of the real number system (real numbers, whole numbers, integers, rational numbers, or irrational numbers) are closed under division by a nonzero number?

   _____

   _____

   _____

   _____

2. Which subset(s) of the real number system (real numbers, whole numbers, integers, rational numbers, or irrational numbers) are closed under multiplication?

   _____

   _____

   _____

   _____

3. Are any of the subsets of the real number system (real numbers, whole numbers, integers, rational numbers, or irrational numbers) not closed under multiplication? Which ones? Explain why.

   _____

   _____

   _____

   _____

4. Are any of the subsets of the real number system (real numbers, whole numbers, integers, rational numbers, or irrational numbers) not closed under division by a nonzero number? Which ones? Explain why.

   _____

   _____

   _____

5. Which pairs of subsets of the real number system have no common elements?

   _____

   _____

   _____

6. If $\sqrt{15} \times a$ is a rational number, what could be the value of a? Explain your reasoning.

   _____

   _____

7. Why is the set of whole numbers not closed under division?

_____

_____

_____

_____

8. The radius of a circle is 7 centimeters. Find the area of the circle to the nearest tenth of a square centimeter. Is the exact area of the circle a rational number or an irrational number? Is the approximate area you found a rational number or an irrational number? Explain your answers.

_____

_____

_____

_____

9. Which number is a rational number?

Ⓐ $\frac{2}{3} + \sqrt{13}$

Ⓑ $\frac{2}{3} \times \sqrt{13}$

Ⓒ $\sqrt{13} + \sqrt{13}$

Ⓓ $\sqrt{13} \times \sqrt{13}$

10. Which number is an irrational number?

Ⓐ $\sqrt{4}$

Ⓑ $\sqrt{5}$

Ⓒ $\sqrt{9}$

Ⓓ $\sqrt{36}$

11. Which number is an integer but not a whole number?

Ⓐ -14

Ⓑ 0

Ⓒ 1.5

Ⓓ 16

Name _____

Step It Out

Learn the Math

> **EXAMPLE 1**   Evaluate each expression.

$$16^{\frac{3}{4}} = \left(16^{\frac{1}{4}}\right)^3$$
$$= \left(\sqrt[4]{16}\right)^3$$
$$= (2)^3$$
$$= 8$$

$$25^{\frac{3}{2}} = \left(25^{\frac{1}{2}}\right)^3$$
$$= \left(\sqrt{25}\right)^3$$
$$= (5)^3$$
$$= 125$$

Do the Math

Evaluate the expression.

$$27^{\frac{2}{3}} = \left(27^{\frac{\square}{\square}}\right)^2$$

$$= \left(\sqrt[3]{\square}\right)^2$$

$$= \left(\square\right)^2$$

$$= \square$$

Learn the Math

EXAMPLE 2 Justify the steps taken to simplify the expression. Assume all variables are positive.

$$\left(36x^2\right)^{\frac{5}{2}} = (36)^{\frac{5}{2}}\left(x^2\right)^{\frac{5}{2}}$$ Power of a Product Property

$$= \left(6^2\right)^{\frac{5}{2}}\left(x^2\right)^{\frac{5}{2}}$$ Rewrite 36 as 6^2.

$$= \left(6^{2\cdot\frac{5}{2}}\right)\left(x^{2\cdot\frac{5}{2}}\right)$$ Power of a Power Property

$$= \left(6^5\right)\left(x^5\right)$$ Simplify exponents.

$$= 7776x^5$$ Rewrite 6^5 as 7776.

Do the Math

Justify the steps taken to simplify the expression. Assume all variables are positive.

$$\left(\frac{8x^6}{27y^3}\right)^{\frac{2}{3}} = \frac{\left(8x^6\right)^{\frac{2}{3}}}{\left(27y^3\right)^{\frac{2}{3}}}$$

[   ]

$$= \frac{(2^3)^{\frac{2}{3}}\left(\boxed{}\right)^{\frac{2}{3}}}{(3^3)^{\frac{2}{3}}\left(\boxed{}\right)^{\frac{2}{3}}}$$

[   ]

$$= \frac{2^2 x^{\boxed{}}}{3^2 y^{\boxed{}}}$$

[   ]

$$= \frac{4x^{\boxed{}}}{9y^{\boxed{}}}$$ Simplify.

Simplify each expression. Assume all variables are positive.

1. $16^{\frac{5}{2}}$

2. $\left(\dfrac{144}{25}\right)^{\frac{3}{2}}$

3. $\left(\dfrac{64x^2}{49y^4}\right)^{-\frac{3}{2}}$

4. $\sqrt{40x^3y^2}$

5. $\left(16x^4y^5\right)^{\frac{1}{4}}$

6. $\left(8x^4y^2\right)^{\frac{2}{3}}$

7. $\sqrt{75x^6y^5}$

8. $\left(\dfrac{12xy^2}{\sqrt{x^3}}\right)^{-2}$

9. **Open Ended** For the expression $x^{\frac{3}{2}}$, is there a difference between doing $\left(\sqrt{x}\right)^3$ or $\sqrt{x^3}$? Explain with examples.

_____

_____

_____

10. **Math on the Spot.** Simplify numerical expressions with nth roots.

   A. $64^{\frac{1}{3}}$

   B. $625^{\frac{1}{4}} + 49^{\frac{1}{2}}$

   _____   _____

   _____   _____

   _____   _____

   _____   _____

11. The time t (in seconds) that it takes for a dropped object to reach the ground is given by $t = \left(\frac{2d}{g}\right)^{\frac{1}{2}}$ where d is the object's initial distance (in feet) above the ground and g is the acceleration due to gravity, equal to about 32 ft/s^2.

   A. What is the time it takes for a dropped object to reach the ground if its initial distance above the ground is 25 feet?

   B. By what factor does the time from Part A increase if the object's initial distance above the ground increases by a factor of 3?

   _____   _____

   _____   _____

   _____   _____

   _____   _____

   _____   _____

12. Which of the following is equivalent to $\left(\frac{27}{y^6}\right)^{-\frac{1}{3}}$?

   (A) $-\frac{3}{y^2}$

   (B) $\frac{y^2}{3}$

   (C) $-\frac{9}{y^2}$

   (D) $\frac{y^2}{9}$

Step It Out

Learn the Math

EXAMPLE 1

You are purchasing a bunch of bananas and decide to measure their mass. The diagram at right represents the measurement taken by observing the bananas on the scale.

What is the most precise answer you can give for the mass of the bananas?

The most precise measurement is 0.75 kilograms because the smallest measurement on the scale is one-tenth of a kilogram and the needle of the scale is not on the line. So, you can estimate that it is between 0.7 and 0.8 kilograms.

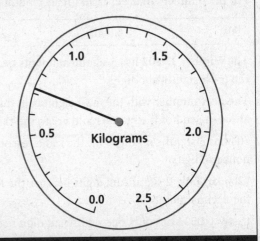

Do the Math

Before placing a specimen in a beaker of water, you are asked to measure the temperature of the water. The thermometer readout is shown. Give your answer to the greatest precision possible.

☐ °C because the scale's smallest marking is ☐ °C and since the needle is not on the line, you can estimate that the answer is between ☐ °C and ☐ °C.

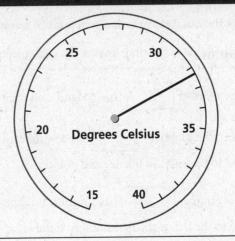

Learn the Math

EXAMPLE 2

Put the numbers in order from greatest number of significant digits to least number of significant digits.

504	0.0003	2.100	7200	37,802

The number 37,802 has 5 significant digits because the zero is between two nonzero digits. Therefore, it has the most significant digits.

The next number with the most significant digits is 2.100. It has 4 significant digits because the two zeros are at the end of the number and are to the right of the decimal point.

504 has 3 significant digits for the same reason as the first number. The zero is between two nonzero digits.

7200 has only 2 significant digits because the two zeros are at the end of the number and are to the left of the decimal point.

Lastly, 0.0003 has only one significant digit because its zeros are to the left of the first nonzero number.

Do the Math

Put the numbers in order from greatest number of significant digits to least number of significant digits.

0.0701	320	1.000	80,000	405.01

The number ⬚ has 5 significant digits because each of its zeros is between nonzero digits.

Next, the number ⬚ has 4 significant digits because the three zeros are at the end of the number and to the right of the decimal point.

The number ⬚ has 3 significant digits. The first two zeros are not significant because they are to the left of the first nonzero number, and the zero between the two nonzero numbers is significant.

The number ⬚ has 2 significant digits because the zero is at the end of the number and is to the left of the decimal point.

Lastly, the number ⬚ has 1 significant digit because all the zeros are at the end of the number and are to the left of the decimal point.

Learn the Math

> **EXAMPLE 3**

You want to know the density of a liquid. You measure its mass to be 30.5 grams and its volume to be 25 mL.

To calculate the density of the liquid you do the following calculation:

$$\rho = \frac{m}{V} = \frac{30.5 \text{ g}}{25 \text{ mL}} = 1.22 \frac{\text{g}}{\text{mL}}$$

Since the measurement of the volume of the liquid has only 2 significant digits, we must round the answer to two significant digits as well. Therefore, the density of the liquid is $1.2 \frac{\text{g}}{\text{mL}}$.

Do the Math

You want to know how far you can travel if you go 65 mph for about 3 hours.

To calculate the distance, you do the following calculation:

$$d = r \cdot t = 65 \frac{\text{miles}}{\text{hour}} \cdot 3 \text{ hours} = \boxed{} \text{ miles}$$

Since the time, 3 hours, has $\boxed{}$ significant digit(s), we must round the answer to $\boxed{}$ significant digit(s) as well. Therefore, the distance traveled is approximately $\boxed{}$ miles.

Learn the Math

> **EXAMPLE 4**

When cooking, we often need to use significant digits to estimate how many items we need to buy.

You are planning to make 9 loafs of banana bread for a school bake sale. The banana bread recipe calls for 4 cups of pureed bananas. You know that 1 banana yields between 0.8 and 0.9 cup of pureed banana.

How many cups of pureed bananas do you need?

$$9 \text{ loafs of banana bread} \cdot \left(\frac{4 \text{ cups of pureed banana}}{1 \text{ loaf of banana bread}} \right) = 36 \text{ cups of pureed banana}$$

Now we must figure out how many bananas you must buy.

Most:		Least:	
$\boxed{\begin{array}{c}\text{Number } x \\ \text{of bananas}\end{array}} \cdot \boxed{\begin{array}{c}0.8 \text{ cup of} \\ \text{pureed banana}\end{array}} = 36 \text{ cups}$		$\boxed{\begin{array}{c}\text{Number } x \\ \text{of bananas}\end{array}} \cdot \boxed{\begin{array}{c}0.9 \text{ cup of} \\ \text{pureed banana}\end{array}} = 36 \text{ cups}$	
$x = \dfrac{36}{0.8} = 45 \approx 50 \left(1 \text{ significant digit}\right)$		$x = \dfrac{36}{0.9} = 40$	

You must now find the average of the most and the least in order to estimate the number of bananas you will need to buy. number of bananas $= \frac{50 + 40}{2} = 45$ bananas

Do the Math

You want to bake 3 apple pies to bring to your Thanksgiving meal. The apple pie recipe calls for $3\frac{1}{2}$ cups of diced apples. You know that 1 apple can yield between 0.6 and 0.8 cup of apples.

How many cups of diced apples do you need?

3 apple pies $\cdot \left(\dfrac{3.5 \text{ cups of diced apples}}{1 \text{ apple pie}} \right) = \boxed{}$ cups of diced apples

Now figure out how many apples you must buy.

Most:	Least:
$\boxed{\begin{array}{c}\text{Number } x \\ \text{of apples}\end{array}} \cdot \boxed{\begin{array}{c}\text{0.6 cup of} \\ \text{diced apples}\end{array}} = \boxed{}$ cups	$\boxed{\begin{array}{c}\text{Number } x \\ \text{of apples}\end{array}} \cdot \boxed{\begin{array}{c}\text{0.8 cup of} \\ \text{diced apples}\end{array}} = 10.5$ cups
$x = \dfrac{10.5}{0.6} = 17.5 \approx \boxed{} \left(1 \text{ significant digit}\right)$	$x = \dfrac{10.5}{\boxed{}} = 13.125 \approx 10 \left(1 \text{ significant digit}\right)$

You must now find the average of the most and the least in order to estimate the number of apples you will need to buy.

number of apples $= \dfrac{\boxed{} + \boxed{}}{2} = \boxed{}$ apples

For the following problems, write the measurement to the appropriate level of precision and explain your reasoning.

1.

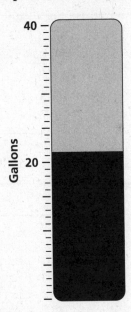

2.

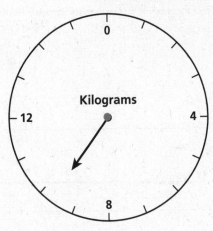

For each problem below, identify the number of significant digits and explain your answer with the appropriate zero rule.

3. 815.0

_____

_____

4. 0.003

_____

_____

5. 602

_____

_____

6. 2100

_____

_____

7. 10.020

_____

_____

8. 0.01500

_____

_____

9. **Open Ended** Can a number be precise but not accurate, or accurate but not precise? Give an example of each.

_____

_____

_____

_____

_____

10. Math on the Spot. Calculate $(30 \text{ m})(2.01 \text{ m})$. Use the correct number of significant digits in the answer.

11. Solve.

$$\left(9.8 \frac{\text{m}}{\text{s}^2}\right) \cdot (2 \text{ s}) = \qquad \frac{61 \text{ g}}{5.75 \text{ mL}} = \qquad 6.5 \text{ ft} + 1.25 \text{ ft} = \qquad 34 \text{ cm} - 8.5 \text{ cm} =$$

12. 500.07 meters has how many significant digits?

(A) 2

(B) 3

(C) 4

(D) 5

13. When multiplying 641.8 ft by 3, what is the answer to the correct level of precision?

(A) 1900 ft

(B) 1925 ft

(C) 1925.4 ft

(D) 2000 ft

14. Which of the following sets of numbers shows a greater level of precision? Explain your reasoning.

Set A

{2.3, 2.5, 2.1, 2.3, 2.4}

Set B

{2.3, 2.3, 1.9, 2.4, 4.2}

_____

_____

_____

_____

15. How many significant digits does 312,400,000.010 have?

(A) 5

(B) 7

(C) 11

(D) 12

© Houghton Mifflin Harcourt Publishing Company

Name _____

Step It Out

Learn the Math

EXAMPLE 1

You have an art project to do for school. You go to the store to buy plywood and acrylic. You buy a total of 6 square feet of plywood and acrylic. If p represents the area of plywood you bought, write and simplify an expression to represent the amount of money you spent at the store, given the information below. Then find the cost if you buy 2 square feet of plywood.

> 32 square feet of plywood $(4 \text{ ft} \times 8 \text{ ft}) = \$15$
>
> 12 square feet of acrylic $(3 \text{ ft} \times 4\text{ft}) = \$43$

First, we must convert the prices above to the cost per square ft.

$$\frac{\$15}{32 \text{ ft}^2} = \frac{\$0.47}{\text{ft}^2} \text{ for plywood}$$

$$\frac{\$43}{12 \text{ ft}^2} = \frac{\$3.58}{\text{ft}^2} \text{ for acrylic}$$

If p represents the area of plywood you bought, and the total area of material bought was 6 ft^2, then the area of acrylic bought would be $6 - p$ ft^2.

To write the expression for the amount of money spent, you must add the cost of the plywood to the cost of the acrylic.

Cost of plywood

Price of plywood $\left(\frac{\$}{\text{ft}^2}\right)$	Area of plywood (ft^2)
$0.47	p

$+$

Cost of acrylic

Price of acrylic $\left(\frac{\$}{\text{ft}^2}\right)$	Area of acrylic (ft^2)
$3.58	$(6 - p)$

Simplify the expression:

$0.47p + 3.58(6 - p)$	Given expression
$0.47p + 21.48 - 3.58p$	Distribute 3.58.
$21.48 - 3.11p$	Combine like terms.

Evaluate the cost if you buy 2 square feet of plywood.

$21.48 - 3.11(2) = 21.48 - 6.22 = 15.26$

You spent $15.26 on 2 square feet of plywood and 4 square feet of acrylic.

Do the Math

Sasha and her friends go for an hour-long drive. For most of the time they are able to travel at the speed limit of 65 mi/h. They hit some traffic and during that time they are only able to drive 20 mi/h. Let t represent the time stuck in traffic in minutes. Write and simplify an expression for the distance Sasha and her friends travel during this trip. Then find the distance if they are stuck in traffic for 10 minutes.

First, we must convert the speeds from $\frac{miles}{hour}$ to $\frac{miles}{min}$.

$$65 \frac{miles}{hour} \left(\frac{1 \ hour}{\boxed{} \ min} \right) = 1.08 \frac{miles}{min}$$

$$20 \frac{miles}{hour} \left(\frac{1 \ hour}{60 \ min} \right) = \boxed{} \frac{miles}{min}$$

If t represents the time stuck in traffic, then $(60 - t)$ represents the time spent traveling at the speed limit.

To write the expression for the distance traveled by Sasha and her friends, you must add the distance traveled while going the speed limit to the distance traveled when stuck in traffic.

Distance traveled at the speed limit

Distance traveled while stuck in traffic

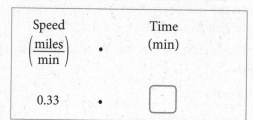

$+$

Simplify the expression:

$1.08(60 - t) + 0.33t$	Given expression
$\boxed{} - 1.08t + 0.33t$	Distribute 1.08.
$64.8 - \boxed{} \ t$	Combine like terms.

Evaluate the distance traveled if Sasha and her friends were stuck in traffic for 10 minutes.

$$64.8 - 0.75 \left(\boxed{} \right) = 57.3$$

Sasha and her friends traveled 57.3 miles.

Name _____

Simplify each of the following expressions.

1. $3(x + 2) - 7 + 4x$

_____

_____

_____

_____

_____

_____

2. $5x + 2(1 + 4x)$

_____

_____

_____

_____

_____

_____

3. $6 + 2x + 3(x + 1)$

_____

_____

_____

_____

_____

_____

_____

4. $3(x + 4) + 2(3 + x) + 7$

_____

_____

_____

_____

_____

_____

_____

5. $2(0.1 + x) - 8(-x - 0.3)$

_____

_____

_____

_____

_____

_____

6. $\frac{3}{4}(x - 1) + 5x + \frac{1}{4}(x + 2)$

_____

_____

_____

_____

_____

_____

7. **Open Ended** When simplifying an algebraic expression, we are allowed to combine "*like terms.*" How do we know when two or more terms are "*like*"?

_____

_____

_____

8. **Critical Reasoning** Consider the following algebraic expression that contains both variable and constant terms: $0.5 + 0.6x - 0.25(0.2 + 5x)$.

   Why can the like terms not yet be combined to simplify the expression? What else needs to be done?

_____

_____

_____

9. **Math on the Spot** Approximately 2000 tires are recycled to produce one lane-mile of asphalt rubber.

   A. Write an expression for the number of tires used to make x lane-miles of asphalt rubber.

   _____

   B. Find the number of tires used to make 11, 50, and 150 lane-miles of asphalt rubber.

   _____

   _____

10. The tuition for a private college is currently $18,000 for each semester. The college will raise tuition by $500 per semester each year.

    A. How much is tuition per year (two semesters)? By how much will tuition increase each year?

    _____

    B. Write an expression for the yearly tuition after x years.

    _____

    C. If a student is paying the current tuition of $18,000 per semester for their first year, how much tuition will the student pay for their senior year (fourth year)? Explain.

    _____

    _____

    _____

11. Which of the following will still have a constant term when the expression is simplified?

    Ⓐ $2(x - 1) + 2$ Ⓒ $-2(x + 1) + 2(x - 1)$

    Ⓑ $3(2 - x) + 6(x - 1)$ Ⓓ $-(x - 1) - (x + 1)$

Step It Out

Learn the Math

EXAMPLE 1 ▸ Solve $-4(-2x+1)+5=3$. Justify your solution steps, and check the solution.

$-4(-2x+1)+5=3$	Given equation
$8x-4+5=3$	Distributive Property
$8x+1=3$	Combine constants.
$8x=2$	Subtraction Property of Equality
$x=0.25$	Division Property of Equality

Check: $-4(-2(0.25)+1)+5\stackrel{?}{=}3$
$-4(0.5)+5\stackrel{?}{=}3$
$-2+5\stackrel{?}{=}3$
$3=3$ ✓

Do the Math

Solve $3(4x-1)+7=1$. Justify your solution steps, and check the solution.

$3(4x-1)+7=1$	Given equation
$12x-\boxed{}+7=1$	Distributive Property
$12x+\boxed{}=1$	Combine constants on the left.
$12x=\boxed{}$	Subtraction Property of Equality
$x=\boxed{}$	Division Property of Equality

Check: $3\left(4\left(\boxed{}\right)-1\right)+7\stackrel{?}{=}1$
$3\left(\boxed{}\right)+7\stackrel{?}{=}1$
$\boxed{}+7\stackrel{?}{=}1$
$\boxed{}=1$ ✓

Learn the Math

EXAMPLE 2 ▸ Solve $2x-\frac{1}{3}(9x+5)=\frac{10}{3}$. Justify your solution steps.

$2x-\frac{1}{3}(9x+5)=\frac{10}{3}$	Given equation
$2x-3x-\frac{5}{3}=\frac{10}{3}$	Distributive Property
$-x-\frac{5}{3}=\frac{10}{3}$	Combine like terms.
$-x=5$	Addition Property of Equality
$x=-5$	Division Property of Equality

Do the Math

Solve $3x-\frac{1}{2}(8x+5)=\frac{3}{2}$. Justify your solution steps.

$3x-\frac{1}{2}(8x+5)=\frac{3}{2}$	Given equation
$3x-\boxed{}-\frac{5}{2}=\frac{3}{2}$	Distributive Property
$\boxed{}-\frac{5}{2}=\frac{3}{2}$	Combine like terms.
$-x=\boxed{}$	
$x=\boxed{}$	

Learn the Math

EXAMPLE 3 Solve $5(x + 2) = -2(3x - 14) + 4$. Justify your solution steps.

$5(x + 2) = -2(3x - 14) + 4$	Given equation
$5x + 10 = -6x + 28 + 4$	Distributive Property
$5x + 10 = -6x + 32$	Combine constants on the right.
$11x + 10 = 32$	Addition Property of Equality
$11x = 22$	Subtraction Property of Equality
$x = 2$	Division Property of Equality

Do the Math

Solve $-2(x + 7) = 4(-3x + 5) + 6$. Justify your solution steps.

Learn the Math

EXAMPLE 4 Ron and Alex canoe toward each other on a river, starting from points 12 miles apart. Ron begins paddling at 9:00 a.m., and Alex begins at 10:00 a.m. Their paddling speeds in still water are 3 mi/h for Ron and 4 mi/h for Alex, but Ron paddles with the current and Alex paddles against it. They meet at 11:00 a.m. What is the current's speed?

Let $c =$ the speed of the current in miles per hour.

Ron's rate (mi/h)		Ron's time (h)		Alex's rate (mi/h)		Alex's time (h)		Distance (mi)
$3 + c$	$\cdot$	2	$+$	$4 - c$	$\cdot$	1	$=$	12

$(3 + c)(2) + (4 - c)(1) = 12$	Write the equation.
$6 + 2c + 4 - c = 12$	Distributive Property
$c + 10 = 12$	Combine like terms.
$c = 2$	Subtraction Property of Equality

The speed of the current is 2 mi/h.

Do the Math

The Robinson and Franklin families are next-door neighbors who decide to drive to an amusement park and spend the day together there. The amusement park is 188 miles away. The Robinson family leaves first and travels at an average speed of 48 mi/h. The Franklin family leaves 30 minutes later and travels at an average speed of 54 mi/h. Does the Franklin family catch up with the Robinson family before the Robinson family reaches the amusement park? Explain.

Solve the equation. Justify your solution steps and check the solution.

1. $8x + 3 = 5x - 3$

_____

_____

_____

_____

_____

_____

2. $4 - 3x = 2x - 11$

_____

_____

_____

_____

_____

_____

3. $-2(3x - 4) + 12 = -16$

_____

_____

_____

_____

_____

_____

4. $0.8 + 0.3(2 - 3x) = 1.4$

_____

_____

_____

_____

_____

_____

5. $\frac{1}{2}(2x - 4) + 2 = 4(x + 2) - 11$

_____

_____

_____

_____

_____

_____

_____

6. $2(x - 3) - 4(x + 3) = -24$

_____

_____

_____

_____

_____

_____

_____

7. Open Ended Explain why you need just the Addition Property of Equality and the Multiplication Property of Equality (and not also the Subtraction Property of Equality and the Division Property of Equality) to solve the equations in this lesson. Give an example to illustrate your reasoning.

_____

_____

_____

8. Math on the Spot The Andersons spend 12% of their budget on travel. Their total budget this year is $1500 more than last year, and this year they plan to spend $5640 on travel. What was their total budget last year?

_____

_____

9. Critique Reasoning While attempting to solve the problem shown at the right, Kevin wrote the following explanation:

> The minute hand of a clock makes 1 revolution in an hour, so it moves through 360° every hour. The hour hand makes only $\frac{1}{12}$ of a revolution in an hour, so it moves through 30° every hour. If I let t represent the time (in hours) since 12:00, then 360t represents the number of degrees through which the minute hand moves and 30t represents the number of degrees through which the hour hand moves. When the minute hand catches up with the hour hand for the first time, it has completed 1 revolution more than the hour hand, so I must subtract 1 from 360t before setting it equal to 30t. So, 360t − 1 = 30t.

The hands of a clock coincide at 12:00. At what time, to the nearest second, do the hands again coincide?

Explain the error in Kevin's reasoning. Then correct the error and finish solving the problem.

_____

_____

_____

10. A group of friends who are going camping decide to take two cars to the campsite. One car leaves 15 minutes before the other and travels at an average speed of 50 miles per hour. The second car travels at an average speed of 55 miles per hour. If t represents the time (in hours) since the first car left, which equation could you use to find the time when the second car catches up with the first (assuming that the cars have not yet reached the campsite)?

Ⓐ $50t = 55(t - 15)$

Ⓑ $50(t - 15) = 55t$

Ⓒ $50t = 55(t - 0.25)$

Ⓓ $50(t - 0.25) = 55t$

Name _____

Step It Out

Learn the Math

EXAMPLE 1 Ahmed has enough chalkboard paint to cover an area of 24 square feet. He plans to use all of the paint to create a rectangular chalkboard on a wall of a room, but he hasn't decided on the chalkboard's dimensions. He calculates several options.

Let the width be 2 feet.

$$A = \ell w$$
$$24 = \ell(2)$$
$$12 = \ell$$

So, the length is 12 feet.

Let the width be 3 feet.

$$A = \ell w$$
$$24 = \ell(3)$$
$$8 = \ell$$

So, the length is 8 feet.

Let the width be 4 feet.

$$A = \ell w$$
$$24 = \ell(4)$$
$$6 = \ell$$

So, the length is 6 feet.

Do the Math

Rose wants to build a wooden storage box in the shape of a rectangular prism. The left and right sides of the box will be squares with an edge length of ℓ feet, and the box will be w feet wide. The surface area S of the box is given by $S = 2\ell^2 + 4w\ell$. Rose plans to paint all six exterior sides of the box but has only enough paint to cover 50 square feet. Complete the calculations below.

Let the edge lengths of the left and right sides be 1 foot.

$$S = 2\ell^2 + 4w\ell$$
$$50 = 2(1^2) + 4w(1)$$
$$50 = \boxed{} + 4w$$
$$\boxed{} = 4w$$
$$\boxed{} = w$$

Let the edge lengths of the left and right sides be 2 feet.

$$S = 2\ell^2 + 4w\ell$$
$$50 = 2(2^2) + 4w(2)$$
$$50 = \boxed{} + 8w$$
$$\boxed{} = 8w$$
$$\boxed{} = w$$

Let the edge lengths of the left and right sides be 3 feet.

$$S = 2\ell^2 + 4w\ell$$
$$50 = 2(3^2) + 4w(3)$$
$$50 = \boxed{} + 12w$$
$$\boxed{} = 12w$$
$$\boxed{} = w$$

Learn the Math

EXAMPLE 2 Rewrite $A = \ell w$ so that it expresses ℓ in terms of A and w.

$A = \ell w$ Given formula

$\dfrac{A}{w} = \ell$ Division Property of Equality

Do the Math

Rewrite $S = 2\ell^2 + 2w\ell$ so that it expresses w in terms of S and ℓ.

$S = 2\ell^2 + 2w\ell$ Given formula

$S - \boxed{} = 2w\ell$ Subtraction Property of Equality

$\dfrac{S - \boxed{}}{\boxed{}} = w$ Division Property of Equality

Learn the Math

EXAMPLE 3 ▷ Solve the literal equation $ax + b = cx$ for x, and justify the solution steps. State any necessary restrictions on the letters representing constants in the equation. Then use the literal equation's solution to solve the specific equations $3x + 5 = 2x$, $-5x + 18 = 4x$, and $4x - 21 = x$.

$ax + b = cx$	Given equation
$b = cx - ax$	Subtraction Property of Equality
$b = (c - a)x$	Distributive Property of Equality
$\dfrac{b}{c - a} = x$	Division Property of Equality You cannot divide by 0, so $c \neq a$.

For the equation
$3x + 5 = 2x$:

$a = 3, b = 5, c = 2$

$x = \dfrac{b}{c - a}$

$= \dfrac{5}{2 - 3}$ Substitute.

$= -5$ Simplify.

For the equation
$-5x + 18 = 4x$:

$a = -5, b = 18, c = 4$

$x = \dfrac{b}{c - a}$

$= \dfrac{18}{4 - (-5)}$ Substitute.

$= 2$ Simplify.

Think of the equation
$4x - 21 = x$ as $4x + (-21) = 1x$.
Then:

$a = 4, b = -21, c = 1$

$x = \dfrac{b}{c - a}$

$= \dfrac{-21}{1 - 4}$ Substitute.

$= 7$ Simplify.

Do the Math

Solve the literal equation $ax = b(x + c)$ for x, and justify the solution steps. State any necessary restrictions on the letters representing constants in the equation. Then use the literal equation's solution to solve the specific equations $2x = 3(x + 1)$, $-4x = 5(x + 9)$, and $x = 6(x - 4)$.

$ax = b(x + c)$	Given equation
$ax = bx + bc$	_____
$ax - bx = bc$	_____
$(a - b)x = bc$	_____
$x = \dfrac{bc}{a - b}$	_____ You cannot divide by 0, so $a \neq \boxed{}$.

For the equation
$2x = 3(x + 1)$:

$x = \dfrac{\boxed{} \cdot \boxed{}}{\boxed{} - \boxed{}} = \boxed{}$

For the equation
$-4x = 5(x + 9)$:

$x = \dfrac{\boxed{} \cdot \boxed{}}{\boxed{} - \boxed{}} = \boxed{}$

For the equation
$x = 6(x - 4)$:

$x = \dfrac{\boxed{} \cdot \boxed{}}{\boxed{} - \boxed{}} = \boxed{}$

Name _____

LESSON 2.3
More Practice

ONLINE
Video Tutorials and
Interactive Examples

Rewrite the formula.

1. **Science** A formula for the work W done to move an object a distance d using a force F in the same direction as the movement is $W = Fd$. Express d in terms of the other variables in the formula.

   _____

2. **Science** Boyle's Law says that the product of the pressure P and volume V of a gas remains constant regardless of how you change the pressure or volume. This law can be expressed as $P_1V_1 = P_2V_2$ for two pressures P_1 and P_2 and corresponding volumes V_1 and V_2. Express P_1 in terms of the other variables in the formula.

   _____

3. **Geometry** The formula for the area A of a kite with diagonal lengths d_1 and d_2 is $A = \frac{1}{2}d_1d_2$. Express d_2 in terms of the other variables and the constant in the formula.

   _____

Solve the literal equation for x. State any necessary restrictions on the letters representing constants in the equation.

4. $ax + bx + c = 0$

5. $a - bx = c$

6. $x - a = b$

   _____   _____   _____

7. $2x - a = x - b$

8. $x - a = b(x - c)$

9. $a(bx + c) = 0$

   _____   _____   _____

10. $ax - bx = c$

11. $a(x - b) - c = d$

12. $a(bx + c) = x$

   _____   _____   _____

13. $x + a = 4x + b$

14. $a = b(cx - d)$

15. $a(bx + c) = d(x + e)$

   _____   _____   _____

16. **Math on the Spot** The formula $C = \frac{5}{9}(F - 32)$ is used to convert temperatures from degrees Fahrenheit to degrees Celsius. Express F in terms of the other variables and constants in the formula.

_____

17. A teacher bases student grades on three exams given during a semester and a final exam at the end of the semester. The scores for all four exams are averaged to determine a student's grade for the semester. Her students typically ask what target score they need on the final exam to achieve a particular average for the semester.

A. Choose letters for all of the variables and constants in this situation. Write an equation relating the variables and constants and then solve the equation to obtain a formula for calculating the target score on the final exam.

_____

_____

_____

B. The teacher wants to put your formula in a spreadsheet. She enters the data for one student as shown below. She must now enter the formula into cell E2 (that is, the cell in column E and row 2). The formula must start with an equals sign, use the cell references for the data in row 2, and use an asterisk to indicate multiplication. Give the formula that the teacher should enter and the result that the spreadsheet will produce.

E2	$\updownarrow$	$\times$ $\checkmark$	fx	$=$	
	A	B	C	D	E
1	Exam 1	Exam 2	Exam 3	Desired semester average	Target score on final exam
2	85	92	88	90	

_____

18. In physics, the average acceleration a of a moving object over a period of time t is defined as $a = \frac{v_1 - v_0}{t}$ where v_0 is the object's initial velocity (the velocity at the beginning of the time period) and v_1 is the final velocity. Which rewritten version of the formula for average acceleration gives v_1 in terms of a, v_0, and t?

Ⓐ $v_1 = a + \dfrac{v_0}{t}$

Ⓒ $v_1 = a + (t + v_0)$

Ⓑ $v_1 = a + \dfrac{t}{v_0}$

Ⓓ $v_1 = at + v_0$

19. Draw arrows from the expressions on the right to the empty boxes on the left to complete the expression obtained from solving the literal equation $a(x + b) = c$ for x. Assume $a \neq c$.

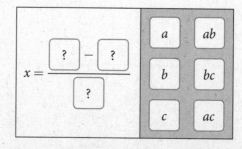

© Houghton Mifflin Harcourt Publishing Company

2.4

Step It Out

Learn the Math

EXAMPLE 1   Solve $4(x - 2) < \frac{1}{2}(4x + 12)$. Justify your solution steps and check the solution.

$4(x - 2) < \frac{1}{2}(4x + 12)$	Given inequality
$4x - 8 < 2x + 6$	Distributive Property
$2x < 14$	Addition Property of Inequality, Subtraction Property of Inequality
$x < 7$	Division Property of Inequality

Check the solution using an x-value that is in the solution set of $x < 7$, such as 2.

$$4(2 - 2) < \frac{1}{2}\left(4(2) + 12\right)$$

$$4(0) < \frac{1}{2}(8 + 12)$$

$$0 < \frac{1}{2}(20)$$

$$0 < 10 \ \checkmark$$

Do the Math

Solve $7(-2x - 1) + 3 \geq 10$. Fill in the blanks below. Justify your solution steps, and check the solution.

Check the solution using a value that is in the solution set.

$7(-2x - 1) + 3 \geq 10$	Given inequality
$-14x - \boxed{} + 3 \geq 10$	Distributive Property
$-14x - \boxed{} \geq 10$	Simplify.
$-14x \geq 14$	$\boxed{}$
$x \leq \boxed{}$	Division Property of Inequality

$$7\left(-2\boxed{} - 1\right) + 3 \overset{?}{\geq} 10$$

$$7\left(\boxed{}\right) + 3 \overset{?}{\geq} 10$$

$$\boxed{} + 3 \overset{?}{\geq} 10$$

$$\boxed{} \geq 10 \ \checkmark$$

Learn the Math

EXAMPLE 2 Fill in the blanks below by choosing the correct letters for the solution steps and justifications.

Solve $3x + \frac{1}{4}(8x - 12) \leq 7$. Then graph the solution.

$3x + \frac{1}{4}(8x - 12) \leq 7$ Given inequality

$3x + 2x - 3 \leq 7$ $\boxed{B}$

   $\boxed{A}$ Simplify.

$5x \leq 10$ $\boxed{D}$

   $\boxed{C}$ Division Property of Inequality

(A) $5x - 3 \leq 7$

(B) Distributive Property

(C) $x \leq 2$

(D) Addition Property of Inequality

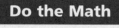

Do the Math

Fill in the blanks below by choosing the correct letters for the solution steps and justifications to solve $\frac{1}{2}(4x - 14) - 6x > 9$. Then graph the solution.

$\frac{1}{2}(4x - 14) - 6x > 9$ Given inequality

   $\boxed{}$ Distributive Property

$-4x - 7 > 9$ $\boxed{}$

$-4x > 16$ $\boxed{}$

   $\boxed{}$ Division Property of Inequality

(A) $x < -4$

(B) Simplify.

(C) $2x - 7 - 6x > 9$

(D) Addition Property of Inequality

© Houghton Mifflin Harcourt Publishing Company

Learn the Math

EXAMPLE 3 An art supply store charges $24 for an easel and $5 for each brush. The local paint store charges $18 for an easel and $6 for each brush. If Meg wants to purchase one easel and several brushes, how many brushes would she need to buy before the total cost of supplies at the art supply store is less expensive than at the paint store?

Let $p = $ the number of paintbrushes.

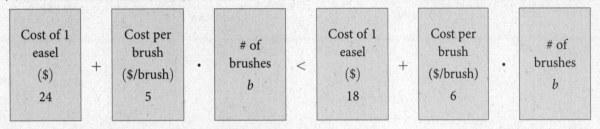

$$24 + 5b < 18 + 6b \qquad \text{Write the inequality.}$$
$$6 + 5b < 6b \qquad \text{Subtraction Property of Inequality}$$
$$6 < b \qquad \text{Subtraction Property of Inequality}$$
$$b > 6 \qquad \text{Write an equivalent inequality.}$$

Meg needs to buy more than 6 brushes before the total cost of an easel and brushes at the art supply store is less expensive than at the paint store.

Do the Math

A. Membership at a gym costs $15 per month. Members pay $5 per class and nonmembers pay $8 per class. After how many classes per month is the total cost with membership less than the total cost of classes without membership? Fill in the blanks below and solve.

Let c = the number of classes.

 + 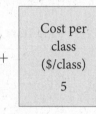 · < 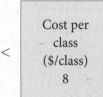 ·

Number of classes
c

$15 + \boxed{} < 8c$ Write the inequality.

$15 < 3c$

$\boxed{}$

Division Property of Inequality

$\boxed{}$

$c > 5$ Write an equivalent inequality.

The total cost of membership and classes will be less than the total cost without a membership after $\boxed{}$ classes.

B. West Side Bike Rentals charges a one-time fee of $5 plus $0.80 per hour. East Side Bike Rentals charges a one-time fee of $8 plus $0.20 per hour. Write and solve an inequality to model when East Side Bike Rentals is a better deal. Show your work, then answer the questions below.

- What is the unknown quantity that the variable represents? _____

- What are the units of the variable? _____

- Could you have written the inequality using either < or >? Explain.

_____

_____

_____

Solve the inequality.

1. $17 > 3(2 + 4x) - (1 - 12x)$

_____

_____

_____

_____

_____

_____

2. $2r - \dfrac{5}{3}r > -\dfrac{1}{3}$

_____

_____

_____

_____

_____

_____

3. $\dfrac{1}{4}(3x + 1) \le x + \dfrac{3}{4}$

_____

_____

_____

_____

_____

_____

4. $-2.7 + 3.1(1 - x) \le 9.7$

_____

_____

_____

_____

_____

_____

5. $x + 8 - 3x \ge 4x - (1 - 3x)$

_____

_____

_____

_____

_____

_____

6. $5(x - 7) - 2(3 - x) < 8$

_____

_____

_____

_____

_____

_____

7. **Open Ended** What extra step do you need to take when using the Multiplication Property of Inequality and the Division Property of Inequality when the coefficient of the variable term is negative? Give an example to illustrate your reasoning.

_____

_____

_____

_____

_____

8. **Math on the Spot** Solve the inequality and graph the solutions.

$$5x - 4 \geq 2x + 11$$

_____

9. **Critique Reasoning** While attempting to solve the problem shown at the right, Christine wrote the following explanation:

$$-2(x - 3) \leq 8$$

I know that when a number is in front of an expression in parentheses, I can use the Distributive Property to multiply the −2 into the parentheses. Instead, I can use the Division Property of Inequality and divide both sides by −2 to get the new inequality $x - 3 \leq -4$. Then all I need to do is use the Addition Property of Inequality to get $x \leq -1$.

Explain the error in Christine's reasoning. Then correct the error and finish solving the problem.

_____

_____

_____

_____

10. Every week Robert rakes leaves for 5 hours and does dishes for x hours. He is paid $7 per hour for each job. He wants to earn at least $56 by the end of the week. Which inequality would model this scenario?

Ⓐ $7(5 + x) \geq 56$

Ⓑ $5 + 7x \geq 56$

Ⓒ $5x + 7x \geq 56$

Ⓓ $5x + 7 \geq 56$

Step It Out

Learn the Math

EXAMPLE 1 ▶ Solve $-2 < 3x + 1 \leq 10$. Then graph the solutions.

$-2 < 3x + 1 \leq 10$	Original inequality
$-2 < 3x + 1$ AND $3x + 1 \leq 10$	Separate into two inequalities.
$-3 < 3x$ AND $3x \leq 9$	Subtraction Property of Inequality
$-1 < x$ AND $x \leq 3$	Division Property of Inequality

Now, graph the solutions to find the **intersection** of the graphs.

-5 -4 -3 -2 -1 0 1 2 3 4 5

-5 -4 -3 -2 -1 0 1 2 3 4 5

-5 -4 -3 -2 -1 0 1 2 3 4 5

The solution is $-1 < x \leq 3$.

Do the Math

Solve $-5 \leq 2x + 3 < 11$. Then graph the solutions.

$-5 \leq 2x + 3 < 11$	Original inequality
$-5 \leq \boxed{}$ AND $2x + 3 < 11$	Separate into two inequalities.
$\boxed{} \leq 2x$ AND $2x < 8$	Subtraction Property of Inequality
$-4 \leq \boxed{}$ AND $x < 4$	Division Property of Inequality

Now, graph the solutions to find the **intersection** of the graphs.

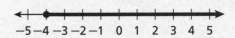

-5 -4 -3 -2 -1 0 1 2 3 4 5

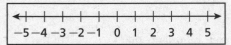

-5 -4 -3 -2 -1 0 1 2 3 4 5

-5 -4 -3 -2 -1 0 1 2 3 4 5

The solution is $\boxed{}$.

Learn the Math

EXAMPLE 2 Solve and graph the solutions for the compound inequality
$$x - 2 \geq -4 \quad \text{AND} \quad 3x < -9.$$

$$x - 2 \geq -4 \quad \text{AND} \quad 3x < -9$$
$$x \geq -2 \quad \text{AND} \quad x < -3$$

Now, graph the solutions to find the **intersection** of the graphs.

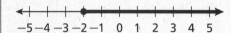

Because this is a compound inequality involving AND, the final graph represents the **intersection** of the previous two graphs. Since there aren't any values that are greater than -2 AND less than -3 (where the two graphs intersect), there is **no solution**.

Do the Math

Solve and graph the solutions for the compound inequality $x + 1 \geq 4 \quad \text{AND} \quad x - 1 < 0$.

$$x + 1 \geq 4 \qquad \text{AND} \qquad \boxed{} < 0$$

$$x \geq \boxed{} \qquad \text{AND} \qquad x < 1$$

Now, graph the solutions to find the **intersection** of the graphs.

Because this is a compound inequality involving AND, the final graph represents the $\boxed{}$ of the

previous two graphs. Since there aren't any values that are greater than or equal to $\boxed{}$ AND less than

$\boxed{}$, there is $\boxed{}$.

Learn the Math

EXAMPLE 3 ▶ Solve and graph the solutions for the compound inequality
$$2x + 1 < -1 \quad \text{OR} \quad 7x + 3 \geq 17.$$

$$2x + 1 < -1 \quad \text{OR} \quad 7x + 3 \geq 17$$
$$2x < -2 \quad \text{OR} \quad 7x \geq 14$$
$$x < -1 \quad \text{OR} \quad x \geq 2$$

Now, graph the solutions to find the **union** of the graphs.

The final graph shows both of the previous graphs because OR represents the **union** of the two graphs.

Do the Math

Solve and graph the solutions for the compound inequality $2x + 3 < 5 \quad \text{OR} \quad 3x - 6 \geq 3$.

$$2x + 3 < 5 \qquad \text{OR} \quad 3x - 6 \geq 3$$
$$2x < \boxed{} \quad \text{OR} \qquad 3x \geq 9$$
$$x < 1 \qquad \text{OR} \qquad x \geq \boxed{}$$

Now, graph the solutions to find the **union** of the graphs.

Because this is a compound inequality involving OR, the final graph represents the $\boxed{}$ of the previous two graphs.

Learn the Math

EXAMPLE 4 ▶ Solve and graph the solutions for the compound inequality
$$x + 3 \leq 5 \quad \text{OR} \quad 3x - 1 \geq -4.$$

$x + 3 \leq 5 \quad \text{OR} \quad 3x - 1 \geq -4$

$\quad x \leq 2 \quad \text{OR} \quad 3x \geq -3$

$\quad x \leq 2 \quad \text{OR} \quad x \geq -1$

The final graph shows both of the previous graphs because OR represents the **union** of the two graphs. In this example, the union of the two graphs generates a graph where the solution is all real numbers.

Do the Math

Solve and graph the solutions for the compound inequality $3x - 6 \leq 9 \quad \text{OR} \quad -2x - 1 \leq -5$.

$3x - 6 \leq 9 \quad \text{OR} \quad -2x - 1 \leq -5$

$3x \leq \boxed{} \quad \text{OR} \quad -2x \leq -4$

$\quad x \leq 5 \quad \text{OR} \quad x \geq \boxed{}$

Because this is a compound inequality involving OR, the final graph represents the $\boxed{}$ of the previous two graphs. In this example, the union of the two graphs generates a graph where the solution

is $\boxed{}$.

Learn the Math

EXAMPLE 5 A manufacturer states that the ideal width of a closet door is 32 inches. The actual width of the door should be within 0.25 inches of the ideal width. Write and graph a compound inequality to represent this situation. What is the range of widths that the closet door manufacturer will accept?

Use a verbal model.

Let w represent the actual width of a closet door. The tolerance (the difference between the actual width and the ideal width), needs to be between -0.25 and 0.25 inches.

Lower bound (inches)		Actual width (inches)		Ideal width (inches)		Upper bound (inches)
-0.25	$\leq$	w	$-$	32	$\leq$	0.25

Write a compound inequality.

$-0.25 \leq w - 32 \leq 0.25$

Write the compound inequality as two inequalities and solve the inequalities.

$-0.25 \leq w - 32$	AND	$w - 32 \leq 0.25$	Separate into two inequalities.
$31.75 \leq w$	AND	$w \leq 32.25$	Addition Property of Inequality
	$31.75 \leq w \leq 32.25$		Rewrite as a compound inequality.

Graph the compound inequality.

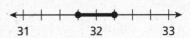

Answer the question.

The closet door manufacturer will accept doors between 31.75 and 32.25 inches wide.

Do the Math

A cookie manufacturer states that the ideal diameter of a chocolate chip cookie is 2.5 inches. The actual diameter of the cookie should be within 0.15 inches of the ideal diameter. Write and graph a compound inequality to represent this situation. What is the range of diameters that the cookie manufacturer will accept?

Use a verbal model.

Let d represent the actual diameter of the cookie. The tolerance (the difference between the actual diameter and the ideal diameter) needs to be between -0.15 and $\boxed{}$ inch.

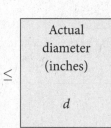 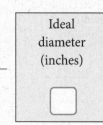 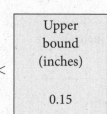

Lower bound (inches)		Actual diameter (inches)		Ideal diameter (inches)		Upper bound (inches)
-0.15	$\leq$	d	$-$	$\boxed{}$	$<$	0.15

Write a compound inequality.

$$-0.15 \leq d - \boxed{} \leq 0.15$$

Write the compound inequality as two inequalities and solve the inequalities.

$-0.15 \leq d - 2.5 \quad \text{AND} \quad d - 2.5 \leq 0.15$ Separate into two inequalities.

$\quad 2.35 < d \qquad\qquad \text{AND} \qquad\qquad d \leq \boxed{}$ Addition Property of Inequality

$\qquad\qquad 2.35 \leq d \leq 2.65$ Rewrite as a compound inequality.

Graph the compound inequality.

Answer the question.

The cookie manufacturer will accept cookie diameters between $\boxed{}$ and 2.65 inches.

Name _____

Solve the inequality. Describe the relationship between the solution and the graphs of the individual inequalities.

1. $r + 5 \leq 1$ OR $r - 1 \geq 1$

_____

_____

_____

_____

_____

2. $3x + 7 > 10x + 14$ AND $10 + 6x \geq 10 + x$

_____

_____

_____

_____

_____

_____

3. $5 \leq x + 7 \leq 12$

_____

_____

_____

_____

_____

4. $-x + 16 \geq 6x + 2$ OR $7x \geq -2x + 9$

_____

_____

_____

_____

_____

5. $-12 - 3s < 0$ AND $5s - 1 < 4$

_____

_____

_____

_____

_____

6. $8 + 2n < 6$ OR $7 - 4n < -5$

_____

_____

_____

_____

_____

7. **Open Ended** Sarah's car gets 24 miles per gallon of gas in the city and 32 miles per gallon on the highway. If her car has a 15-gallon gas tank, write a compound inequality to describe the range of distances, in miles, that her car can travel using a full tank of gas.

_____

_____

_____

8. **Math on the Spot** Write a compound inequality to represent the given recommended level, and graph the solutions.

   A. The recommended pH level for a saltwater fish tank is between 8.3 and 8.5, inclusive.

   _____

   _____

   B. The recommended calcium level for a saltwater fish tank is between 350 and 450 parts per million, exclusive.

   _____

   _____

9. **Critique Reasoning** Debbie wrote a compound inequality that generated the following graph:

$$-5\ -4\ -3\ -2\ -1\quad 0\quad 1\quad 2\quad 3\quad 4\quad 5$$

   She says the compound inequality is $x \leq -2$ AND $x \geq 1$. Is she correct? If not, correct the errors and rewrite the inequalities.

   _____

   _____

   _____

10. The community pool currently has 13,000 gallons of water in it. The pool service wants it to have at least 15,500 gallons but less than 21,000 gallons. Which compound inequality represents the number of gallons of water the pool service should add to the pool?

   Ⓐ $15,500 \leq x + 13,000 < 21,000$

   Ⓑ $15,500 \geq x + 13,000 \leq 21,000$

   Ⓒ $15,500 < x - 13,000 < 21,000$

   Ⓓ $15,500 \leq x + 13,000 \leq 21,000$

Step It Out

Learn the Math

EXAMPLE 1 Andrea plans to buy several shirts and pairs of pants for a new job. Shirts sell for $5 each and pairs of pants sell for $8 each. Andrea has $120 and she plans to spend all of it on clothes.

The linear equation that models this situation is $5x + 8y = 120$, where x represents the number of shirts Andrea buys and y represents the number of pairs of pants she buys.

Identify and interpret the intercepts in the context of this problem.

To find the x-intercept, let $y = 0$.	To find the y-intercept, let $x = 0$.
$5x + 8y = 120$	$5x + 8y = 120$
$5x + 8(0) = 120$	$5(0) + 8y = 120$
$5x = 120$	$8y = 120$
$x = 24$	$y = 15$

The x-intercept is $(24, 0)$. It means that Andrea can buy 24 shirts if she doesn't buy any pairs of pants. The y-intercept is $(0, 15)$. It means that Andrea can buy 15 pairs of pants if she doesn't buy any shirts.

The graph of the linear equation is given.

All points on the line are solutions to $5x + 8y = 120$. However, not all of the points make sense in the context of this problem. Identify one point that is a solution in this context and explain why it makes sense. Identify another point that is *not* a solution in this context and explain why it does not make sense.

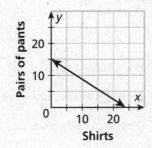

The point $(8, 10)$ is a solution to $5x + 8y = 120$ because $5(8) + 8(10) = 120$. This means that Andrea can buy 8 shirts and 10 pairs of pants for $120.

The point $(6, 11.25)$ is a solution to $5x + 8y = 120$ because $5(6) + 8(11.25) = 120$. It does not make sense in the context of this problem because Andrea cannot buy 11.25 pairs of pants.

Do the Math

Dennis goes to a local electronics store to purchase movies and video games. Movies sell for $10 each and video games sell for $12 each. Dennis has $180 to spend and he plans to spend all of it on the movies and video games.

The linear equation that models this situation is $10x + 12y = \boxed{}$, where

x represents the number of movies Dennis purchases and y represents the number of video games Dennis purchases.

Identify and interpret the intercepts in the context of this problem.

To find the x-intercept, let _____.

$$10x + 12y = 180$$

$$10x + \boxed{}\left(\boxed{}\right) = 180$$

$$\boxed{} = 180$$

$$x = \boxed{}$$

To find the y-intercept, let _____.

$$10x + 12y = 180$$

$$\boxed{}\left(\boxed{}\right) + 12y = 180$$

$$\boxed{} = 180$$

$$y = \boxed{}$$

The x-intercept is $\left(\boxed{}, \boxed{}\right)$. It means that Dennis can purchase $\boxed{}$ movies if he doesn't purchase any video games. The y-intercept is $\left(\boxed{}, \boxed{}\right)$. It means that

Dennis can purchase _____ if he doesn't purchase any _____.

The graph of the linear equation is given.

Identify two points that are solutions in this context and explain why they makes sense.

The points $\left(\boxed{}, \boxed{}\right)$ and $\left(\boxed{}, \boxed{}\right)$ are solutions to

$10x + 12y = 180$. These points make sense because

_____

_____

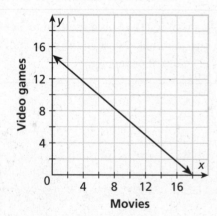

Identify a point that is *not* a solution in this context and explain why it does not make sense.

The point $\left(\boxed{}, \boxed{}\right)$ is a solution to $10x + 12y = 180$, but it does not make sense in the context of this problem because _____

_____

Name _____

LESSON 3.1
More Practice

[Ed] **ONLINE**
Video Tutorials and
Interactive Examples

Determine whether each equation is linear.

1. $x^2 + 5y = 8$

2. $7x + 3y = 21$

_____

3. $4x + 6y^2 = 15$

4. $8x - 3y = -6$

_____

Determine whether the point $(4, -5)$ is on the graph of each equation.

5. $3x + 2y = 4$

6. $2x + 3y = -7$

_____

7. $y = 4x - 21$

8. $y = 6x - 15$

_____

9. $\frac{1}{5}y = 7 - \frac{5}{2}x$

10. $\frac{3}{4}x + \frac{2}{10}y = 2$

_____

Determine the x- and y-intercepts for each indicated line.

11. $2x - 4y = 8$

12. $4x + y = -5$

_____

13. $14x - 7y = -14$

14. $2x + 6y = 10$

_____

15. The dollar amount y that remains to be repaid on a loan x months after the loan is issued is represented by $y = -1000x + 8000$.

A. What is the initial balance on the loan? Explain.

_____

B. How much is repaid each month? Explain.

_____

C. How many months will it take for the loan to be repaid? Explain.

_____

_____

16. Math on the Spot Devon is recording the daytime temperature. The temperature is increasing at a constant rate of 2 °F per hour. The temperature was 54 °F when he started recording. Write an equation in standard form to model the linear situation.

_____

17. Critique Reasoning DeShawn says that because x represents the horizontal axis, the graph of $x = 4$ is a horizontal line. Camden says that DeShawn is incorrect. With whom do you agree? Explain.

_____

_____

18. Open Ended How can you tell by looking at an equation whether its graph will be a vertical line, a horizontal line, or a slanted line?

_____

_____

_____

19. Which line has an x-intercept of -3?

  Ⓐ $x + 2y = 3$ Ⓒ $3x + 2y = -9$

  Ⓑ $2x + y = -3$ Ⓓ $4x = -3$

20. What are the x-intercept and y-intercept of the graph?

  Ⓐ $(-3, 4.5)$ and $(4.5, -3)$

  Ⓑ $(-3, 0)$ and $(0, 4.5)$

  Ⓒ $(3, -4.5)$ and $(-4.5, 3)$

  Ⓓ $(0, -3)$ and $(4.5, 0)$

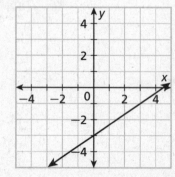

Step It Out

Learn the Math

EXAMPLE 1 ▶ The slope of a line represents the *average rate of change* of a function. Slope is often expressed as *rise over run*. The phrase *rise over run* can help you remember the slope formula.

$$\text{slope} = \frac{\text{rise}}{\text{run}} = \frac{\text{change in } y\text{-values}}{\text{change in } x\text{-values}} = \frac{y_2 - y_1}{x_2 - x_1}$$

$$\text{slope} = \frac{y_2 - y_1}{x_2 - x_1} = \frac{5 - 3}{5 - 0} = \frac{2}{5}$$

The slope, or average rate of change, of this line is $\frac{2}{5}$.

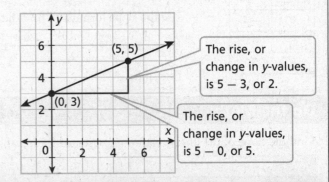

The rise, or change in *y*-values, is 5 − 3, or 2.

The rise, or change in *y*-values, is 5 − 0, or 5.

Do the Math

Use the slope formula to find the slope between points *D* and *E*, between points *E* and *F*, and between points *D* and *F*. What do you notice?

For points *D* and *E*:

$$\text{slope} = \frac{y_2 - y_1}{x_2 - x_1} = \frac{3 - (-1)}{-1 - (-3)} = \frac{3 + 1}{-1 + 3} = \frac{4}{2} = \boxed{}$$

For points *E* and *F*:

$$\text{slope} = \frac{y_2 - y_1}{x_2 - x_1} = \frac{5 - \boxed{}}{0 - \boxed{}} = \frac{\boxed{}}{0 + \boxed{}} = \frac{\boxed{}}{1} = \boxed{}$$

For points *D* and *F*:

$$\text{slope} = \frac{y_2 - y_1}{x_2 - x_1} = \frac{\boxed{} - \boxed{}}{\boxed{} - \boxed{}} = \frac{\boxed{} + \boxed{}}{\boxed{} + \boxed{}} = \frac{\boxed{}}{\boxed{}} = \boxed{}$$

The slope between each pair of points is $\boxed{}$. This shows that the average

rate of change of the function is $\boxed{}$.

Learn the Math

EXAMPLE 2 You can also find the slope of a linear relation when it is represented in a table of values.

x	y
−2	−10
0	−4
5	11
8	20

Choose any two ordered pairs from the table.

$(-2, -10)$ and $(8, 20)$

Use the slope formula to find the slope between the two points.

$$\frac{y_2 - y_1}{x_2 - x_1} = \frac{20 - (-10)}{8 - (-2)} = \frac{20 + 10}{8 + 2} = \frac{30}{10} = 3$$

The slope is 3.

Do the Math

Find the slope of the linear relation represented in the table.

x	−3	−1	5	7
y	13	5	−19	−27

Learn the Math

EXAMPLE 3 If you know the slope of a line and any point on the line, you can create a graph of the line.

A line has a *y*-intercept of $(0, 6)$ and a slope of $-\frac{4}{3}$. To graph the line, first plot the given point.

Because $-\frac{4}{3} = \frac{-4}{3}$, the *rise* is −4 and the *run* is 3. So, from the point $(0, 6)$, move *down* 4 units and *right* 3 units to locate another point on the line. Finally, draw a line through $(0, 6)$ and $(3, 2)$.

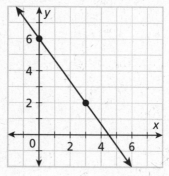

Do the Math

A line has a slope of $\frac{2}{7}$ and passes through the point $(-3, -2)$. Create a graph of the line.

First, plot the point _____.

The rise is ☐ and the run is ☐.

So, from $(-3, -2)$, move _____ 2 units and _____ 7 units to locate another point on the line. Finally, draw a line through $(-3, -2)$ and _____.

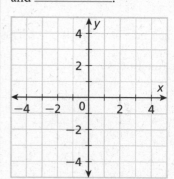

Name _____

Determine the slope of each line.

1.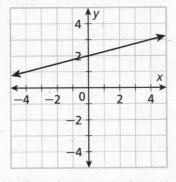

_____

2.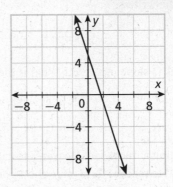

_____

Determine the slope of the line described in each table.

3.

x	y
2	1
4	7
6	13
8	19

_____

4.

x	y
−3	15
1	9
3	6
7	0

_____

5.

x	y
1	0
2	−2
3	−4
4	−6

_____

6.

x	y
−2	3
2	0
6	−3
10	−6

_____

Determine the slope of a line containing the two points.

7. $(2, 4)$ and $(6, -3)$

_____

8. $(-5, 1)$ and $(-1, 9)$

_____

Apply the slope to the point given to determine a second point that is on the line.

9. $m = \frac{1}{2}$ through $(2, 1)$

_____

10. $m = -4$ through $(-3, 7)$

_____

11. Critique Reasoning Danika wants to calculate the slope between the points $(12, 2)$ and $(8, 5)$. She writes:

$$\text{slope} = \frac{(8 - 12)}{(5 - 2)} = -\frac{4}{3}$$

Why is Danika's slope incorrect? What is the actual slope between $(12, 2)$ and $(8, 5)$?

_____

_____

12. Evan is running a marathon. He wants to calculate his average speed between two checkpoints. He reaches the 3-mile checkpoint after 0.75 hour and the 18-mile checkpoint after 2 hours. What is Evan's average speed, in miles per hour, between the two checkpoints?

_____

_____

13. Math on the Spot The graph shows the value of a computer after x months. Find the slope of the line and explain what the slope represents.

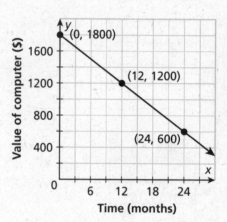

_____

_____

14. Which describes the graph of $\frac{1}{4}x = -y + 6$?

(A) a line with a y-intercept of $\frac{1}{4}$ and a positive slope

(B) a line with a y-intercept of -6 and a positive slope

(C) a line with a y-intercept of 4 and a negative slope

(D) a line with a y-intercept of 6 and a negative slope

15. Which equation represents a line with a y-intercept of 5 and a slope of -2?

(A) $y = 5x - 2$

(B) $x = 5y - 2$

(C) $y + 2x = 5$

(D) $x - 2y = 5$

Step It Out

Learn the Math

EXAMPLE 1 ▷ Brianna purchased a small laptop computer for $550.00. She signed up for an interest-free payment plan where she will pay $50 per month until the computer is paid off. Write a function to determine how long it will take Brianna to pay off the computer. Use A to represent the amount of money and t to represent the time in months.

Because the original loan amount is $550 and the amount Brianna owes for the laptop decreases by $50 each month, the situation can be modeled by the equation $A(t) = 550 - 50t$.

A graph of the function can help you to analyze Brianna's situation.

From the graph, you can see that the original loan amount of $550 is represented by the y-intercept, $(0, 550)$.

The graph is a series of discrete points because Brianna only makes a payment once a month and the loan amount decreases by exactly $50 with each payment.

You can also see from the graph that after 11 months, the loan amount decreases to $0. It takes Brianna 11 months to pay off the loan, and the domain of this situation is integers from 0 to 11 months.

The value of the loan at 0 months is $A(0) = 550 - 50(0)$, or $550. The value of the loan at 11 months is $A(11) = 550 - 50(11) = 550 - 550$, or $0. So, the range is multiples of $50 from $0 to $550.

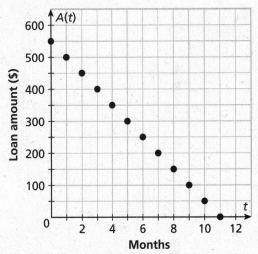

You can use either the equation or the graph to answer other questions about Brianna's loan.

Next, find how long it takes Brianna to pay off at least half of the loan.

Half of the loan amount of $550 is $275. The points on the graph closest to $275 are $(5, 300)$ and $(6, 250)$. At $(5, 300)$, Brianna still has more than half of the loan left to pay. It takes her 6 months to pay off at least half of the loan.

To use the equation to find how long, substitute 275 for $A(t)$ and solve for t.

$$A(t) = 550 - 50t$$
$$275 = 550 - 50t$$
$$-275 = -50t$$
$$5.5 = t$$

Because Brianna only makes payments once per month, it will take her 6 months to pay off at least half the loan.

Do the Math

Jamil boards a train and is 900 miles from his destination. The train travels at an average speed of 75 miles per hour. Write and graph a function that shows how far Jamil is from his final destination. Use t to represent the time in hours and D to represent the distance in miles.

The distance from the final destination is ☐ miles. After each hour, Jamil's

distance from his destination decreases by ☐ miles. An equation that models

Jamil's distance from his destination is _____ .

Complete the table of values and make a graph to analyze the situation.

t	D(t)
0	☐
1	☐
2	☐
3	☐
4	☐

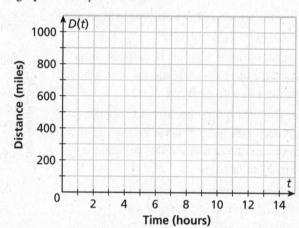

Jamil's distance from his destination when he boards the train is represented by

the y-intercept, (☐ , ☐).

The graph is a [set of points / solid line] because _____

_____ .

It takes Jamil ☐ hours to reach his destination. The domain of this

situation is _____ hours.

The distance at 0 hours is $D(0) = 900 -$ ☐ (0), or ☐ miles. The distance

at ☐ hours is $D($☐$) = 900 - 75($☐$)$, or ☐ miles. The range

is _____ miles.

Find how far Jamil is from his destination after he has been on the train for 4 hours.

When ☐ $= 4$, $y =$ ☐. After 4 hours, Jamil is ☐ miles from his destination.

Determine whether each relation is a function.

1. $(4, 2), (2, -1), (0, -4), (2, -7), (4, -10)$

2. $(-1, 4), (1, -4), (0, 0), (-1, -4), (2, 4)$

For each function, evaluate $f(-2)$, $f(2)$, and $f(5)$.

3. $f(x) = -2x + 8$

$f(-2) = $ _____

$f(2) = $ _____

$f(5) = $ _____

4. $f(x) = x^2 + 4x + 2$

$f(-2) = $ _____

$f(2) = $ _____

$f(5) = $ _____

5. $f(x) = \dfrac{x + 4}{3}$

$f(-2) = $ _____

$f(2) = $ _____

$f(5) = $ _____

6. $f(x) = -\dfrac{12}{x}$

$f(-2) = $ _____

$f(2) = $ _____

$f(5) = $ _____

7. **Math on the Spot** Give the domain and range of each relation. Tell whether the relation is a function. Explain.

A.

Date	Pairs of shoes sold	Total sales
9/25	53	$345
9/26	62	$981
9/27	53	$674

B.

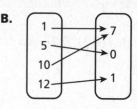

_____   _____

_____   _____

_____   _____

_____   _____

C.

_____

_____

_____

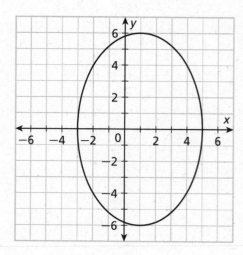

8. **Open Ended** Explain how the vertical line test demonstrates whether the graph of a relation is a function.

_____

_____

_____

9. A local fitness center offers a membership with an application fee of $14.95 and a membership fee of $9.95 per month. A new center offers an application fee that is $5.50 less than its competitor, but a membership fee that is $1.00 more per month. Which function models the cost of a membership at the new center?

Ⓐ $f(x) = 14.95 + 9.95x$

Ⓒ $f(x) = 9.45 + 10.95x$

Ⓑ $f(x) = 9.45 + 9.95x$

Ⓓ $f(x) = 14.45 + 10.95x$

Name _____

Step It Out

Learn the Math

EXAMPLE 1 ▸ At an entertainment center, Dwayne loaded a game pass with $30.00. Each time Dwayne inserts the card to play a game, $1.25 is deducted from the card. Write a linear function for the amount A, in dollars, left on the game pass after Dwayne plays x games.

To write a linear function, determine the slope and the y-intercept of the function.

You can interpret slope as the rate of change.

Since the value on the game pass *decreases*, the slope is negative. The value decreases by $1.25 each time Dwayne plays a game, so the slope of the linear function is -1.25.

The y-intercept is the value of a function when $x = 0$.

The value on the game pass when Dwayne has played 0 games is $30.00, so the y-intercept is 30.

Use the slope and the y-intercept to write the linear function.

$A(x) = 30 - 1.25x$

What are the domain and the range for the general function $A(x)$?

Both the domain and the range of $A(x) = 30 - 1.25x$ are all real numbers.

What are the domain and the range in the context of this real-world problem?

The domain, which represents the number of games Dwayne can play, is the whole number values between $x = 0$ and $x = 24$. The range, which represents the amount of money on Dwayne's game pass, is the y-values of the function evaluated for each domain value. The range is 0, 1.25, 2.50, ..., 27.50, 28.75, 30.00.

Graph the function as a set of discrete points. The graph is a discrete set of points because Dwayne can only play a whole number of games.

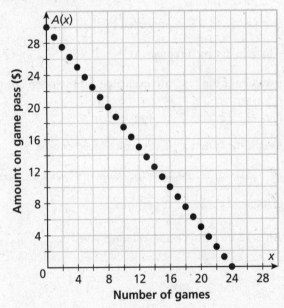

Do the Math

Gwen opens a savings account with $50.00. Over the next year, she plans to deposit $10.00 each month into the account. Write a linear function for the amount A, in dollars, in Gwen's account after x months.

Because the amount in Gwen's savings account is increasing, the slope is _____.

The amount is increasing by ☐ each month, so the slope of the function is ☐.

The opening value of Gwen's savings account is ☐, so the y-intercept is ☐.

Use the slope and the y-intercept to write the linear function.

$A(x) = $ ☐ $+$ ☐ x

What are the domain and the range for the general function $A(x)$?

The domain and the range of $A(x) = $ ☐ $+$ ☐ x are _____.

What are the domain and the range in the context of this real-world problem?

In the context of Gwen's saving account, the domain is the number of _____

in a year, and it is represented by the _____ values from $x = $ ☐ to $x = $ ☐.

The range, which represents the _____ of Gwen's savings account, is the

y-values of the function evaluated for each domain value. The range is 50,

☐, ☐, ..., 150, ☐, ☐.

Graph the function. The graph should consist

of _____ because the value of Gwen's account only

changes _____ per month.

After 12 months, Gwen will have saved _____.

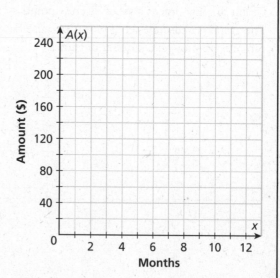

Name _____

Graph each linear function.

1. $f(x) = 3x + 4$

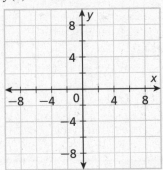

2. $f(x) = -3$

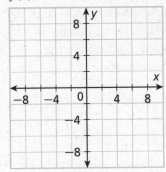

3. $f(x) = -2x - 5$

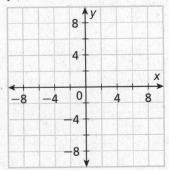

4. $f(x) = \frac{2}{5}x + 6$

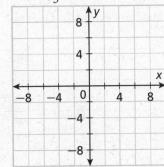

5. $f(x) = -4x + 2$

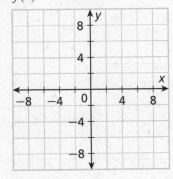

6. $f(x) = -\frac{4}{3}x - 3$

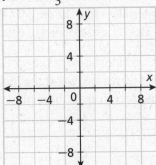

7. Math on the Spot Jack rents a space at a farmers' market and pays the market manager $6.50 for each gourd he sells. The amount Jack pays each day is given by $f(x) = 6.50x$, where x is the number of gourds sold. Graph this function and give its domain and range.

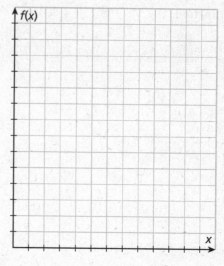

Domain: _____

Range: _____

8. Open Ended What conditions must be met for the graph of a linear function to pass through every quadrant except for Quadrant II? Explain.

_____

_____

_____

_____

9. Model with Mathematics As a member of a dance committee, you are developing a formula that models the total profit P, for selling x tickets to the dance. A committee determines that the cost of a DJ and security for a 3-hour dance will be about $400.00. Tickets are sold for $10.00 each.

Write a linear function that models the total profit made from the dance. Interpret the slope and the x- and y-intercepts of the function. State the domain and the range of the function and interpret them in the context of the problem.

_____

_____

_____

_____

_____

10. Which of the following are linear functions? Select all that apply.

Ⓐ $f(x) = 2x^2 - 1$

Ⓑ $f(x) = 3 - 4x$

Ⓒ $f(x) = 7x$

Ⓓ $f(x) = 2x + 5^2$

Ⓔ $f(x) = 5$

Ⓕ $f(x) = x^2 - 4x + 6$

© Houghton Mifflin Harcourt Publishing Company

Name _____

Step It Out

Learn the Math

EXAMPLE 1 Determine the maximum and minimum value of the function on the interval $-1 \leq x \leq 3$.

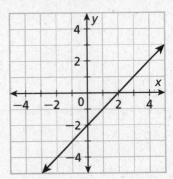

The graph of the function is increasing over the entire interval, so find the value of the function at the endpoints of the interval.

$$f(-1) = -3 \qquad f(3) = 1$$

The minimum value on the interval is -3 and the maximum value is 1.

Do the Math

Determine the maximum and minimum value of the function on the interval $-2 \leq x \leq 2$.

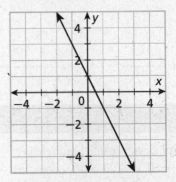

The graph of the function is _____ over the entire interval, so find the value of the function at the endpoints of the interval.

$$f(-2) = \boxed{} \qquad f\left(\boxed{}\right) = \boxed{}$$

The minimum value on the interval is $\boxed{}$ and the maximum value is $\boxed{}$.

Learn the Math

EXAMPLE 2 Describe the characteristics of the function $f(x) = 3x + 4$.

The slope of the function is 3, which is positive, so the function is increasing.

The function has a zero when $f(x) = 0$.

$3x + 4 = 0$

$\quad 3x = -4$

$\quad\ x = -\dfrac{4}{3}$

So, the function has a zero when $x = -\dfrac{4}{3}$.

The y-intercept is the value of the function when $x = 0$.

$f(0) = 3(0) + 4 = 4$

The y-intercept is $y = 4$.

Do the Math

Describe the characteristics of the function $f(x) = -2x + 2$.

The slope of the function is $\boxed{}$, which is _____, so

the function is _____.

A. Find the zero.

The function has a zero when $x = \boxed{}$.

B. Find the y-intercept.

The y-intercept is $y = \boxed{}$.

Learn the Math

EXAMPLE 3 This year, Lake City has received 20 inches of rain. Today it rained 0.25 inch per hour for 8 hours. A function that models the total rainfall is $R(t) = 0.25t + 20$, with a domain from $t = 0$ to $t = 8$. What are the characteristics of this function?

The slope is positive, so the function is increasing. The minimum value is 20 and the maximum value is 22. The y-intercept is 20. There are no zeros on this domain.

Do the Math

The total rainfall for Fairview can be modeled by the function $R(t) = 0.2t + 23$, with a domain from $t = 0$ to $t = 12$.

A. Is the function increasing or decreasing?

B. What are the maximum and minimum values of this function on the given domain?

C. What are the y-intercept and the zero for this function, if any?

Give the end behavior indicated for each function.

1. $f(x) = 3x + 2$ for $x \to -\infty$

_____

2. $f(x) = -2x + 5$ for $x \to -\infty$

_____

3. $f(x) = \frac{3}{5}x - 2$ for $x \to +\infty$

_____

4. $f(x) = -x + 8$ for $x \to +\infty$

_____

Give the equation that has the indicated characteristics.

5. a function that has a zero at 5 and a slope of -3

_____

6. a function that has a zero at 1 and a slope of 2

_____

7. a function that has a zero at -4 and a slope of -1

_____

8. a function that has a zero at 6 and a slope of 2

_____

Determine the extreme values for each function on the interval $-3 \leq x \leq 4$, and include if any extreme values found are maximum or minimum values.

9. $f(x) = 4x + 1$

_____

10. $f(x) = -3$

_____

11. $f(x) = -\frac{1}{3}x + 7$

_____

12. $f(x) = -3x - 8$

_____

Determine the zeros for each function.

13. $f(x) = 5x - 10$

_____

14. $h(x) = -\frac{3}{4}x + 6$

_____

15. $g(x) = 4x + 20$

_____

16. $f(x) = \frac{1}{2}x - 3$

_____

17. Open Ended A car dealer starts the month with 120 cars. The dealer sells 3 cars each day. The number of cars remaining on any day can by modeled by the function $f(x) = 120 - 3x$. What should the domain of the function be if you want to know the number of cars remaining on any day during the month? What are the maximum and minimum values during the month?

_____

_____

_____

_____

18. Francis received some money for his birthday. He spends the same amount of money each week on trading cards. The following graph shows the amount of money he has at the end of each week. What are the domain and the range of the function? What is the slope of the function? What are the y-intercept and the zero of the function?

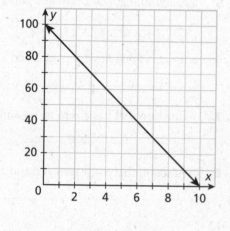

_____

_____

_____

19. Critique Reasoning Jackson states that the function does not have a maximum value. Carson disagrees and says the maximum is 0.5. Who is correct? Explain your reasoning.

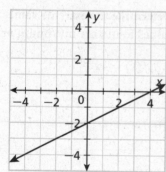

_____

_____

_____

_____

20. A family takes a road trip. When they start the trip, their car has 4524 miles on the odometer. They travel at a constant speed of 60 miles per hour. Which function represents the number of miles on the odometer after h hours?

Ⓐ $m(h) = 60h$

Ⓑ $m(h) = 60h + 4524$

Ⓒ $m(h) = 4524h$

Ⓓ $m(h) = 4524h + 60$

Name _____

Step It Out

Learn the Math

EXAMPLE 1 ▶ Chloe starts a savings account with $250. Each month she will deposit $40 in the account for 12 months.

A. Write a function to represent this situation, using A to represent the amount in the account and m to represent the number of months.

The initial value is $250 and the rate of change is $40 per month. The function is $A(m) = 40m + 250$.

B. State the domain and range of the function in this situation.

The problem states that Chloe will deposit $40 each month for 12 months. So, the domain is integer values from 0 to 12. The value of the function when $m = 0$ is $40(0) + 250 = 250$.

The value of the function when $m = 12$ is $40(12) + 250 = 730$. So, the range is integers from 250 to 730, in steps of 40.

C. How much money is in the account after 7 months?

Evaluate the function when $m = 7$.

$A(m) = 40(7) + 250 = 280 + 250 = 530$

After 7 months, Chloe has $530 in her savings account.

Do the Math

A math club has 24 members at the beginning of the school year. Four more people join the club each month for 8 months.

A. Write a function to represent this situation, using T to represent the total number of members in the math club and m to represent the number of new members who join the club.

Initial value: ☐ members

Rate of change: ☐ members per month

Function: $T(m) = $ ☐ $m + $ ☐

B. State the domain and range of the function in this situation.

Domain: _____

Range: _____

C. How many people are in the club after 5 months?

Find the value of ☐ when ☐ equals ☐ .

$T(m) = $ ☐ (☐) $ + $ ☐ $ = $ ☐

The number of people after 5 months is ☐ .

Learn the Math

EXAMPLE 2 A bookstore receives a shipment of a new book. Each week after receiving the shipment, they sell 14 copies of the book. After 4 weeks, the bookstore has 64 copies of the book in stock. Write an equation in slope-intercept form that represents this situation.

The slope is -14 books per week.

A point in this situation is $(4, 64)$.

Use the point-slope form of the equation of a line.

$y - y_1 = m(x - x_1)$ Point-slope form

$y - 64 = -14(x - 4)$ Substitute.

$y - 64 = -14x + 56$ Distributive Property

$y = -14x + 120$ Addition Prop. of Equality

Do the Math

Anita is draining her pool. The pool is draining at a rate of 20 gallons per minute. After draining for 35 minutes, there are still 14,300 gallons of water in the pool. Write an equation in slope-intercept form that represents this situation.

The slope is $\boxed{}$ gallons per minute.

A point in this situation is $\left(\boxed{}, \boxed{}\right)$.

$y - y_1 = m(x - x_1)$ _____

$y - \boxed{} = \boxed{}\left(x - \boxed{}\right)$ Substitute.

$y - \boxed{} = \boxed{}\,x + \boxed{}$ _____

$y = \boxed{}\,x + \boxed{}$ _____

Learn the Math

EXAMPLE 3 Eric borrowed money to buy a phone. He is paying the money back that he owes by paying the same amount each month. After 6 months, he owes $505. After 12 months, he owes $385. Write a function to represent this situation. How much money does Eric owe after 16 months?

Two points on the graph of this function are $(6, 505)$ and $(12, 385)$. Use these points to find the slope.

$$m = \frac{y_2 - y_1}{x_2 - x_1} = \frac{385 - 505}{12 - 6} = \frac{-120}{6} = -20$$

Now use the point-slope form to write an equation for the function.

$y - y_1 = m(x - x_1)$ Point-slope form

$y - 505 = -20(x - 6)$ Substitute.

$y - 505 = -20x + 120$ Distributive Property

$y = -20x + 625$ Addition Property of Equality

Substitute 16 for x to find how much money Eric owes after 16 months.

$y = -20(16) + 625 = -320 + 625 = 305$

After 16 months, Eric still owes $305 for his phone.

Do the Math

Michael joins a book club. He receives the same number of books each month. After 8 months, he has 29 books. After 11 months, he has 38 books. Write a function to represent this situation. How many books does Michael have after 20 months?

Name _____

Use the point-slope form of a linear equation to write the equation of the line.

1. $m = 2$ through $(3, -5)$

_____
_____
_____
_____

2. $m = -1$ through $(-2, 1)$

_____
_____
_____
_____

3. $m = -\frac{2}{3}$ through $(7, 3)$

_____
_____
_____
_____
_____

4. $m = \frac{1}{4}$ through $(-8, 6)$

_____
_____
_____
_____
_____

5. through $(4, 4)$ and $(-2, 8)$

_____
_____
_____
_____

6. through $(1, 3)$ and $(7, -3)$

_____
_____
_____
_____

7. through $(1, -4)$ and $(5, -4)$

_____
_____
_____
_____

8. through $(-4, -2)$ and $(8, -6)$

_____
_____
_____
_____

9. **Open Ended** Describe a situation that can be modeled by an equation with a positive slope.

_____

_____

_____

10. **Math on the Spot** Write an equation in point-slope form for the line with the given slope that contains the given point.

slope $= \frac{4}{3}$; $(-1, 0)$

_____

_____

11. Devon wants to buy a computer for $1000 but does not have enough money. He has $680 in his savings account. He is going to save $60 each month until he has enough money to buy the computer. Write a function to model this situation. How many months will Devon need to save until he has enough money to buy the computer? Explain how you can find this answer.

_____

_____

_____

12. A farmer collected some eggs and is packing them in cartons of 12. After the farmer packed 14 cartons, there are still 312 eggs left to package. Write a function to model the number of eggs left to be packed after packing x cartons. How many cartons can the farmer package?

_____

_____

_____

13. Which function is represented by the graph?

Ⓐ $y = 2.5x + 10$

Ⓑ $y = -2.5x + 10$

Ⓒ $y = 2.5x + 4$

Ⓓ $y = -2.5x + 4$

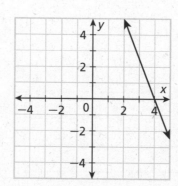

Name _____

Step It Out

Learn the Math

EXAMPLE 1 Identify the transformation shown in each graph.

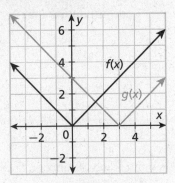

The graph of function *g* is the graph of function *f* shifted to the right.

To shift a graph to the right, subtract a constant from the domain.

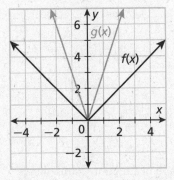

The graph of function *g* is narrower than the graph of function *f*.

To make a graph narrower, multiply the range by a value greater than 1.

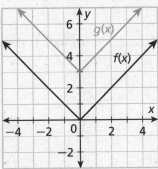

The graph of function *g* is the graph of function *f* shifted up.

To shift a graph up, add a constant to the range.

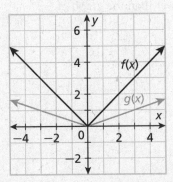

The graph of function *g* is wider than the graph of function *f*.

To make a graph wider, multiply the range by a value less than 1.

Do the Math

Identify the transformation shown in each graph.

A.

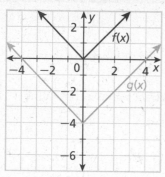

The graph of function *g* is the graph of function *f* shifted down.

To shift a graph down, _____ a constant from the

_____ .

B.

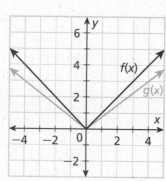

The graph of function *g* is wider than the graph of function *f*.

To make a graph wider, _____ the _____

by a value _____ than 1.

C.

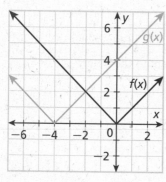

The graph of function *g* is the graph of function *f* shifted to the left.

To shift a graph to the left, _____ a constant to the

_____ .

D.

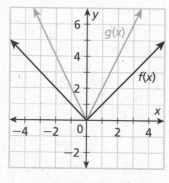

The graph of function *g* is narrower than the graph of function *f*.

To make a graph narrower, _____ the

_____ by a value _____ than 1.

Describe how the graph of function *g* is different from the graph of function *f*. Then identify the transformation that produces that change.

1.

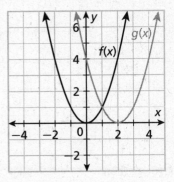

_____
_____
_____
_____

2.

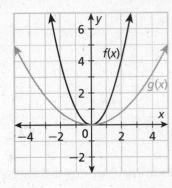

_____
_____
_____
_____

3.

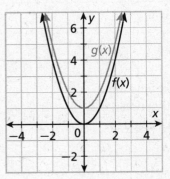

_____
_____
_____
_____

4.

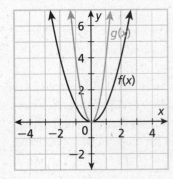

_____
_____
_____
_____

5. How is the graph of $g(x) = f(x) - 10$ related to the graph of function f?

_____
_____

6. How is the graph of $g(x) = \frac{1}{10} f(x)$ related to the graph of function f?

_____
_____

7. **Use Structure** Why does adding a positive value to the domain of a function shift the graph of the function to the left? Use the functions $f(x) = x^2$ and $g(x) = (x + 2)^2$ to explain.

_____

_____

_____

_____

_____

8. **Critique Reasoning** Riley says that the graph of $k(x) = g(x) + \frac{1}{2}$ is narrower than the graph of function g because $\frac{1}{2}$ is less than 1. Is Riley correct? If so, explain why. If not, describe the graph of function k.

_____

_____

_____

_____

_____

9. **Reason** Gina is analyzing the graphs of function f and function g, where function g is a transformation of function f. She draws several vertical line segments between the two graphs and finds that the length of each line segment is 6 units. What could the transformation be? Explain your reasoning.

_____

_____

_____

_____

_____

10. Function j is a transformation of function f that changes the shape of the graph of function f. Which equation could be the equation for function j?

Ⓐ $j(x) = f\left(x + \frac{3}{4}\right)$

Ⓑ $j(x) = f(x) - 5$

Ⓒ $j(x) = f(x - 8)$

Ⓓ $j(x) = \frac{1}{3}f(x)$

© Houghton Mifflin Harcourt Publishing Company

Step It Out

Learn the Math

> **EXAMPLE 1** In each graph, function g represents a transformation of $f(x) = x$. Identify the transformation of function f and give the transformed function.

The slope of function g is $\frac{1}{2}$. When the slope is a fraction less than 1, the graph is compressed. Function g represents a compression by a factor of $\frac{1}{2}$.

$g(x) = \frac{1}{2}f(x)$

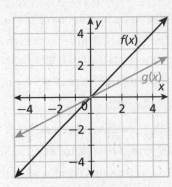

The slope of function g is -3, and the y-intercept of function g is 4 more than the y-intercept of function f.

Function g represents a reflection, a stretch by a factor of 3, and then a translation up 4 units.

$g(x) = -3f(x) + 4$

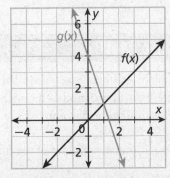

Do the Math

Function g represents a transformation of $f(x) = x$. Identify the transformation of function f and give the transformed function.

The slope of function g is $\boxed{}$.

The y-intercept of function g is $\boxed{}$ more than the y-intercept of function f.

Function g represents a _____ by a factor of $\boxed{}$

and then a _____ up $\boxed{}$ unit(s).

$g(x) = \boxed{}\, f(x) + \boxed{}$

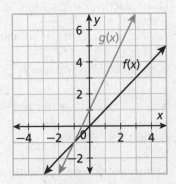

Learn the Math

EXAMPLE 2 Jasmine started saving for new headphones with $20 that she earned from babysitting. She saves an additional $8 each week. Function g models the amount of money Jasmine has saved after x weeks.

A. What transformations of the function $f(x) = x$ does function g represent?

The $8 that Jasmine saves each week represents a slope of 8, so function g represents a stretch by a factor of 8.

The initial $20 represents a y-intercept of 20, so function g is a vertical translation up 20 units.

B. What function represents $g(x)$?

To stretch by a factor of 8, multiply the range by 8.

To translate up 20 units, add 20 to the range.

$g(x) = 8f(x) + 20$

Do the Math

A scuba diver starts 2 feet below the ocean surface and descends at a rate of 45 feet per minute. Function d models the scuba diver's depth from the ocean surface x minutes after beginning the descent.

A. What transformations of the function $f(x) = x$ does function d represent?

Since the scuba diver is descending at a rate of 45 feet per minute, the slope is $\boxed{}$.

Function d is a _____ across the x-axis and a _____ by a

factor of $\boxed{}$.

The scuba diver starts 2 feet below the ocean surface, which represents a

_____ of $\boxed{}$. Function d is a vertical _____ down $\boxed{}$ units.

B. What function represents $d(x)$?

To _____ across the x-axis and _____ by a factor of $\boxed{}$,

multiply the range by $\boxed{}$.

To translate down $\boxed{}$ units, _____ $\boxed{}$ from the range.

$d(x) = \boxed{} f(x) - \boxed{}$

Describe the transformations of the parent linear function shown in the graph. Give the equation for the transformed function.

1. _____
_____
_____
_____
_____

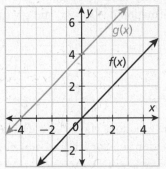

2. _____
_____
_____
_____
_____

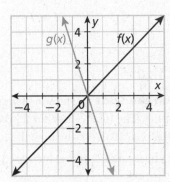

3. _____
_____
_____
_____
_____

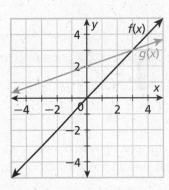

Describe the graph of each linear function by identifying the transformation(s) of the parent linear function.

4. $g(x) = 2x$

_____
_____
_____

5. $j(x) = -x + 11$

_____
_____
_____

6. $t(x) = \dfrac{9}{10}x - \dfrac{1}{10}$

_____
_____
_____

7. $h(x) = -10x + 3$

_____
_____
_____

8. Mr. Juarez pays a security deposit of $800 when he signs a lease for a new apartment. He pays $1250 per month to rent the apartment. The function h gives the total amount Mr. Juarez has paid for the apartment after x months. Describe function g as a transformation of $f(x) = x$, and give an equation for $h(x)$.

_____

_____

_____

9. Add the functions $g(x) = -\frac{2}{3}x$ and $h(x) = -6$ to make the new function $j(x)$. Write the function rule for $j(x)$ and describe the new function as a transformation of $f(x) = x$.

_____

_____

_____

10. Math on the Spot A pizzeria charges $10 for a large cheese pizza plus $0.50 per topping. The total charge for a pizza with x toppings is given by the function $f(x) = 0.50x + 10$. Describe how the following changes affect the graph.

A. The cheese pizza's cost is increased to $14.

_____

_____

B. The charge per topping is raised to $1.00.

_____

_____

11. Which equation represents a vertical compression by a factor of $\frac{1}{3}$, a reflection across the x-axis, and a translation down 7 units of $f(x) = x$?

Ⓐ $h(x) = \frac{1}{3}x + 7$

Ⓑ $h(x) = -7x - \frac{1}{3}$

Ⓒ $h(x) = -x - \frac{7}{3}$

Ⓓ $h(x) = -\frac{1}{3}x - 7$

12. For what values of a and b does $h(x) = ax + b$ represent a vertical stretch by a factor of 2 and a translation up 5 units of $f(x) = x$?

Ⓐ $a = \frac{1}{2}, b = 5$

Ⓑ $a = 2, b = 5$

Ⓒ $a = \frac{1}{2}, b = -5$

Ⓓ $a = 2, b = -5$

© Houghton Mifflin Harcourt Publishing Company

Step It Out

Learn the Math

EXAMPLE 1 ▶ What function shown has the least output for $x = -4$?

$f(x) = 3x + 1$

$h(x) = \left\{ (0, -2), (1, 1), (2, 4), (3, 7), (4, 10) \right\}$

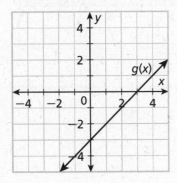

$j(x)$					
x	0	1	2	3	4
y	3	5	7	9	11

f:

$f(-4) = 3(-4) + 1$

$= -12 + 1$

$= -11$

h:

Write an equation for the function.

Use $(0, -2)$ and $(1, 1)$ to find the slope:

$m = \dfrac{y_2 - y_1}{x_2 - x_1} = \dfrac{1 - (-2)}{1 - 0} = 3$

When $x = 0$, $y = -2$. So, $b = -2$.

Write the equation: $h(x) = 3x - 2$

Evaluate $h(-4)$: $h(-4) = 3(-4) - 2 = -14$

g:

Use the graph to write an equation.

The line passes through $(0, -3)$ and $(2, -1)$. Find the slope:

$m = \dfrac{y_2 - y_1}{x_2 - x_1} = \dfrac{-1 - (-3)}{2 - 0} = 1$

The graph intersects the y-axis at $(0, -3)$, so $b = -3$.

Write the equation: $g(x) = x - 3$

Evaluate $g(-4)$: $g(-4) = -4 - 3 = -7$

j:

Look for a pattern in the table.

As x decreases by 1, y decreases by 2.

$j(-1) = 1$

$j(-2) = -1$

$j(-3) = -3$

$j(-4) = -5$

The function with the least output for $x = -4$ is function h.

Do the Math

What function shown has the greatest output for $x = 8$?

$f(x) = \frac{1}{2}x + 5$

$h(x) = \left\{ (0, -5), (1, -3), (2, -1), (3, 1), (4, 3) \right\}$

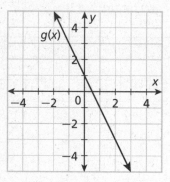

		$j(x)$			
x	0	1	2	3	4
y	3	2	1	0	−1

f:

$f(8) = \frac{1}{2}\left(\boxed{}\right) + 5 = \boxed{}$

h:

Use the points $\left(0, \boxed{}\right)$ and $\left(1, \boxed{}\right)$.

$m = \dfrac{\boxed{} - \boxed{}}{1 - 0} = \boxed{}$ and $b = \boxed{}$.

The equation is $h(x) = \boxed{}x + \boxed{}$.

$h(8) = \boxed{}(8) + \boxed{} = \boxed{}$

g:

The line passes through $\left(0, \boxed{}\right)$ and $\left(1, \boxed{}\right)$.

$m = \dfrac{\boxed{} - \boxed{}}{1 - 0} = \boxed{}$ and

$b = \boxed{}$.

The equation is $g(x) = \boxed{}x + \boxed{}$.

$g(8) = \boxed{}(8) + \boxed{} = \boxed{}$.

j:

As x increases by 1, y _____ by $\boxed{}$.

$j(5) = \boxed{}$

$j(6) = \boxed{}$

$j(7) = \boxed{}$

$j(8) = \boxed{}$

The function with the greatest output for $x = 8$ is function $\boxed{}$.

Name _____

Use the function models for Problems 1–4.

$f(x) = \{(0, 4,), (1, 7), (2, 10), (3, 13), (4, 16)\}$

g(x)					
x	0	1	2	3	4
y	8	8.5	9	9.5	10

$j(x) = -4x$

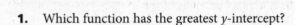

1. Which function has the greatest y-intercept?

2. Which function has the least x-intercept?

3. Which function has the least output for $x = -10$?

4. Which function has the greatest slope?

Use the function models for Problems 5–8.

$g(x) = \frac{3}{2}x + 1$

$h(x) = \{(0, -0.5), (1, -1), (2, -1.5), (3, -2), (4, -2.5)\}$

f(x)	
x	y
0	-1.5
1	1.5
2	4.5
3	7.5
4	10.5

5. Which function has the least output for $x = -3$?

6. Which function has the greatest x-intercept?

7. Which function has the greatest output for $x = 0.5$?

8. Which function has the least y-intercept?

9. **Reason** The function f is given by the equation $f(x) = -4x - 7$, and the graph of function g passes through the points $(0, -7)$ and $(2, -3)$. Without writing an equation or evaluating a function, how could you determine which function has a greater output for $x = 12$? Explain your reasoning.

_____

_____

_____

10. **Math on the Spot** A student is saving money at a rate of $5 per week, as described by the function f. Another student is saving money as shown in the table. Find and compare the rates of change and initial values of the linear functions in terms of the situation they model.

Student 1

$f(x) = 5x + 50$

Student 2

Time (weeks)	0	1	2	3
Account balance ($)	20	30	40	50

_____

_____

11. Talia and Jason leave their homes at the same time and bike at a constant rate to school. Talia's distance in kilometers from the school after x minutes is given by $t(x) = -0.2x + 1.9$. Jason's distance in kilometers from the school after x minutes is given by $j(x) = \{(0, 4.5), (1, 4.2), (2, 3.9)\}$. Who reaches the school first? Explain how you know.

_____

_____

_____

12. Three amusement parks charge an entrance fee and a fee for each ride. The total cost for x rides at Extreme Fun is given by the function $f(x) = 5x + 12$. At Rides Galore, the entrance fee is $30 and the total cost of 4 rides is $42. The total cost of rides at Coasters and More is given by $c(x) = \{(0, 10), (1, 16), (2, 22)\}$. Which of the following correctly lists the amusement parks from least cost to greatest cost based on the total cost of 8 rides?

Ⓐ Extreme Fun, Rides Galore, Coasters and More

Ⓑ Rides Galore, Extreme Fun, Coasters and More

Ⓒ Rides Galore, Coasters and More, Extreme Fun

Ⓓ Coasters and More, Extreme Fun, Rides Galore

© Houghton Mifflin Harcourt Publishing Company

Step It Out

Learn the Math

EXAMPLE 1

A. Is $g(x) = \frac{2}{3}x + \frac{2}{3}$ the inverse of $f(x) = \frac{3}{2}x - 1$?

Determine whether $f(g(x)) = x$ and $g(f(x)) = x$.

$$f(g(x)) = f\left(\frac{2}{3}x + \frac{2}{3}\right) \qquad\qquad g(f(x)) = g\left(\frac{3}{2}x - 1\right)$$

$$= \frac{3}{2}\left(\frac{2}{3}x + \frac{2}{3}\right) - 1 \qquad\qquad = \frac{2}{3}\left(\frac{3}{2}x - 1\right) + \frac{2}{3}$$

$$= x + 1 - 1 \qquad\qquad\qquad = x - \frac{2}{3} + \frac{2}{3}$$

$$= x \qquad\qquad\qquad\qquad\qquad = x$$

Since $f(g(x)) = x$ and $g(f(x)) = x$, function g is the inverse of function f.

B. Is $g(x) = -\frac{1}{2}x + 3$ the inverse of $f(x) = -2x - 3$?

Determine whether $f(g(x)) = x$ and $g(f(x)) = x$.

$$f(g(x)) = f\left(-\frac{1}{2}x + 3\right)$$

$$= -2\left(-\frac{1}{2}x + 3\right) - 3$$

$$= x - 6 - 3$$

$$= x - 9$$

Since $f(g(x)) \neq x$, you do not need to evaluate $g(f(x))$. Function g is not the inverse of function f.

Do the Math

A. Is $g(x) = \frac{1}{2}x - 2$ the inverse of $f(x) = 2x + 1$?

$f(g(x)) = f\left(\frac{1}{2}x - 2\right)$

$g(f(x)) = g(2x + 1)$

$= \boxed{}\left(\frac{1}{2}x - 2\right) + \boxed{}$

$= \boxed{}(2x + 1) - \boxed{}$

$= \boxed{} - \boxed{} + \boxed{}$

$= \boxed{} + \boxed{} - \boxed{}$

$= \boxed{}$

$= \boxed{}$

Since $f(g(x))\ \boxed{}\ x$ and $g(f(x))\ \boxed{}\ x$, function g _____ the inverse of function f.

B. Is $g(x) = \frac{1}{5}x + \frac{2}{5}$ the inverse of $f(x) = 5x - 2$?

$f(g(x)) = f\left(\frac{1}{5}x + \frac{2}{5}\right)$

$g(f(x)) = g(5x - 2)$

$= \boxed{}\left(\frac{1}{5}x + \frac{2}{5}\right) - \boxed{}$

$= \boxed{}(5x - 2) + \boxed{}$

$= \boxed{} + \boxed{} - \boxed{}$

$= \boxed{} - \boxed{} + \boxed{}$

$= \boxed{}$

$= \boxed{}$

Since $f(g(x))\ \boxed{}\ x$ and $g(f(x))\ \boxed{}\ x$, function g _____ the inverse

of function f.

Name _____

LESSON 5.4
More Practice

ONLINE
Video Tutorials and
Interactive Examples

1. Use the function in the table.

x	f(x)
0	−4
3	−2
6	0
9	2

A. Function g is the inverse of function f. Complete the table of values for g(x).

x	g(x)

B. The function $f(x) = \frac{2}{3}x - 4$ is represented in the table. Find an equation for g(x).

_____

_____

_____

_____

2. Use the set of ordered pairs to answer the questions.

$$f(x) = \left\{(-8, 0), (-4, 3), (0, 6), (4, 9), (8, 12)\right\}$$

A. What is the function rule modeled by the ordered pairs?

_____

B. What is the function rule for the inverse of f?

_____

_____

_____

_____

3. Verify that $g(x) = 2x - 8$ is the inverse of $f(x) = \frac{1}{2}x + 4$.

_____

_____

_____

_____

4. Which functions shown in the graph are inverses of each other? Explain how you know.

_____

_____

_____

_____

_____

5. The amount of water, in gallons, remaining in a tank x minutes after the plug is removed is given by the function $w(x) = -4x + 200$. Write the inverse of function w and explain what the inverse function represents.

_____

_____

_____

_____

6. Reason What is the relationship between the slopes of linear functions that are inverses of each other? Explain your reasoning and give an example to support your answer.

_____

_____

_____

_____

7. The function $f(x) = 5x - 25$ gives the profit Janna makes from a craft sale, where x is the number of pottery bowls she sells. Which function is the inverse of function f?

Ⓐ $g(x) = x + 25$

Ⓑ $g(x) = x - 5$

Ⓒ $g(x) = \frac{1}{5}x + 5$

Ⓓ $g(x) = \frac{1}{5}x + 25$

8. Function g is the inverse of $f(x) = \frac{3}{4}x + \frac{1}{2}$. If the equation for g is written as $g(x) = ax + b$, what are the values of a and b?

Ⓐ $a = -\frac{3}{4}, b = -\frac{1}{2}$

Ⓑ $a = \frac{4}{3}, b = -\frac{2}{3}$

Ⓒ $a = -\frac{4}{3}, b = \frac{2}{3}$

Ⓓ $a = -\frac{3}{4}, b = 2$

Step It Out

Learn the Math

EXAMPLE 1 The scatter plot for the data of ice cream sales is shown. Estimate a line of best fit for the data.

Choose any two points that look like they would be on a line through the data: (50, 55) and (90, 195).

Use the two points to calculate the slope:

$$m = \frac{195 - 55}{90 - 50} = \frac{140}{40} = \frac{7}{2}.$$

Use the point-slope form to write an equation. Use either of the two points used to determine the slope for (x_1, y_1) in the formula.

$$y - 195 = \frac{7}{2}(x - 90) \rightarrow y = \frac{7}{2}x - 120$$

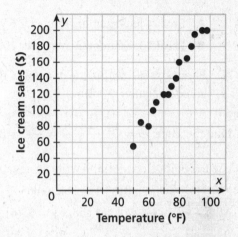

In this situation, the slope suggests that for every 1 degree rise in temperature, the number of ice cream sales increases by 3.5.

Do the Math

The scatter plot for the data relating the temperature to the amount of Ava's gas bill is shown. Estimate a line of best fit for the data.

The scatter plot shows a _____

correlation. As the temperature increases, the monthly

gas bill _____.

Use the points (15, 260) and (70, 40) to find the slope

of the line of best fit:

$$m = \frac{260 - \boxed{}}{15 - \boxed{}} = \frac{\boxed{}}{\boxed{}} = \boxed{}.$$

Use the point-slope form to write an equation:

$$y - \boxed{} = \boxed{}\left(x - \boxed{}\right).$$

The line in slope-intercept form is $y = \boxed{}x + \boxed{}$. For approximately every 1 degree rise in temperature,

Ava's gas bill _____ by approximately $\boxed{}$.

Learn the Math

EXAMPLE 2 The scatter plot and line of fit show how Joe's monthly rent increases over the years. The domain of the model is $1 \leq x \leq 8$.

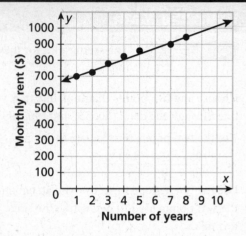

A. Predict Joe's monthly rent after 6 years.

B. Predict Joe's monthly rent after 10 years.

A. Because 6 falls within the domain of the model, this is an *interpolation* problem.

Find the slope: $m = \dfrac{945 - 700}{8 - 1} = \dfrac{245}{7} = 35$.

Use the point-slope form to write an equation. Then rewrite the equation in slope-intercept form.

$y - 945 = 35(x - 8) \rightarrow y = 35x + 665$

After 6 years, Joe will pay about $y = 35(6) + 665 = \$875$ per month in rent.

B. The same model can be used to predict Joe's monthly rent after 10 years. Because 10 falls outside of the domain of the model, this is an *extrapolation* problem.

After 10 years, Joe will pay about $y = 35(10) + 665 = \$1015$ per month in rent.

Do the Math

The scatter plot and line of fit for Grant's credit card balance are shown. Predict Grant's balance after 5 months and after 10 months.

The domain of the model is $\boxed{} \leq x \leq \boxed{}$.

Because 5 falls _____ the domain,

predicting the balance after 5 months is an example

of _____. Because 10 falls

_____ the domain, predicting the balance

after 10 months is an example of _____.

Use the points $(1, 3700)$ and $(9, 1300)$ to find the slope:

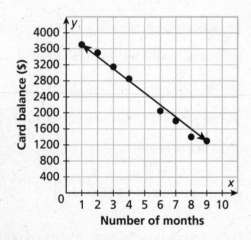

$m = \dfrac{3700 - \boxed{}}{1 - \boxed{}} = \dfrac{\boxed{}}{\boxed{}} = \boxed{}$. Write an equation in point-slope form:

$y - \boxed{} = \boxed{}\left(x - \boxed{}\right)$. The line in slope-intercept form is $y = \boxed{} x + \boxed{}$.

Grant's balance after 5 months is about $\$\boxed{}$. Grant's balance after 10 months will be about $\$\boxed{}$.

Name _____

Describe the type of correlation in the data. Justify your answer.

1.

x	−3	1	0	4	7	9	13
y	3	3	7	11	17	23	36

2.

x	−7	−2	3	8	13	23	38
y	52	39	40	27	19	−3	−9

For each graph, estimate the value of the correlation coefficient *r*. Tell whether it would be *close to −1*, *close to −0.5*, *close to 0*, *close to 0.5*, or *close to 1*.

3.

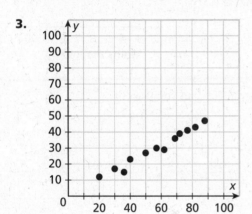

4.

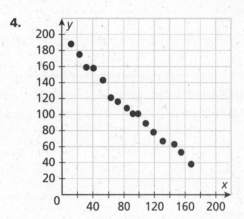

5.

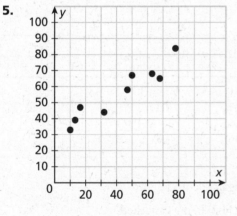

6.

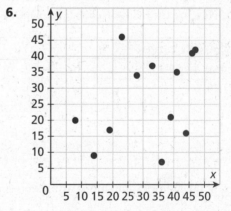

7. Math on the Spot The scatter plot shows a relationship between the total amount of hours worked by a waiter and the total amount he earned in tips. Based on this relationship, predict the total amount he will earn in tips if he works 8 hours.

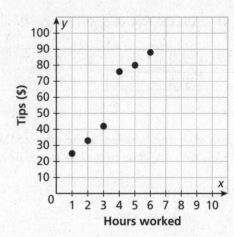

_____

_____

_____

_____

8. Open Ended When writing the equation of a line of fit, what strategies can you use to pick two points from which to write the equation?

_____

_____

_____

_____

_____

9. Use Structure Melanie conducted a survey to determine whether there is a correlation between the number of children in a family and the number of pets in the family. How are the data correlated? Explain.

Number of children	1	3	3	2	1	4	3	2	2
Number of pets	4	2	0	4	0	2	5	0	6

_____

_____

_____

10. Which of the following situations would you expect to have a negative correlation?

Ⓐ amount of snow in inches from a storm and the chance of school being cancelled

Ⓑ the number of minutes studying for a math test and the grade on the math test

Ⓒ number of miles driven in a car and the gallons of gasoline in the tank

Ⓓ the chance of rain tomorrow and the number of text messages sent tomorrow

Step It Out

Learn the Math

EXAMPLE 1 ▶ Ms. Prada asked the students in her math class to keep track of the amount of time they spent studying throughout a unit. She entered that data, along with the students' unit test scores, in the table below.

Hours per week spent studying	0	2.5	4	5	5.5	8	10
Score on unit test (percent)	30	50	61	73	68	82	95

Use a statistical software package and linear regression to find an equation for the line of best fit for the data. Use the number of hours for x_1 and the score for y_1. The linear regression feature will yield the information on the right.

From the regression, the equation of the approximate line of best fit is $y = 6.301x + 34.068$.

The correlation coefficient r is about 0.98, which indicates a very strong correlation between the amount of time students spent studying and their scores on the unit test. Therefore, the line fits the data well and can be used to make predictions.

$\checkmark \ y_1 \sim mx_1 + b$

Statistics   Residuals
$r^2 = 0.9686$ e_1 PLOT
$r = 0.9842$

Parameters
$m = 6.30075$ $b = 34.0677$

Do the Math

Ms. Prada decides to compare her students' missing assignments and their homework grades. The table shows the data she collected.

Number of missing assignments	0	1	3	4	5	8	10
Homework grade (percent)	100	90	75	70	67	59	55

Use a statistical software package and linear regression to find an equation for the line of best fit for the data. Use the _____ for x_1 and the _____ for y_1.

The equation of the approximate line of best fit is $y = \boxed{} x + \boxed{}$.

The correlation coefficient is approximately $\boxed{}$, which indicates a _____ correlation.

This line _____ be used to make predictions.

Learn the Math

EXAMPLE 2 ▶ The data show the prices of houses, in thousands, and their areas, in square feet.

Area (square feet)	1050	1400	1495	1600	1710	1850	2350
Price ($1000s)	200	250	220	300	280	310	400

Use a statistical software package to find the equation of the line of best fit for the data. Interpret the correlation coefficient. Then use the regression plot with the line of best fit to estimate the price of a house that is 2000 square feet.

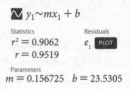

$y_1 \sim mx_1 + b$

Statistics
$r^2 = 0.9062$
$r = 0.9519$

Residuals
e_1 **PLOT**

Parameters
$m = 0.156725$ $b = 23.5305$

Using the area for x_1 and the price for y_1, the approximate equation for the line of best fit is
$y = 0.157x + 23.531$.

The correlation coefficient is about 0.95, which indicates that this equation is a good fit for the data and can be used to make predictions.

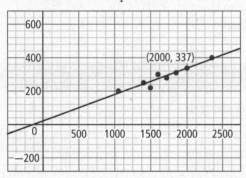

The price of a 2000-square-foot house is approximately $337,000.

Do the Math

Home prices in Denver have been increasing over the last several years. The data show the median sale prices in January of every year since 2012. Use a statistical software package to find the equation of the line of best fit for the data. Interpret the correlation coefficient. Then use the regression plot with the line of best fit to estimate the median sale price of a house in Denver in 2019.

Year	2012	2013	2014	2015	2016	2017	2018
Median sale price ($1000s)	212	249	255	285	327	359	402

For each table of data, compare the two given lines of fit. Identify which line is a better fit by calculating and plotting the residuals.

1.
x	3	6	9	12
y	0	17	11	24

$y = 2.2x - 3.5$
$y = 2.8x - 3$

2.
x	1	2	3	4
y	5	7	6	9

$y = 1.1x + 4$
$y = x + 5$

3.
x	2	4	6	8
y	197	140	150	126

$y = -11x + 205$
$y = -10x + 204$

For each table of data, compare the two given lines of fit. Identify which line is a better fit by calculating the sum of the squared residuals.

4.
x	1	2	3	4
y	205	175	234	268

$y = 14.4x + 157$
$y = 12.4x + 159$

5.
x	1	2	3	4
y	20	28	42	70

$y = 16x - 1$
$y = 16.4x - 1$

6.
x	2	4	6	8
y	210	176	133	101

$y = -18.5x + 247.5$
$y = -18x + 245.5$

7. Use the data shown and the line of fit $y = 4x + 5$ to complete the problem.

x	2	4	6	8	10	12	14
y	14	20	31	38	47	55	63

Use a spreadsheet to create a table like the one shown.

	A	B	C	D	E
1	x	y (Actual)	y (Predicted)	Residual	Residual Squared
2	2	14			
3	4	20			
4	6	31			
5	8	38			
6	10	47			
7	12	55			
8	14	63			
9					

A. What formulas could you enter into cells C2, D2, and E2 to calculate the predicted y-value, the residual, and the residual squared, respectively?

_____

B. Interpret the meaning of the sum of the squared residuals.

_____

8. **Math on the Spot** The table shows the number of passes received and the number of touchdowns scored during one season for 8 receivers in a high-school football league. Find the equation of the line of best fit. Interpret the meaning of the slope and y-intercept. Use the equation to predict the number of touchdowns scored by a receiver who received 36 passes.

Passes	Touchdowns
25	8
30	10
20	6
18	7
32	8
24	7
30	12
28	9

_____

_____

_____

9. Which statement would help you decide if a line of fit is a good fit for a set of data?

Ⓐ A scatter plot of the x-values and their corresponding residuals is random and loose.

Ⓑ The sum of the squared residuals is close to zero.

Ⓒ The line of best fit passes through the origin.

Ⓓ A scatter plot of the x-values and their corresponding residuals is not random.

© Houghton Mifflin Harcourt Publishing Company

Step It Out

Learn the Math

EXAMPLE 1 Given the arithmetic sequence 27, 22, 17, 12, 7, ..., write a recursive rule and graph the sequence.

Organize the terms in a table.

Position, n	1	2	3	4	5
Term, $f(n)$	27	22	17	12	7

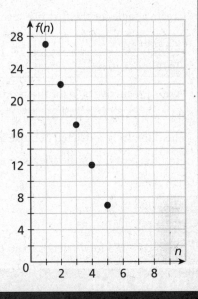

Identify the first term.

$f(1) = 27$

Identify the common difference.

Ensure that

$f(2) - f(1) = f(3) - f(2) = f(4) - f(3) = f(5) - f(4)$.

$22 - 27 = 17 - 22 = 12 - 17 = 7 - 12 = -5$

The common difference is -5.

The recursive rule, $f(n) = f(n - 1) + d$, for $n \geq 2$ for this sequence is $f(1) = 27$ and $f(n) = f(n - 1) - 5$, for $n \geq 2$.

Use the ordered pairs from the table, $(n, f(n))$, to graph the sequence.

Do the Math

Given the arithmetic sequence -4, 13, 30, 47, 64, ..., write a recursive rule and graph the sequence.

Organize the terms in a table.

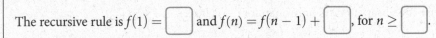

Position, n	1	2	3	4	5
Term, $f(n)$	-4				

The first term is $f(1) = \boxed{}$.

The common difference is $f(4) - f(3) = \boxed{}$.

The recursive rule is $f(1) = \boxed{}$ and $f(n) = f(n - 1) + \boxed{}$, for $n \geq \boxed{}$.

Use the ordered pairs from the table, $(n, f(n))$, to graph the sequence.

Learn the Math

EXAMPLE 2 A group of 12 friends are camping and they decide to rent kayaks. At most, only 10 of the friends want to do the kayak trip. The cost to rent one kayak is $25 and there is a $10 fee for each additional kayak rented. Each kayak fits one person.

Model this situation using an arithmetic sequence.

Create a table for the first five terms.

Kayaks, n	1	2	3	4	5
Total cost, $f(n)$	25	35	45	55	65

Write a recursive rule for the model.

$f(1) = 25$ and $f(n) = f(n-1) + 10$, for $2 \leq n \leq 10$

The domain is restricted because at most 10 of the friends want to go on the kayak trip.

Find the cost if 7 of the friends decide to go on the trip.

$f(5) = 65$

$f(6) = 65 + 10 = 75$

$f(7) = 75 + 10 = 85$

It will cost $85 for 7 friends to go on the kayak trip.

Do the Math

While on vacation, the Martinez family decides to use the telescope at an observatory for stargazing. They are not sure how long they'll stay, but the observatory is open for 12 hours. It costs $15 to use a telescope for 1 hour and $7 for each additional hour.

Model this situation using an arithmetic sequence. Find the cost of using the telescope for 9 hours.

Create a table for the first five terms.

Telescopes, n	1	2	3	4	5
Total cost, $f(n)$	☐	☐	☐	☐	☐

$f(1) = \boxed{}$ and $f(n) = f(n-1) + \boxed{}$, for $\boxed{} \leq n \leq \boxed{}$

The domain is restricted because the observatory is only open for $\boxed{}$ hours.

It will cost $\boxed{}$ to use the telescope for 9 hours.

Write the first five terms of each arithmetic sequence.

1. $f(1) = 13$ and $f(n) = f(n - 1) - 6$, for $n \geq 2$ _____

2. $f(1) = -7$ and $f(n) = f(n - 1) + 2$, for $n \geq 2$ _____

3. $f(1) = 22$ and $f(n) = f(n - 1) + 9$, for $n \geq 2$ _____

4. $f(1) = -11$ and $f(n) = f(n - 1) - 5$, for $n \geq 2$ _____

Write the recursive rule for the sequence shown in each table.

5.

Position, n	1	2	3	4	5
Term, $f(n)$	5	18	31	44	57

6.

Position, n	1	2	3	4	5	6	7
Term, $f(n)$	65	54	43	32	21	10	−1

7.

Position, n	1	2	3	4	5	6	7
Term, $f(n)$	−9	6	21	36	51	66	81

8.

Position, n	1	2	3	4	5	6	7	8
Term, $f(n)$	17	13	9	5	1	−3	−7	−11

Find the 7th term for each of the sequences.

9. $-1, 7, 15, 23, \ldots$

10. $1, 15, 29, 43, \ldots$

11. $-3, 4, 11, 18, \ldots$

12. $29, 17, 5, -7, \ldots$

13. **Open Ended** Write a real-world problem that can be represented by the sequence $f(1) = 1000$ and $f(n) = f(n-1) - 50$, for $n \geq 2$. Evaluate $f(8)$ and explain what it means in the context of your situation.

_____

_____

_____

_____

_____

14. **Critique Reasoning** Joe says that the ninth term of the arithmetic sequence $-2, 9, 20, 31, \ldots$ will have a negative value. Sarah disagrees. With whom do you agree? Explain.

_____

_____

_____

_____

15. An air hockey game costs \$2 for the first round and \$0.50 for each additional round. Write a recursive formula that models this situation. How much will it cost to play 7 rounds?

_____

_____

16. Which arithmetic sequence can be represented by the recursive rule $f(1) = 16$ and $f(n) = f(n-1) - 7$, for $n \geq 2$?

Ⓐ $16, 23, 30, 37, 44, \ldots$

Ⓑ $16, 9, 2, -5, -12, \ldots$

Ⓒ $-7, 9, 25, 41, 57, \ldots$

Ⓓ $-7, -23, -39, -55, -71, \ldots$

17. What is the 5th term of the arithmetic sequence defined by the recursive rule $f(1) = 5$ and $f(n) = f(n-1) + 10$, for $n \geq 2$?

Ⓐ 35

Ⓑ 40

Ⓒ 45

Ⓓ 50

Name _____

Step It Out

Learn the Math

EXAMPLE 1 ▶ Write the explicit rule of the arithmetic sequence in the table.

n	1	2	3	4	5
$f(n)$	18	30	42	54	66

Find the common difference.

$d = 30 - 18 = 12$

$f(n) = f(1) + d(n - 1)$

$f(n) = 18 + 12(n - 1)$, for $n \geq 1$

Graph the sequence.

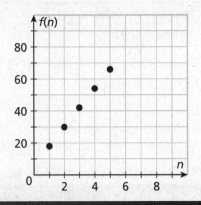

Do the Math

Write the explicit rule of the arithmetic sequence in the table. Then graph the sequence.

n	1	2	3	4	5
$f(n)$	27	33	39	45	51

$d = \boxed{} - \boxed{} = \boxed{}$

$f(n) = \boxed{} + \boxed{}(n - 1)$, for $n \geq 1$

Learn the Math

EXAMPLE 2 ▶ Write the explicit rule of the arithmetic sequence in the graph.

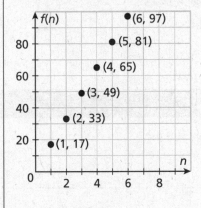

$d = 33 - 17 = 16$

$f(n) = 17 + 16(n - 1)$, for $n \geq 1$

Do the Math

Write the explicit rule of the arithmetic sequence in the graph.

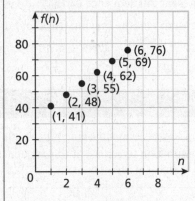

$d = 48 - 41 = \boxed{}$

$f(n) = \boxed{} + \boxed{}(n - 1)$, for $n \geq 1$

Learn the Math

EXAMPLE 3 A T-shirt printing company creates a table that shows the total cost to order T-shirts, including shipping. How much does it cost to order 7 T-shirts?

Number of T-shirts, (n)	1	2	3	4	5	...
Total cost, $f(n)$	27	48	69	90	111	...

You can use an arithmetic sequence to model this situation. Write an explicit rule for the sequence.

$f(1) = 27, d = 48 - 27 = 21$

$f(n) = 27 + 21(n - 1)$, for $n \geq 1$

Evaluate the function when $n = 7$.

$f(7) = 27 + 21(7 - 1) = 27 + 21(6) = 153$

It will cost $153 to order 7 T-shirts.

Do the Math

A bricklayer charges the following amounts for their work. What is the total amount the bricklayer charges for 8 hours of work?

Number of hours, (n)	1	2	3	4	5	...
Total cost, $f(n)$	130	210	290	370	450	...

Learn the Math

EXAMPLE 4 A moving truck rental company charges $29.95 to rent a truck, plus $0.99 for each whole mile driven. Write a function to represent this sequence. What is the total cost to rent a moving truck and drive it 36 miles?

The cost to rent a truck and drive it 1 mile is $29.95 + $0.99 = $30.94. So, $f(1) = 30.94$.

The common difference is 0.99.

A function to represent this sequence is $f(n) = 30.94 + 0.99(n - 1)$, for $n \geq 1$.

To find the total cost to rent the moving truck and drive it 36 miles, find $f(36)$.

$f(36) = 30.94 + 0.99(36 - 1) = 30.94 + 0.99(35) = 65.59$

The total cost is $65.59.

Do the Math

It costs $8 to rent a locker at an amusement park, plus $1.50 for each hour you use the locker. Write a function to represent this sequence. What is the total cost to rent a locker for 6 hours?

© Houghton Mifflin Harcourt Publishing Company

Name _____

LESSON 7.2
More Practice

ONLINE
Video Tutorials and
Interactive Examples

Write a recursive rule and an explicit rule for the arithmetic sequence in the table or graph. Find $f(11)$.

1.

n	1	2	3	4	5
$f(n)$	15	22	29	36	43

_____

_____

_____

2.

n	1	2	3	4	5
$f(n)$	72	61	50	39	28

_____

_____

_____

3.

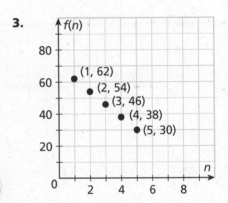

_____

_____

_____

4.

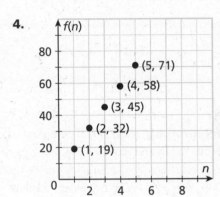

_____

_____

_____

5.

n	1	2	3	4	5
$f(n)$	63	67	71	75	79

_____

_____

_____

6.

n	1	2	3	4	5
$f(n)$	52	75	98	121	144

_____

_____

_____

7. **Open Ended** Write a real-word situation that could be modeled by the arithmetic sequence $f(n) = 100 + 25n$, for $n \geq 1$.

_____

_____

_____

8. **Math on the Spot** The graph shows how the cost of a safari adventure depends on the number of passengers. Write an explicit rule for the sequence of costs.

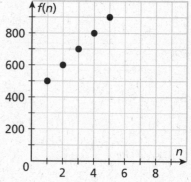

_____

_____

_____

9. **Critique Reasoning** A car rental company charges $30 per day to rent a car plus a $50 deposit. Kevin and Suzanne are writing explicit rules for this sequence. Kevin says the explicit rule is $f(n) = 50 + 30(n - 1)$. Suzanne says the explicit rule is $f(n) = 80 + 30(n - 1)$. Who is correct? Explain your reasoning.

_____

_____

_____

10. A salesperson earns a one-time bonus of $2000 when starting the job and a monthly salary of $3500. Write an explicit rule for the amount of money the salesperson has earned since starting the job. How much money has the salesperson earned after 9 months?

_____

_____

_____

11. An internet service provider charges a one-time fee of $35 to install internet service. The monthly fee for their service is $60. Which function is an explicit rule for the total amount paid for internet service after n months?

Ⓐ $f(n) = 60 + 35(n - 1)$

Ⓑ $f(n) = 35 + 60(n - 1)$

Ⓒ $f(n) = 95 + 35(n - 1)$

Ⓓ $f(n) = 95 + 60(n - 1)$

Name _____

Step It Out

Learn the Math

EXAMPLE 1 ▶ The graph of a piecewise-defined function is shown. Write the function that is graphed.

Find the equation of the first segment.

$$m = \frac{5 - 8}{3 - 0} = -1, b = 8$$

$$y = mx + b$$

$$y = -x + 8$$

Find the equation of the second segment.

$$y = c$$

$$y = 3$$

Find the equation of the third segment.

$$m = \frac{10 - 8}{10 - 6} = 0.5$$

$$y - y_1 = m(x - x_1)$$

$$y - 10 = 0.5(x - 10)$$

$$y - 10 = 0.5x - 5$$

$$y = 0.5x + 5$$

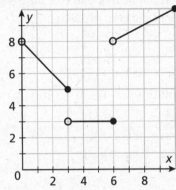

Use the equations for each segment to write the piecewise-defined function with the appropriate domain interval.

$$f(x) = \begin{cases} -x + 8 & \text{if } 0 < x \leq 3 \\ 3 & \text{if } 3 < x \leq 6 \\ 0.5x + 5 & \text{if } 6 < x \leq 10 \end{cases}$$

Do the Math

The graph of a piecewise-defined function is shown. Write the function that is graphed.

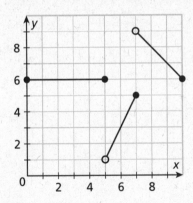

Learn the Math

EXAMPLE 2 — Parking lot A charges $2.50 to park for up to one hour, and $1.50 for each additional hour. Write a function that represents this situation. How much does it cost to park for 5.5 hours?

This situation can be modeled by a piecewise-defined function. Let t represent the time parked, in hours. Let C represent the cost, in dollars.

$$C(t) = \begin{cases} 2.50 & \text{if } 0 < t \le 1 \\ 4.00 & \text{if } 1 < t \le 2 \\ 5.50 & \text{if } 2 < t \le 3 \\ 7.00 & \text{if } 3 < t \le 4 \\ 8.50 & \text{if } 4 < t \le 5 \\ 10.00 & \text{if } 5 < t \le 6 \\ \vdots \end{cases}$$

To find the cost to park for 5.5 hours, find the domain interval that includes 5.5.

5.5 is in the interval $5 < t \le 6$, so $C(5.5) = 10.00$.

It costs $10.00 to park in parking lot A for 5.5 hours.

Do the Math

Parking lot B charges $3.50 to park for up to one hour, and $1.00 for each additional hour. Write a function that represents this situation. How much does it cost to park for 5.5 hours? Which lot should you use if you are going to park for 5.5 hours?

$$C(t) = \begin{cases} \boxed{} & \text{if } 0 < t \le 1 \\ \boxed{} & \text{if } \boxed{} < t \le 2 \\ \boxed{} & \text{if } 2 < t \le 3 \\ \boxed{} & \text{if } 3 < t \le 4 \\ \boxed{} & \text{if } 4 < t \le \boxed{} \\ \boxed{} & \text{if } 5 < t \le 6 \\ \vdots \end{cases}$$

$C(5.5) = \boxed{}$

It costs $\boxed{}$ to park in parking lot B for 5.5 hours. You should park in parking lot $\boxed{}$.

Name _____

LESSON 8.1
More Practice

 ONLINE
Video Tutorials and
Interactive Examples

Evaluate each function for $x = -2$, $x = 1$, and $x = 4$.

1. $g(x) = \begin{cases} 2x - 6 & \text{if } x < 1 \\ x + 8 & \text{if } 1 \leq x < 4 \\ -3x + 2 & \text{if } x \geq 4 \end{cases}$

_____

_____

2. $f(x) = \begin{cases} 4 & \text{if } x < 0 \\ 2x & \text{if } 0 \leq x < 5 \\ -x + 4 & \text{if } x \geq 5 \end{cases}$

_____

_____

Graph each function.

3. $f(x) = \begin{cases} -2x & \text{if } x < 1 \\ 0.5x + 1 & \text{if } x \geq 1 \end{cases}$

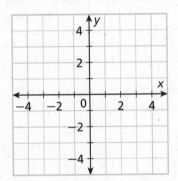

4. $f(x) = \begin{cases} -3 & \text{if } x < 2 \\ x + 2 & \text{if } x \geq 2 \end{cases}$

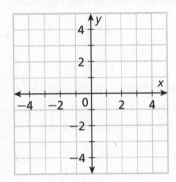

Write a piecewise-defined function for each graph.

5.

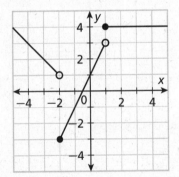

_____

_____

6.

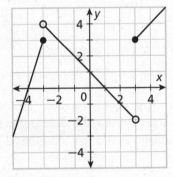

_____

_____

7. A consignment shop is selling a chair for $120. At the end of each week, the price of the chair is decreased by $10 until the chair is sold. Write a piecewise-defined function for this situation. How much does the chair sell for if it is sold 5 weeks and 2 days after it is put on sale?

_____

_____

_____

8. **Math on the Spot** Margaret is competing in a 100-mile adventure race. She kayaks 20 miles in 2 hours, then mountain bikes 75 miles in 3 hours, and finally she runs 5 miles in 1 hour. Sketch a graph of Margaret's distance versus time. Then write a piecewise-defined function for the graph.

_____

_____

9. **Critique Reasoning** Mario reads a sign at a bicycle rental shop. The sign says that bicycle rentals are $25 for the first hour and $20 for each hour after that. He writes the following piecewise-defined function for this situation.

$$f(x) = \begin{cases} 25x & \text{if } 0 < x \le 1 \\ 20x + 5 & \text{if } x > 1 \end{cases}$$

Explain the error in Mario's reasoning. Then write a piecewise-defined function that represents this situation.

_____

_____

_____

_____

10. A hotel rents a large conference room. The rate for the conference room is $30 per hour, or $200 for the entire day. Any duration greater than 6 hours is considered a full day. Write a piecewise-defined function that represents this situation.

_____

_____

_____

_____

11. A baker makes loaves of bread. The baker makes 8 loaves at a time and it takes 45 minutes for each loaf to bake. How many loaves will the baker have finished after 4.5 hours of baking?

Ⓐ 48

Ⓒ 24

Ⓑ 40

Ⓓ 8

Step It Out

Learn the Math

EXAMPLE 1 ▶ Construct the function of the form $g(x) = a|x - h| + k$ for the given graph.

The graph of the parent function $f(x) = |x|$ is translated *right* 4 units, so $h = 4$, and *down* 2 units, so $k = -2$.

The graph is not stretched or compressed, so $a = 1$ or $a = -1$.

The graph *is* reflected over the x-axis, so $a = -1$.

The absolute value function graphed is $g(x) = -|x - 4| - 2$.

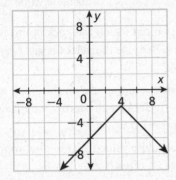

Do the Math

Construct the function of the form $g(x) = a|x - h| + k$ for the given graph.

The graph of the parent function $f(x) = |x|$ is translated

_____ 4 units, so $h = $ ☐, and _____ 1 unit,

so $k = $ ☐.

The slope between $(-4, 1)$ and $(-2, 5)$ is

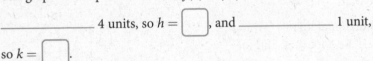

$m = \dfrac{5 - \boxed{}}{-2 - \boxed{}} = \dfrac{\boxed{}}{\boxed{}} = \boxed{}$. Therefore, the graph is

vertically _____ by a factor of ☐ and $|a| = $ ☐. The

graph _____ reflected over the x-axis, so the sign of a is

_____.

The absolute value function graphed is $g(x) = \boxed{} \left| x - \boxed{} \right| + \boxed{}$,

which can be simplified to $g(x) = \boxed{} \left| x + \boxed{} \right| + \boxed{}$.

Learn the Math

EXAMPLE 2 In a game of hockey, Claude hits the puck against a wall of the ice rink. The puck is located at the point $(-8, 2)$ before Claude hits it. The puck banks off the wall at $(-4, 6)$ and comes to a rest at $(4, -2)$. Graph the path described and write an absolute value function that models the path of the puck.

The point at which the puck bounces off the wall, $(-4, 6)$, is the vertex. Because the vertex is given by the point (h, k), $h = -4$ and $k = 6$.

The slopes of the rays on the graph are 1 and -1, so $a = 1$ or $a = -1$. Because the vertex is a maximum and the V-shape opens downward, $a = -1$.

The absolute value function that models the path of the puck is $g(x) = -|x + 4| + 6$.

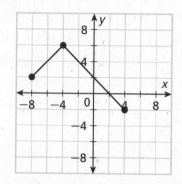

Do the Math

Suppose Claude had hit the hockey puck from $(-8, 2)$ against the opposite wall of the ice rink and it came to rest in the same place. Graph the path described and write an absolute value function that models the path of the puck when it hits the opposite wall.

The opposite wall is represented by the horizontal line $y = -6$. The slopes of the two rays of the graph will be opposites, and the y-coordinate of the vertex will be $\boxed{}$.

To meet these conditions, the vertex, or the point at which the puck bounces off the wall, must be $\left(\boxed{}, \boxed{} \right)$. It follows that $h = \boxed{}$ and $k = \boxed{}$. The slopes of the rays on the graph are $\boxed{}$ and $\boxed{}$, so $a = \boxed{}$ or $a = \boxed{}$. Because the vertex is a _____ and the V-shape opens _____, $a = \boxed{}$.

The absolute value function that models the path of the puck is

$g(x) = \boxed{} \left| x - \boxed{} \right| + \boxed{}$.

Name _____

LESSON 8.2
More Practice

ONLINE
Video Tutorials and
Interactive Examples

Determine the values of *a*, *h*, and *k* for each function.

1. $f(x) = -3|x + 7| - 10$

2. $f(x) = |x - 14| + 8$

_____   _____

Determine the vertex of each function.

3. $f(x) = |x + 9| + 13$

4. $f(x) = |x - 11| - 15$

_____   _____

Write the equations of the following graphs in the form $f(x) = |x - h| + k$.

5.

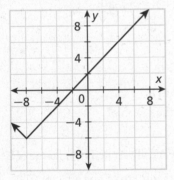

6.

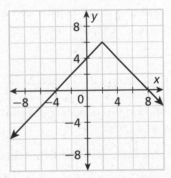

_____   _____

7. **Math on the Spot** Perform each transformation. Then graph.

A. Reflect the graph of $f(x) = |x - 2| - 3$ across the *x*-axis.

B. Stretch the graph of $f(x) = |x| + 1$ vertically by a factor of 2.

C. Compress the graph of $f(x) = |x - 2| + 1$ horizontally by a factor of 0.25.

A.

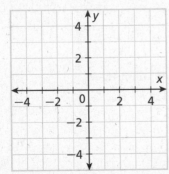

B.

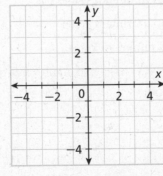

C.

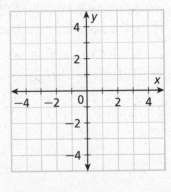

8. **Open Ended** Without graphing, explain how you could obtain the graph of $g(x) = |x - 7| + 5$ from the graph of $f(x) = -|x + 3| - 2$.

_____

_____

_____

_____

9. Gina kicks a ball at $(-1, 0.5)$ and the ball bounces off a wall, represented by the line $y = -2$, at point $(4, -2)$.

   A. Explain how you can use the transformation of the graph $f(x) = |x|$ to write a function to describe the path of the ball.

   _____

   _____

   _____

   _____

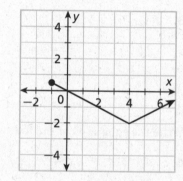

   B. If the ball continues along its path, will it get to Andre, who is standing at $(11, 2)$? Explain how you know.

   _____

   _____

10. Which of the following sequences transforms the graph of $f(x) = |x|$ into the graph of $g(x) = -2|x - 4| + 7$?

   Ⓐ Reflect f across the x-axis, translate 4 units right and 7 units up, and vertically stretch by a factor of 2.

   Ⓑ Reflect f across the x-axis, translate 4 units left and 7 units up, and vertically stretch by a factor of 2.

   Ⓒ Reflect f across the x-axis, translate 4 units right and 7 units up, and horizontally compress by a factor of 2.

   Ⓓ Reflect f across the x-axis, translate 7 units right and 4 units down, and vertically stretch by a factor of 2.

11. The function $f(x)$ has a maximum value of 5 and has no minimum value. Which is a true statement about $g(x) = -f(x + 5) + 5$?

   Ⓐ $g(x)$ has a maximum value but no minimum value.

   Ⓑ $g(x)$ has a minimum value but no maximum value.

   Ⓒ $g(x)$ has a maximum value and a minimum value.

   Ⓓ It cannot be determined whether $g(x)$ has a maximum value or a minimum value.

Step It Out

Learn the Math

EXAMPLE 1 ▸ The absolute value of a number is defined as its distance from 0. So, $|2| = 2$ and $|-2| = 2$ because both 2 and -2 are two units from 0 on the number line.

A. Solve $|4x| + 2 = 6$ algebraically.

$$|4x| + 2 = 6$$

$$|4x| + 2 - 2 = 6 - 2 \qquad \text{Isolate the absolute value expression by subtracting 2 from both sides.}$$

$$|4x| = 4 \qquad \text{Simplify.}$$

This means the expression within the absolute value symbols, $4x$, can either equal 4 or -4 because both $|4|$ and $|-4|$ equal 4.

$$4x = 4 \quad \text{OR} \quad 4x = -4 \qquad \text{Write both cases.}$$

$$x = 1 \quad \text{OR} \quad x = -1 \qquad \text{Divide both sides of each equation by 4.}$$

The solutions to $|4x| + 2 = 6$ are 1 and -1.

B. Solve $|9x| + 8 = 2$ algebraically.

$$|9x| + 8 = 2$$

$$|9x| + 8 - 8 = 2 - 8 \qquad \text{Isolate the absolute value expression by subtracting 8 from both sides.}$$

$$|9x| = -6 \qquad \text{Simplify.}$$

Because absolute value represents a distance, an absolute value expression can never be negative. So, this equation has no solution.

Do the Math

Solve $2 = -4 + |12x|$ algebraically.

$$2 = -4 + |12x|$$

$$\boxed{} = |12x| \qquad \text{Isolate the absolute value expression by adding } \boxed{} \text{ to both sides.}$$

$$\boxed{} = 12x \quad \text{OR} \quad \boxed{} = 12x \qquad \text{Write both cases.}$$

$$\boxed{} = x \quad \text{OR} \quad \boxed{} = x \qquad \text{Divide both sides of each equation by } \boxed{}.$$

The solutions to $2 = -4 + |12x|$ are $\boxed{}$ and $\boxed{}$.

Learn the Math

EXAMPLE 2 The inequality $|ax + b| < c$ where $c > 0$ is equivalent to the compound inequality $-c < ax + b < c$.

We-Ship-It charges $5 to ship any package that is within 0.2 pound of 5 pounds. Use an absolute value inequality to determine the acceptable weights of packages that can be shipped for $5.

The situation can be modeled by $|x - 5| \leq 0.2$, where x represents the weight of the package, because the absolute value of the difference between the actual weight of the package and 5 pounds cannot exceed 0.2 pound.

$$|x - 5| \leq 0.2$$

$-0.2 \leq x - 5 \leq 0.2$	Rewrite the absolute value inequality as a compound inequality.
$+5 \quad +5 \quad +5$	Add 5 to all parts of the inequality.
$4.8 \leq x \leq 5.2$	Simplify.

To be shipped for $5, a package must weigh between 4.8 pounds and 5.2 pounds.

Do the Math

An online math program will score answers as correct if they are within 0.02 of the exact answer. For one problem, the exact answer is 2.83. What answers will the program score as correct?

The situation can be modeled by $\left| x - \boxed{} \right| \leq 0.02$, where x represents the value of a student's answer, because the absolute value of the difference between the student's answer and the exact answer cannot exceed $\boxed{}$.

$$\left| x - \boxed{} \right| \leq 0.02$$

$\boxed{} \leq x - \boxed{} \leq \boxed{}$	Rewrite the absolute value inequality as a compound inequality.
$+ \boxed{} \quad + \boxed{} \quad + \boxed{}$	Add $\boxed{}$ to all parts of the inequality.
$\boxed{} \leq x \leq \boxed{}$	Simplify.

For this problem, a student must enter a value between $\boxed{}$ and $\boxed{}$ for the program to score it as correct.

Solve each equation graphically.

1. $|x + 2| = 5$

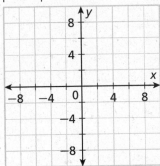

2. $|x - 2| - 4 = -2$

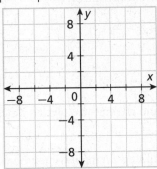

Solve each equation algebraically.

3. $|2 + x| - 3 = 6$

4. $|8x| + 5 = 1$

Solve each inequality algebraically.

5. $|3 + x| - 2 \leq 6$

6. $3|x| + 1 < 16$

7. **Math on the Spot** Solve the absolute value equations.

A. $|x + 5| - 1 = -1$

B. $9 + |x + 2| = 0$

8. The speedometer in Erin's car is accurate within 2 miles per hour. It currently reads 56 mph. Write and solve an absolute value inequality to represent the situation. At what speeds could Erin be driving?

_____

_____

_____

9. Noah writes and attempts to solve an absolute inequality to model the following situation.

Volunteers building a ramp must use boards within 0.35 centimeter of 122 centimeters. What lengths are acceptable for the boards used to build the ramp?

Noah's work:

$$|x - 122| \geq 0.35$$

$$0.35 \geq x - 122 \geq 0.35$$

$$122.35 \geq x \geq 122.35$$

What mistakes did Noah make?

_____

_____

_____

10. Consider the absolute value equation $a|x + b| + c = d$. Write an equation or inequality to describe when the equation has one solution and when the equation has no solutions.

_____

_____

_____

11. Which equation can be solved using the graph?

Ⓐ $|x - 4| - 5 = -1$

Ⓑ $|x + 4| - 5 = 1$

Ⓒ $|x - 4| + 5 = -1$

Ⓓ $|x + 4| + 5 = 1$

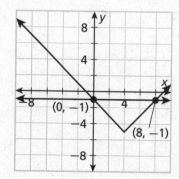

Step It Out

Learn the Math

EXAMPLE 1 Samantha buys square cakes and circular cakes for her birthday party. She buys 10 cakes with a total of 78 pieces. Each square cake is cut into 9 pieces and each circular cake is cut into 7 pieces. How many of each type of cake did Samantha buy?

Define the variables.

Let $x =$ the number of square cakes, and let $y =$ the number of circular cakes.

Model the system algebraically.

$x + y = 10$ $\qquad$ $9x + 7y = 78$

Write the linear equations in slope-intercept form.

$x + y = 10$ $\qquad$ $9x + 7y = 78$

$\quad y = -x + 10$ $\qquad\quad$ $7y = -9x + 78$

$\qquad\qquad\qquad\qquad\qquad y = -\dfrac{9}{7}x + \dfrac{78}{7}$

Graph the system $\begin{cases} y = -x + 10 \\ y = -\dfrac{9}{7}x + \dfrac{78}{7} \end{cases}.$

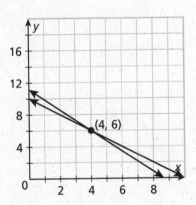

Samantha bought 4 square cakes and 6 circular cakes.

Do the Math

Andrew uses both rectangular and circular baking sheets to make cookies. He can make 177 cookies on his 17 baking sheets. He can fit 9 cookies on each circular baking sheet and 12 cookies on each rectangular baking sheet. How many of each type of baking sheet does Andrew use?

Let x = the number of circular baking sheets and y = the number of rectangular baking sheets. Model the system algebraically.

$x + y = \boxed{}$ $\qquad$ $9x + \boxed{}y = 177$

Write the linear equations in slope-intercept form.

$x + y = \boxed{}$ $\qquad$ $9x + \boxed{}y = 177$

$y = \boxed{} + \boxed{}$ $\qquad$ $\boxed{}y = \boxed{}x + 177$

$$y = \frac{\boxed{}}{\boxed{}}x + \frac{\boxed{}}{\boxed{}}$$

Graph the system $\begin{cases} y = \boxed{} + \boxed{} \\ y = \dfrac{\boxed{}}{\boxed{}}x + \dfrac{\boxed{}}{\boxed{}} \end{cases}$.

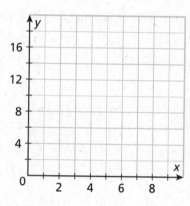

Andrew uses _____ circular baking sheets and _____ rectangular baking sheets.

Solve the system of linear equations by graphing.

1. $\begin{cases} y = x + 5 \\ y = 2x + 6 \end{cases}$

2. $\begin{cases} -3x + y = 1 \\ 3 = -5x + y \end{cases}$

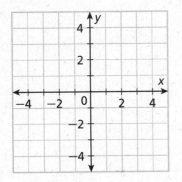

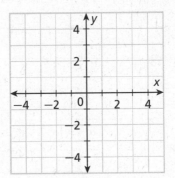

3. $\begin{cases} -x - 3y = -6 \\ 2y + x = 6 \end{cases}$

4. $\begin{cases} y = 2x - 3 \\ -8x + 2y = -2 \end{cases}$

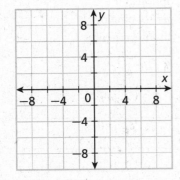

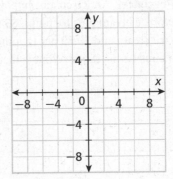

5. $\begin{cases} y = \dfrac{3}{2}x + 5 \\ -2x + 3y = 0 \end{cases}$

6. $\begin{cases} -2x + y = 1 \\ -4x + 8y = -16 \end{cases}$

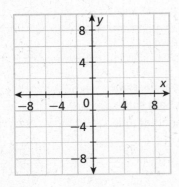

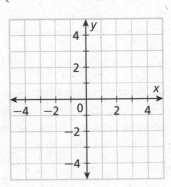

7. **Math on the Spot** Funtime Carnival charges a $3.00 entrance fee and $1.00 per ride. Crazy Carnival charges a $5.00 entrance fee and $0.50 per ride. For how many rides will the total charge be the same at both places? What is that cost? Write a system of equations and solve the system by graphing.

_____

_____

_____

_____

_____

_____

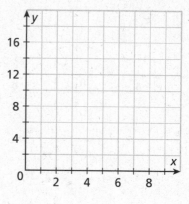

8. **Attend to Precision** An ice cream shop owner considers two pricing options for serving a cup of ice cream plus toppings: $3 for the ice cream and $0.75 per topping or $4.50 for the ice cream and $0.50 per topping. For how many toppings will the price of the ice cream cups be the same? What is that price?

_____

_____

_____

_____

9. **Open Ended** Explain the possible results when solving any system of two linear equations by graphing.

_____

_____

_____

10. Sam and Tyrone are running on a trail. Sam reaches the 4th mile marker at the same time that Tyrone reaches the 1st mile marker. From the 4th mile marker, Sam runs another mile every 10 minutes. From the 1st mile marker, Tyrone runs another mile every 6 minutes. After how many minutes will Sam and Tyrone meet?

Ⓐ 60 minutes

Ⓑ 45 minutes

Ⓒ 36 minutes

Ⓓ 40 minutes

© Houghton Mifflin Harcourt Publishing Company

Name _____

Step It Out

Learn the Math

EXAMPLE 1 Use the substitution method to solve the system of equations.

$$\begin{cases} y = 4x + 5 \\ 6x + 3y = 24 \end{cases}$$

Choose the equation that is already solved for y.

First, substitute $4x + 5$ into the second equation for y and solve for x. Then, substitute $\frac{1}{2}$ for x in either of the original equations and solve for y.

Step 1

$$6x + 3(4x + 5) = 24$$
$$6x + 12x + 15 = 24$$
$$18x + 15 = 24$$
$$18x = 9$$
$$x = \frac{1}{2}$$

Step 2

$$y = 4x + 5$$
$$y = 4\left(\frac{1}{2}\right) + 5$$
$$y = 2 + 5$$
$$y = 7$$

The solution of the system is the ordered pair $\left(\frac{1}{2}, 7\right)$.

Do the Math

Use the substitution method to solve the system of equations.

$$\begin{cases} 4x - 5y = -27 \\ x = 3y - 12 \end{cases}$$

Choose the equation that is already solved for x.

First, substitute $\boxed{}$ into the first equation for $\boxed{}$ and solve for y. Then, substitute $\boxed{}$ for y in either of the original equations and solve for $\boxed{}$.

$$4\left(\boxed{}\right) - 5y = -27$$
$$\boxed{} - \boxed{} - 5y = -27$$
$$\boxed{}\, y - \boxed{} = -27$$
$$\boxed{}\, y = \boxed{}$$
$$y = \boxed{}$$

$$x = 3y - 12$$
$$x = 3\left(\boxed{}\right) - 12$$
$$x = \boxed{} - \boxed{}$$
$$x = \boxed{}$$

The solution of the system is the ordered pair $\left(\boxed{}, \boxed{}\right)$.

Learn the Math

EXAMPLE 2 A community organization sponsored a trip to a baseball game, offering bleacher seats for $20 and grandstand seats for $30. The organization sold $2600-worth of seating and 100 people attended the game. How many tickets did they sell for each type of seat?

Use a verbal model to write each equation. Let x = number of bleacher tickets sold and y = number of grandstand tickets sold.

Number of bleacher tickets sold		Number of grandstand tickets sold		Number of people who bought tickets		Value of bleacher tickets sold		Value of grandstand tickets sold		Total value of tickets sold
	+		=				+		=	
x	+	y	=	100		$20x$	+	$30y$	=	2600

The system of equations is $\begin{cases} x + y = 100 \\ 20x + 30y = 2600 \end{cases}$.

Use substitution to solve. $\begin{aligned} x + y &= 100 \\ y &= 100 - x \end{aligned}$

Substitute $100 - x$ for y in the second equation and solve for x.

$20x + 30(100 - x) = 2600$

$20x + 3000 - 30x = 2600$

$-10x + 3000 = 2600$

$-10x = -400$

$x = 40$

Substitute this value into the other equation and solve for y.

$y = 100 - x$

$y = 100 - 40$

$y = 60$

The community organization sold 40 tickets for bleacher seats and 60 tickets for grandstand seats.

Do the Math

A teen center is sponsoring a trip to the seaside for the day. The center can take 55 people (including drivers) in 8 vehicles. Cars can hold 5 people and vans can hold 8 people. How many of each type of vehicle will the teen center use for the trip? Let x represent the number of cars and y the number of vans.

The system of equations is $\begin{cases} x + y = \boxed{} \\ \boxed{}x + \boxed{}y = \boxed{} \end{cases}$.
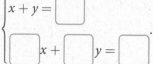

The teen center will use cars and vans.

Name _____

LESSON 9.2
More Practice

ONLINE
Video Tutorials and
Interactive Examples

Solve the system by substitution.

1. $\begin{cases} y = 6 \\ 4x - 8y = 0 \end{cases}$

2. $\begin{cases} y = 3x \\ 7x + 10y = 111 \end{cases}$

3. $\begin{cases} y = x - 4 \\ 6x - 5y = 17 \end{cases}$

4. $\begin{cases} x = 3y + 5 \\ 8x - 3y = -44 \end{cases}$

5. $\begin{cases} x + y = 10 \\ 2x + 7y = 35 \end{cases}$

6. $\begin{cases} 5x + y = 28 \\ 4x - 5y = 34 \end{cases}$

7. **Math on the Spot** A quilt designer is creating a new pattern on the computer and needs to know the coordinates of the point where the line connecting point A to point B will intersect the line connecting points C and D. At what point do the two lines intersect?

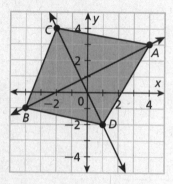

_____

8. **Open Ended** Write one substitution for x and one substitution for y that you could use to solve the system below. Solve the system using both of your substitutions.

$$\begin{cases} 2x + y = 14 \\ x + y = 8 \end{cases}$$

_____

_____

_____

_____

_____

9. Charlie has 6 more quarters than dimes in a jar and a total of $9.20. Which system of equations can be used to determine the number of each type of coin Charlie has if $q = $ the number of quarters and $d = $ the number of dimes?

Ⓐ $\begin{cases} q = d + 6 \\ 10d + 25q = 920 \end{cases}$

Ⓑ $\begin{cases} d = q + 6 \\ 10d + 25q = 920 \end{cases}$

Ⓒ $\begin{cases} d + q = 6 \\ 10d + 25q = 920 \end{cases}$

Ⓓ $\begin{cases} q = d + 920 \\ 10d + 25q = 6 \end{cases}$

Name _____

Step It Out

Learn the Math

EXAMPLE 1 Use elimination to solve the system.

$$\begin{cases} 5x + 3y = 3 \\ x + 3y = -9 \end{cases}$$

Subtract the equations to eliminate y. Then solve for x.

$$\begin{aligned} 5x + 3y &= 3 \\ -(x + 3y &= -9) \\ \hline 4x \quad\quad &= 12 \\ x &= 3 \end{aligned}$$

Substitute 3 for x in either original equation and solve for y.

$$\begin{aligned} 5x + 3y &= 3 \\ 5(3) + 3y &= 3 \\ 15 + 3y &= 3 \\ 3y &= -12 \\ y &= -4 \end{aligned}$$

The solution is $(3, -4)$.

Do the Math

Use elimination to solve the system.

$$\begin{cases} 4x + y = 10 \\ -4x + 2y = 8 \end{cases}$$

Add the equations to eliminate x. Then solve for y.

$$\begin{aligned} 4x + \;\; y &= 10 \\ + (-4x + 2y &= 8) \\ \hline \boxed{}\, y &= \boxed{} \\ y &= \boxed{} \end{aligned}$$

Substitute _____ for y in either original equation and solve for x.

$$\begin{aligned} 4x + y &= 10 \\ 4x + \boxed{} &= 10 \\ 4x &= \boxed{} \\ x &= \boxed{} \end{aligned}$$

The solution is $\left(\boxed{}, \boxed{} \right)$.

Learn the Math

EXAMPLE 2 Solve the system of equations. What does the result tell you about the solution(s) of the system?

$$\begin{cases} 2x - 4y = 9 \\ 2x - 4y = -9 \end{cases}$$

Subtract the equations.

$$\begin{aligned} 2x - 4y &= 9 \\ -(2x - 4y &= -9) \\ \hline 0 &= 18 \end{aligned}$$

The system has no solution.

Do the Math

Solve the system of equations. What does the result tell you about the solution(s) of the system?

$$\begin{cases} -x + 3y = 6 \\ x - 3y = -6 \end{cases}$$

Add the equations.

$$\begin{aligned} -x + 3y &= 6 \\ + (x - 3y &= -6) \\ \hline \boxed{} &= \boxed{} \end{aligned}$$

The system has _____ solution(s).

Learn the Math

EXAMPLE 3   A school sells adult and student tickets for a football game for different prices. Wes buys 2 adult tickets and 4 student tickets and pays a total of $36. Mary buys 4 adult tickets and 4 student tickets and pays a total of $52. What is the price of a student ticket and an adult ticket?

Write a system of equations.

$$\begin{cases} 2a + 4s = 36 \\ 4a + 4s = 52 \end{cases}$$

Subtract the equations to eliminate s. Then solve for a.

$$
\begin{aligned}
2a + 4s &= 36 \\
-(4a + 4s &= 52) \\
\hline
-2a \qquad &= -16 \\
a &= 8
\end{aligned}
$$

Substitute 8 for a in either original equation and solve for s.

$$
\begin{aligned}
2a + 4s &= 36 \\
2(8) + 4s &= 36 \\
16 + 4s &= 36 \\
4s &= 20 \\
s &= 5
\end{aligned}
$$

Adult tickets cost $8 and student tickets cost $5.

Do the Math

Franklin has a total of 18 pennies and nickels worth 78 cents. How many pennies and how many nickels does Franklin have?

Write a system of equations.

$$\begin{cases} p + n = 18 \\ \boxed{}\,p + \boxed{}\,n = 78 \end{cases}$$

Solve the system of equations.

Franklin has $\boxed{}$ pennies and $\boxed{}$ nickels.

© Houghton Mifflin Harcourt Publishing Company

Name _____

Use elimination to solve the system.

1. **Math on the Spot** $\begin{cases} 2x + 5y = 4 \\ 2x - y = -8 \end{cases}$

2. $\begin{cases} 2x - 4y = 12 \\ 2x - 4y = 10 \end{cases}$

_____

_____

_____

_____

_____

3. $\begin{cases} 7x - 3y = -2 \\ 4x - 3y = -14 \end{cases}$

4. $\begin{cases} 4x + 2y = -2 \\ -4x - y = 7 \end{cases}$

_____

_____

_____

_____

_____

_____

5. $\begin{cases} 6x - 5y = 15 \\ -6x + 5y = -15 \end{cases}$

6. $\begin{cases} x + 3y = -9 \\ -x + y = 5 \end{cases}$

_____

_____

_____

_____

_____

_____

7. **Open Ended** Write a system of two linear equations in two variables that you can solve by subtracting the equations and that results in a solution of $(3, 1)$.

_____

_____

_____

8. Kellen is playing a board game with a six-sided number cube. Every time he rolls an even number, he moves ahead 4 spaces. Every time he rolls an odd number, he moves back 1 space. After rolling the number cube 8 times, he has moved ahead a total of 17 spaces. How many times has he rolled an even and an odd number on the number cube?

_____

_____

_____

9. Jillian and Jacob are playing a game where they have to collect blue and yellow tokens. Blue and yellow tokens are worth a different amount of points. Jillian has collected 4 blue tokens and 7 yellow tokens and has 95 points. Jacob has collected 4 blue tokens and 3 yellow tokens and has 75 points. How many points are a blue token and a yellow token worth?

_____

_____

_____

10. **Construct Arguments** Kelly is solving the following system of equations.

$$\begin{cases} 8x - y = 12 \\ -8x - y = -20 \end{cases}$$

She states that the system has no solution because, after adding the equations, she has $0 = -8$. Explain the error Kelly made. Then solve the system of equations.

_____

_____

_____

_____

11. Drew and Nick are selling two different types of raffle tickets for their math club. One raffle ticket is for a computer and the other is for a gift card. The tickets are different prices. Drew sells 8 tickets for the computer and 5 tickets for the gift card and receives $50. Nick sells 8 tickets for the computer and 11 tickets for the gift card and receives $62. How much does each type of ticket cost?

(A) computer tickets $8, gift card tickets $5

(B) computer tickets $8, gift card tickets $11

(C) computer tickets $5, gift card tickets $2

(D) computer tickets $2, gift card tickets $5

9.4

Step It Out

Learn the Math

EXAMPLE 1 ▶ Solve the linear system using the elimination method.

$$\begin{cases} 3x - 2y = -10 \\ 2x + 5y = -13 \end{cases}$$

Study the coefficients. Notice that multiplying the first equation by 5 and the second equation by 2 causes the coefficients of y to be opposites. Similarly, multiplying the first equation by 2 and the second equation by -3 causes the coefficients of x to be opposites. Either of these two options will result in one of the variables being eliminated.

$$\begin{cases} 5(3x - 2y = -10) \\ 2(2x + 5y = -13) \end{cases} \rightarrow \begin{cases} 15x - 10y = -50 \\ 4x + 10y = -26 \end{cases}$$

Add the equations to eliminate y. Then solve for x.

$$\begin{array}{r} 15x - 10y = -50 \\ + (4x + 10y = -26) \\ \hline 19x \qquad = -76 \\ x = -4 \end{array}$$

Substitute -4 for x in either original equation and solve for y.

$$\begin{array}{r} 3x - 2y = -10 \\ 3(-4) - 2y = -10 \\ -12 - 2y = -10 \\ -2y = 2 \\ y = -1 \end{array}$$

The solution is $(-4, -1)$.

Do the Math

Solve the linear system using the elimination method. $\begin{cases} 6x + 4y = -8 \\ 3x + 5y = -19 \end{cases}$

Since 3 is a factor of 6, multiplying the second equation by $\boxed{}$ will result in the coefficients of x being

opposites. In this case, it _____ necessary to multiply the first equation by a number in order to eliminate a variable.

Rewrite the system:

$$\begin{cases} 6x + 4y = -8 \\ \boxed{}(3x + 5y = -19) \end{cases} \Rightarrow \begin{cases} 6x + 4y = -8 \\ \boxed{}x + \boxed{}y = \boxed{} \end{cases}.$$

The solution is $\left(\boxed{}, \boxed{} \right)$.

Learn the Math

EXAMPLE 2 A school is selling tickets to a play. The tickets cost $8 for students and $12 for adults. The total number of tickets sold is 180. The total amount earned from selling the tickets is $1740. How many student and adult tickets were sold?

Write a system of equations.

$$\begin{cases} a + s = 180 \\ 12a + 8s = 1740 \end{cases}$$

Rewrite the first equation in this system by multiplying.

$$\begin{cases} -8(a + s = 180) \\ 12a + 8s = 1740 \end{cases} \rightarrow \begin{cases} -8a - 8s = -1440 \\ 12a + 8s = 1740 \end{cases}$$

Add the equations to eliminate s. Then solve for a.

$$\begin{array}{r} -8a - 8s = -1440 \\ + (12a + 8s = 1740) \\ \hline 4a = 300 \\ a = 75 \end{array}$$

Substitute 75 for a in either original equation and solve for s.

$$a + s = 180$$
$$75 + s = 180$$
$$s = 105$$

75 adult tickets and 105 student tickets were sold for the play.

Do the Math

Jessica sells small and large flower arrangements. One month, she sold 16 small and 7 large arrangements and earned $485. Another month, she sold 12 small and 5 large arrangements and earned $355. What does Jessica charge for small and large flower arrangements?

Write a system of equations.

$$\begin{cases} \boxed{}\,s + \boxed{}\,l = 485 \\ \boxed{}\,s + \boxed{}\,l = 355 \end{cases}$$

Solve the system of equations by first multiplying _____ by a factor in order to eliminate a variable.

Jessica charges $ $\boxed{}$ for a small arrangement and $ $\boxed{}$ for a large arrangement.

Name _____

LESSON 9.4
More Practice

ONLINE
Video Tutorials and
Interactive Examples

Use elimination to solve the system.

1. $\begin{cases} 4x - y = 8 \\ 2x - 3y = -16 \end{cases}$

_____
_____
_____
_____
_____
_____

2. $\begin{cases} -3x + 5y = 14 \\ x - 3y = -6 \end{cases}$

_____
_____
_____
_____
_____
_____

3. $\begin{cases} -2x - 4y = 2 \\ 3x - 5y = 30 \end{cases}$

_____
_____
_____
_____
_____
_____

4. $\begin{cases} 5x + 4y = -2 \\ -4x - 3y = 3 \end{cases}$

_____
_____
_____
_____
_____
_____

5. $\begin{cases} -2x + 6y = 22 \\ -3x + 4y = 13 \end{cases}$

_____
_____
_____
_____
_____
_____

6. $\begin{cases} 5x - 3y = -2 \\ 3x + 7y = -54 \end{cases}$

_____
_____
_____
_____
_____
_____

7. Open Ended Write a system of two linear equations in two variables that you can solve by elimination by multiplying first and that results in a solution of $(2, -5)$.

_____

_____

_____

8. Math on the Spot Doug has 45 coins worth $9.00. The coins are all quarters and dimes. How many of each type of coin does Doug have?

_____

_____

_____

9. Michael and Eric are purchasing music. Each album costs the same amount, and each song costs the same amount. Michael purchases 5 albums and 9 songs and spends $58.50. Eric purchases 2 albums and 20 songs and spends $48. How much do albums and songs cost?

_____

_____

_____

_____

10. Critique Reasoning Geno is solving the following system of equations.

$$\begin{cases} 5x - 2y = 14 \\ 4y + 3y = 21 \end{cases}$$

He states that he can solve the system by multiplying the first equation by 3 and the second equation by 2 and then add the equations. Is he correct? Explain your reasoning.

_____

_____

_____

_____

11. Andrew and Manny are filling buckets of water. Andrew has filled 8 large buckets and 6 small buckets. Manny has filled 14 large buckets and 3 small buckets. The total amount of water Andrew has collected is 58 gallons. The total amount of water Manny has collected is 79 gallons. How much water does a large bucket hold? How much water does a small bucket hold?

Ⓐ A large bucket holds 5 gallons and a small bucket holds 3 gallons.

Ⓑ A large bucket holds 3 gallons and a small bucket holds 5 gallons.

Ⓒ A large bucket holds 40 gallons and a small bucket holds 18 gallons.

Ⓓ A large bucket holds 70 gallons and a small bucket holds 9 gallons.

Name _____

Step It Out

Learn the Math

EXAMPLE 1 It is possible to write a linear inequality based on a graph.

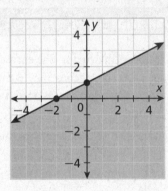

To write the inequality, determine the equation for the boundary line and the inequality symbol.

The boundary line has a y-intercept at -3 and a slope of $-\frac{4}{1}$, or -4. The equation is $y = -4x - 3$.

The shading is below the line, and the boundary line is dashed. The inequality is $y < -4x - 3$.

Check this inequality using substitution.

A point in the solution region should make the inequality true.	A point on the boundary line should make the inequality false. Points on boundary lines that are dashed are not part of the solution region.	A point not in the solution region should make the inequality false.
$(-2, -2)$ is in the solution region.	$(0, -3)$ is on the boundary line.	$(0, 0)$ is not in the solution region.
$(-2) < -4(-2) - 3$	$(-3) < -4(0) - 3$	$(0) < -4(0) - 3$
$-2 < 5$	$-3 < -3$	$0 < -3$
true	false	false

Do the Math

The equation of the line is $y = \boxed{} x + \boxed{}$.

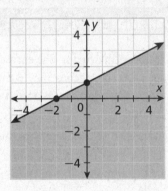

The shading is _____ the line, and the boundary line is

_____.

The inequality is $\boxed{}$.

The point $(0, 0)$ is in the solution region and should make

the inequality _____. Test this point to check that the inequality is correct.

© Houghton Mifflin Harcourt Publishing Company

Learn the Math

EXAMPLE 2 Phoebe has up to $80 to spend every month on fitness. Her favorite classes at the local recreation center are cycling and yoga. Phoebe pays $6 each time she attends a cycling class and $8 each time she attends a yoga class.

Write a linear inequality to describe this situation. Let x represent the number of cycling classes and y represent the number of yoga classes that Phoebe attends. The total cost of cycling classes is $6 \cdot x$, and the total cost of yoga classes is $8 \cdot y$. The inequality $6x + 8y \leq 80$ represents this situation.

Rewrite the inequality in slope-intercept form.

$$6x + 8y \leq 80 \rightarrow y \leq -\frac{3}{4}x + 10$$

Graph the boundary line. The boundary line should be solid because Phoebe can spend $80 on classes. Shade below the line to show the region up to $80.

Phoebe takes 4 cycling classes and decides to take only yoga classes for the rest of the month. How many yoga classes can she attend?

The point $(4, 7)$ lies on the boundary line.

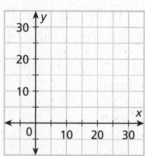

Phoebe checks that this point is a solution to her inequality.

$$6x + 8y \leq 80$$
$$6(4) + 8(7) \leq 80$$
$$24 + 56 \leq 80$$
$$80 \leq 80$$

Since the inequality is true, Phoebe can take up to 7 yoga classes during the rest of the month.

Do the Math

Keri is a fitness instructor. She earns $20 for each cycling class she teaches and $25 for each yoga class she teaches. She wants to earn at least $500 each month. Let x equal the number of cycling classes and y equal the number of yoga classes that Keri teaches in one month.

Write an inequality that describes this situation.

$\boxed{}x + \boxed{}y \geq \boxed{}$.

Graph the inequality.

If Keri teaches 18 cycling classes and 8 yoga classes, will she meet her financial goal? Explain.

Name _____

LESSON 10.1
More Practice

ONLINE
Video Tutorials and
Interactive Examples

Match each equation with the correct graph.

1. $y > 2x + 3$ _____

2. $y \leq 2x + 3$ _____

3. $y < 2x + 3$ _____

4. $y \geq 2x + 3$ _____

A.
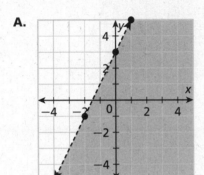

B.
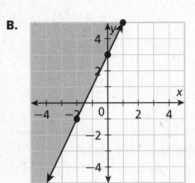

C.
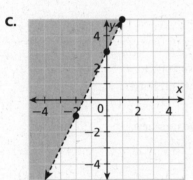

D.
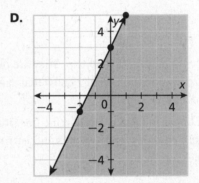

Tell whether each ordered pair is a solution of the inequality.

5. $4x - 2y > 10; (1, 3)$ _____

6. $x + 4y < 0; (0, 0)$ _____

7. $x \geq -9; (-9, 2)$ _____

8. $y < 7; (5, 12)$ _____

9. $3x - y \leq 3; (2, -6)$ _____

10. $-2x - 5y > 7; (-1, -10)$ _____

Determine whether each ordered pair is a solution of the inequality graphed.

11. $(2, -2)$ _____

12. $(0, -2)$ _____

13. $(-6, 0)$ _____

14. $(6, 7)$ _____

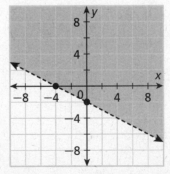

15. Open Ended Use the graph shown.

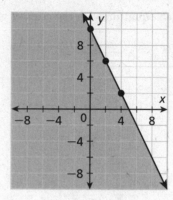

A. What inequality symbol is indicated by the graph? _____

B. Write the linear inequality that is represented by the graph.

_____

C. Describe a situation that might be represented by the graph.

_____

_____

16. Math on the Spot The Hungarian club needs to earn at least $175 from a bake sale to fund their Goulash Festival. They are selling croissants for $2.00 each and loaves of French bread for $5.00 each. Write a linear inequality to describe the situation and graph the solutions.

_____

17. Jude's family is planning a road trip. They are planning a budget and have $600 to spend on accommodations. They know that campsites cost $20 per night and hotel rooms cost $140 per night.

A. Write a linear inequality to describe this situation. Let x represent the number of nights that Jude's family camps and let y represent the number of nights that Jude's family stays in a hotel.

_____

B. Describe the boundary line of the graph of the inequality.

_____

C. Interpret the point $(16, 2)$. Is this a valid solution for the situation?

_____

D. Jude's family wants to take the longest vacation possible. Suggest a solution.

_____

18. Which inequality has the same graph as the inequality $-6x + y > 20$?

Ⓐ $-6x + y < -20$ Ⓒ $y > -6x + 20$

Ⓑ $y > 6x + 20$ Ⓓ $y < 6x + 20$

19. Which ordered pair is NOT in the solution region of the inequality $\frac{1}{2}x + 4y \leq 8$?

Ⓐ $(0, 2)$ Ⓒ $(0, 16)$

Ⓑ $(16, 0)$ Ⓓ $(8, 1)$

Step It Out

Learn the Math

EXAMPLE 1 ▷ Use the graph to write a system of linear inequalities and identify the solution region.

The solution region is the region where the shading for the two inequalities in the system overlap.

Identify the y-intercept and the slope of each of the boundary lines. Then write the equation of each boundary line in slope-intercept form. $y = 3x + 6$ and $y = -2x - 4$

Use the direction of the shading and whether the boundary lines are solid or dashed to write the system of inequalities.

$$\begin{cases} y \le 3x + 6 \\ y > -2x - 4 \end{cases}$$

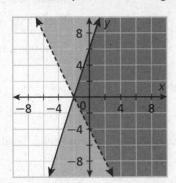

The point $(0, 0)$ is in the overlapping shaded region. The table verifies that this is the only region that satisfies the system.

Point	$y \le 3x + 6$	$y > -2x - 4$	$\begin{cases} y \le 3x + 6 \\ y > -2x - 4 \end{cases}$
$(0, 0)$	True	True	True
$(0, 10)$	False	True	False
$(-6, 0)$	False	False	False
$(0, -8)$	True	False	False

Do the Math

Use the graph to write a system of linear inequalities.

The boundary lines in slope-intercept form are

$y = \boxed{}x + \boxed{}$ and $y = \boxed{}x - \boxed{}$.

The system of inequalities is: $\begin{cases} \boxed{} \\ \boxed{} \end{cases}$.

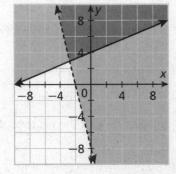

Which of the following points is in the solution region of the system: $(-6, 0)$, $(0, 0)$, $(0, 6)$, or $(-6, 6)$?

The point $\left(\boxed{}, \boxed{} \right)$ satisfies the system of linear inequalities.

Learn the Math

EXAMPLE 2 Victor is attending a local fair and wants to go on at least 12 rides. The spinning rides cost $2.00 each, and the roller coasters cost $3.00 each. Victor has $30. Write a system of inequalities and create a graph to model all the combinations of spinning rides and roller coasters Victor can ride.

Let $x =$ the number of spinning rides and let $y =$ the number of roller coasters.

$$\begin{cases} x + y \geq 12 \\ 2x + 3y \leq 30 \end{cases} \Rightarrow \begin{cases} y \geq 12 - x \\ y \leq -\frac{2}{3}x + 10 \end{cases}$$

Both boundary lines are solid. Shade above $y = 12 - x$ and shade below $y = -\frac{2}{3}x + 10$.

Although there are points with fractional coordinates included in the overlapping shaded region, it only makes sense for Victor to ride whole numbers of rides. The ordered pairs in the form of (spinning rides, roller coasters) show the numbers of rides Victor can ride: $(6, 6)$, $(7, 5)$, $(8, 4)$, $(9, 3)$, $(9, 4)$, $(10, 2)$, $(10, 3)$, $(11, 1)$, $(11, 2)$, $(12, 0)$, $(12, 1)$, and $(12, 2)$.

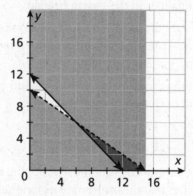

Do the Math

The director of a summer camp is planning a pizza and movie night. She has $110 and plans to buy at least 12 pizzas. Small pizzas cost $8.00, and large pizzas cost $10.00. Write a system and create a graph to model all the combinations of small and large pizzas the director can buy.

Let $x =$ the number of small pizzas and $y =$ the number of large pizzas.

$$\begin{cases} x + y \boxed{} 12 \\ \boxed{}x + \boxed{}y \leq \boxed{} \end{cases} \Rightarrow \begin{cases} \boxed{} \\ \boxed{} \end{cases}$$

For the first line, plot the y-intercept at $\boxed{}$ and use the slope to plot the next point at $\left(\boxed{}, \boxed{}\right)$. Make the line _____ and shade _____ the line. For the second line, plot the y-intercept at $\boxed{}$ and use the slope to plot the next point at $\left(\boxed{}, \boxed{}\right)$. Make the line _____ and shade _____ the line.

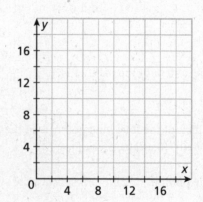

It only makes sense for the director to order _____.
The ordered pairs in the form of (small pizzas, large pizzas) that show the numbers of pizzas she can order are

_____

Name _____

Write a system of inequalities for each graph.

1.

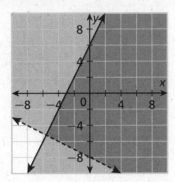

2.

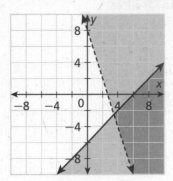

_____   _____

Graph each system of linear inequalities.

3. $\begin{cases} y \geq 4 \\ x < -2 \end{cases}$

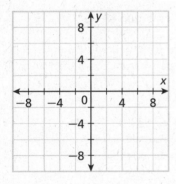

4. $\begin{cases} 4x + 5y \leq 40 \\ y < 3x - 4 \end{cases}$

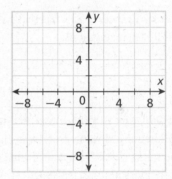

5. Math on the Spot Graph the following systems of linear inequalities.

A. $\begin{cases} y \geq x + 2 \\ y \leq x - 3 \end{cases}$

B. $\begin{cases} y < x + 3 \\ y \geq x - 1 \end{cases}$

C. $\begin{cases} y \geq -\dfrac{1}{3}x + 1 \\ y \geq -\dfrac{1}{3}x - 2 \end{cases}$

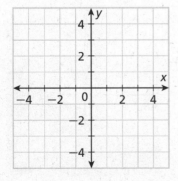

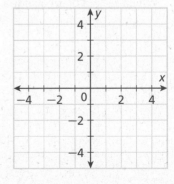

© Houghton Mifflin Harcourt Publishing Company

6. **Open Ended** Write a system of linear inequalities where the solution region lies entirely within Quadrant I.

_____

7. **Critique Reasoning** Frances is trying to determine whether the pair $(3, -2)$ is a solution of the system of linear inequalities.

$$\begin{cases} 2x - 4y \geq 8 \\ 3x + 2y < 5 \end{cases}$$

Her work is shown below:

$2x - 4y \geq 8$ $3x + 2y = 5$

$2(3) - 4(-2) \overset{?}{\geq} 8$ $3(3) + 2(-2) \overset{?}{=} 5$

$6 + 8 \overset{?}{\geq} 8$ $9 - 4 \overset{?}{=} 5$

$14 \geq 8$ $5 = 5$

$(3, -2)$ _satisfies both inequalities, so it is a solution._

Explain the error Frances made. Correctly determine whether $(3, -2)$ is a solution of the system of linear inequalities.

_____

8. Ursula is participating in a fundraiser, selling calendars and mugs. She is trying to sell at least 50 items and wants to raise at least $140.00. The calendars cost $10.00 each, and the mugs cost $7.00 each. Which system of inequalities models the possible number of calendars and mugs Ursula can sell?

Ⓐ $\begin{cases} x + y \geq 50 \\ 7x + 10y \geq 140 \end{cases}$ Ⓒ $\begin{cases} x + y \geq 140 \\ 7x + 10y \geq 50 \end{cases}$

Ⓑ $\begin{cases} x + y \geq 50 \\ 7x + 10y \leq 140 \end{cases}$ Ⓓ $\begin{cases} x + y \geq 140 \\ 7x + 10y \leq 50 \end{cases}$

9. Which system of inequalities is shown by the graph?

Ⓐ $\begin{cases} y \geq -x + 3 \\ y > \frac{1}{2}x - 2 \end{cases}$ Ⓒ $\begin{cases} y \geq -x + 3 \\ y < \frac{1}{2}x - 2 \end{cases}$

Ⓑ $\begin{cases} y \leq -x + 3 \\ y > \frac{1}{2}x - 2 \end{cases}$ Ⓓ $\begin{cases} y \leq -x + 3 \\ y < \frac{1}{2}x - 2 \end{cases}$

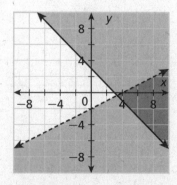

Step It Out

Learn the Math

EXAMPLE 1 ▶ Noah purchases a photograph for $100. The artist assures Noah that the photograph will increase in value at a rate of 5% each year.

This situation can be modeled by an exponential growth function. There is an initial amount and a growth rate. In exponential growth situations, replace the base b in an exponential function with the growth factor.

Exponential function: $f(x) = a(b)^x$

Exponential growth function: $f(x) = a(1 + r)^x$

In the exponential growth function, a represents the initial amount, r represents the growth rate, and x represents time. Write an exponential growth function to represent this situation.

$f(x) = a(1 + r)^x$

$f(x) = 100(1 + r)^x$ Replace a with the initial amount.

$f(x) = 100(1 + 0.05)^x$ Replace r with the growth rate. Make sure to write the percent as a decimal.

$f(x) = 100(1.05)^x$ Simplify the equation.

Use the exponential growth function to find the value of the photograph in 8 years. Use substitution and a calculator to find the value to the nearest hundredth.

$f(x) = 100(1.05)^x$

$f(8) = 100(1.05)^8$ Replace x with the amount of time in years.

$f(8) \approx 147.75$

The value of the photograph in 8 years will be about $147.75.

The y-intercept of the graph of the exponential growth function, $(0, 100)$, shows the initial value of the photograph.

The graph of the exponential growth function shows the continued growth of the value of the photograph over time. Based on the graph, the photograph will have a value of about $265 after 20 years and $432 after 30 years.

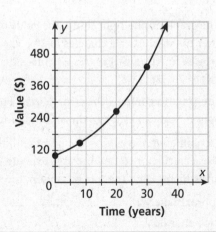

Do the Math

A. You have $500 to start an investment account. The bank offers a savings account with an annual interest rate of 3.5%.

Write an exponential growth function that represents this situation.

$$f(x) = a(1 + r)^x$$

Replace a with the initial amount. Replace r with the growth rate. Make sure to write the percent as a decimal. Simplify the equation. The exponential growth function that

represents the situation is $f(x) = $ [   ].

The graph shows the exponential growth function that represents your situation. The initial investment of $500 is shown on the graph by the _____.

You plan to take your money out of the savings account after 15 years. You can estimate the amount of money in your account at this time by the point with the

[ ]-value of 15.

Use a calculator to find the approximate value of your investment after 15 years. Round to the nearest hundredth. After 15 years, the amount of your

investment is approximately $ [   ].

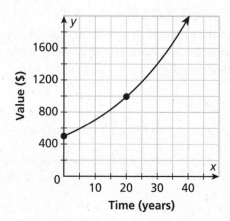

B. When you arrive at your bank, they have a special offer: Earn a 7% interest rate on your initial investment of $500 for the first 5 years, and then a 2% interest rate after that. The exponential growth function that represents the first 5 years of your

investment in this situation is $f(x) = $ [   ].

Use a calculator to find the approximate value of your investment after 5 years. Round to the nearest hundredth. After 5 years, the amount of your investment is

approximately $ [   ].

C. The graph on the right shows the value of your investment after the interest rate changes to 2%. The exponential growth function that represents this situation is $f(x) = 701.28(1.02)^x$.

You want to compare the two options. For the second option, you can estimate the amount of money in your

account after 15 years by the point with the x-value of [ ].

Use a calculator to find the approximate value of your investment. With the second option, the value is

approximately $ [   ]. So, the _____ option is

the better deal.

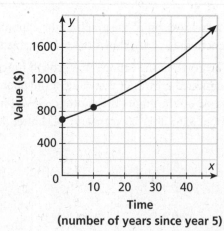

For each function of the form $y = ab^x$, **identify** a **and** b.

1. $f(x) = 3(2)^x$ _____

2. $g(x) = 3^x$ _____

3. $h(x) = 0.5(4)^x$ _____

Identify the characteristics of the function $f(x) = 4(2)^x$.

4. What is the y-intercept of the function? _____

5. What is the domain of the function? _____

6. What is the range of the function? _____

7. As x increases without bound, what will happen to the graph of the function?

_____

8. As x decreases without bound, what will happen to the graph of the function?

_____

9. Create a table of values for each exponential growth function for x-values from -3 to 3.

   A. $g(x) = 4^x$

   B. $f(x) = 2(2)^x$

   C. Based on the tables completed in parts A and B, which function increases at a faster rate, $g(x) = 4^x$ or $f(x) = 2(2)^x$? Explain.

_____

Identify the characteristics of each function graphed.

10.

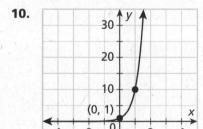

_____

_____

_____

11.

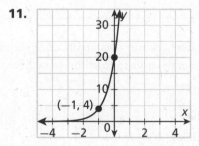

_____

_____

_____

12. Jackson invests \$12,000 in a savings plan that offers 3% annual interest. The exponential growth function $f(x) = a(1 + r)^x$ can represent this situation.

A. What is the value of r? _____

B. What is the value of a? _____

C. Write the exponential growth function that models Jackson's investment.

_____

D. How much will Jackson's investment be worth after 5 years? _____

13. Math on the Spot The original value of a painting is \$1200, and the value increases by 6% each year. Write an exponential growth function to model this situation. Then find the value of the painting in 15 years.

_____

_____

_____

14. An app store opened in 2018, and consumers downloaded one million apps. The owner of the app store predicts that the number of app downloads (in millions) will increase at a rate of about 30% per year.

A. Use $x = 0$ to represent the year 2018. What x-value represents the year 2028?

_____

B. Write an exponential growth function that represents this situation.

_____

C. Use a calculator to estimate the number of app downloads in the year 2028.

_____

D. Is an exponential growth function a reasonable model for this situation? Explain.

_____

_____

15. Your bank offers a savings plan with a 2.5% annual interest. You have \$1000 to invest. Which exponential growth function represents this situation?

Ⓐ $f(x) = 1000(1.25)^x$

Ⓑ $f(x) = 1.25(1000)^x$

Ⓒ $f(x) = 1000(1.025)^x$

Ⓓ $f(x) = 1.025(1000)^x$

16. Choose the statement that describes a characteristic of the graph of the exponential function $f(x) = 4(3)^x$.

Ⓐ The graph includes the point $(0, 3)$.

Ⓑ As x increases without bound, the graph of the function will decrease.

Ⓒ As x decreases without bound, the graph of the function will increase.

Ⓓ The graph has a y-intercept at $(0, 4)$.

© Houghton Mifflin Harcourt Publishing Company

Name _____

Step It Out

Learn the Math

EXAMPLE 1 John plays trumpet in the marching band. He purchased a new trumpet valued at $2500. The value of the trumpet decreases at a rate of 15% each year. What will John's trumpet be worth after 5 years?

Because the value of the trumpet decreases by a given percentage each year, this situation can be modeled by an exponential decay function.

The standard form of an exponential decay function is $f(x) = a(1 - r)^x$. Write the function that models the situation.

$$f(x) = a(1 - r)^x$$

$$f(x) = 2500(1 - 0.15)^x$$

$$f(x) = 2500(0.85)^x$$

Graph the function.

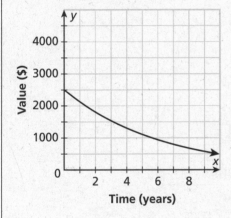

Use the graph to estimate the value of the trumpet after 5 years.

From the graph, the value of the trumpet after 5 years will be about $1100.

Evaluate $f(5)$ to determine the actual value of the trumpet after 5 years.

$$f(x) = 2500(0.85)^x$$

$$f(5) = 2500(0.85)^5$$

$$f(5) = 1109.26$$

The actual value of the trumpet after 5 years is $1109.26.

Do the Math

Maria purchased a new pickup truck that is valued at $25,000. The value of the truck decreases at a rate of 20% each year. What will Maria's truck be worth after 7 years?

Because the value of the truck decreases by a given percentage each year, this situation can be modeled by an exponential _____ function.

The standard form of an exponential decay function is $f(x) = \boxed{}\left(1 - \boxed{}\right)^x$.

The function that models this situation is $f(x) = \boxed{}\left(\boxed{}\right)^x$.

Graph the function.

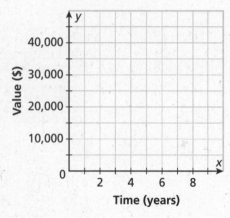

Time (years)

From the graph, the value of Maria's truck after 7 years will be about $\boxed{}$.

Evaluate $f\left(\boxed{}\right)$ to determine the actual value of Maria's truck after 7 years.

After 7 years, Maria's truck will be worth $\boxed{}$.

ONLINE
Video Tutorials and
Interactive Examples

For each function of the form $y = ab^x$, identify a and b.

1. $f(x) = 5\left(\dfrac{1}{2}\right)^x$ $a = \boxed{}$, $b = \boxed{}$

2. $g(x) = 12.75(0.6)^x$ $a = \boxed{}$, $b = \boxed{}$

Graph each function.

3. $f(x) = 8\left(\dfrac{1}{2}\right)^x$

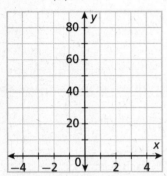

4. $g(x) = 6(0.7)^x$

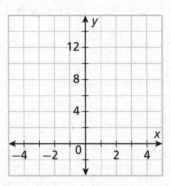

5. $f(x) = 5\left(\dfrac{1}{5}\right)^x$

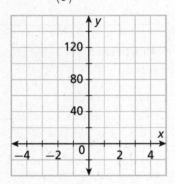

6. $g(x) = 60(0.4)^x$

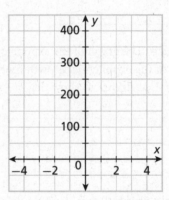

Write a function in the form $f(x) = a\left(\dfrac{1}{3}\right)^x$ that is modeled by each graph.

7.

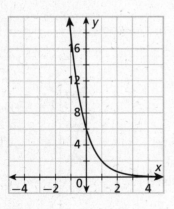

$f(x) =$ _____

8.

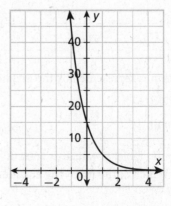

$f(x) =$ _____

9. **Math on the Spot** The population of a town is decreasing at a rate of 2% per year. In 2000 there were 1100 people. Write an exponential decay function to model this situation. Then find the population in 2009.

_____

10. **Open Ended** In Lakeview, 57 families had babies in 2018, and 43 new families moved into the town. Yet statistics show that the population of Lakeview is consistently declining by 3% per year. Explain how this is possible.

_____

_____

_____

_____

11. In Baron, the population is 1600 and decreases at an annual rate of 4% each year. In Manchester, the population is 3600 and decreases at an annual rate of 7% each year. Which town will have the larger population after 10 years? By how many more people?

_____

_____

12. **Use Structure** The graph of the exponential decay function $f(x) = 2\left(\frac{1}{2}\right)^x$ is a reflection of the graph of the exponential growth function $g(x) = 2(2)^x$. This is true because $g(-x) = f(x)$. Use algebra to show that $g(-x) = f(x)$.

_____

_____

_____

13. **Critique Reasoning** Reese says that the function $f(x) = 500(0.15)^x$ models a population that has an initial population of 500 and decreases at a decay rate of 15% each year for x years. Is Reese correct? If not, what is Reese's error?

_____

_____

14. Which function is represented by the graph?

Ⓐ $f(x) = 500(0.5)^x$ Ⓒ $f(x) = 200(0.4)^x$

Ⓑ $f(x) = 500(0.4)^x$ Ⓓ $f(x) = 200(0.5)^x$

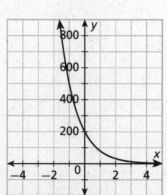

15. A new computer tablet is valued at $600. Its value decreases by an annual rate of 25%. Which of the following equations models the value of the tablet after 5 years?

Ⓐ $f(5) = 600(0.25)^5$ Ⓒ $f(5) = 0.25(600)^5$

Ⓑ $f(5) = 600(0.75)^5$ Ⓓ $f(5) = 0.75(600)^5$

Name _____

Step It Out

Learn the Math

EXAMPLE 1 ▶ The population of a city is 24,000, and the population decreases by 1.5% each year. Write functions to model the annual decrease, the monthly decrease, and the decrease per decade.

Write a function to model the annual decrease.

The value of a is 24,000, and the value of b is $1 - 0.015 = 0.985$.

$f(t) = 24,000(0.985)^t$, where t is the time in years

Write a function to model the monthly decrease.

One month is $\frac{1}{12}$ of a year, so multiply t by $\frac{1}{12}$ in the annual decrease model and then simplify.

$f(t) = 24,000(0.985)^{\frac{t}{12}} = 24,000\left(0.985^{\frac{1}{12}}\right)^t \approx 24,000(0.9987)^t$, where t is the time in months

Write a function to model the decrease each decade.

One decade is 10 years, so multiply t by 10 in the annual decrease model and then simplify.

$f(t) = 24,000(0.985)^{10t} = 24,000\left(0.985^{10}\right)^t \approx 24,000(0.8597)^t$, where t is the time in decades

Do the Math

The population of a different city is 45,600, and the population is decreasing by 2% each year. Write functions to model the annual decrease, the monthly decrease, and the decrease per decade.

The value of a is [ ], and the value of b is [ ].

Annual decrease:

$f(t) = $ [ ]([ ])^t, where t is the time in years

Monthy decrease:

$f(t) = $ [ ]([ ])$^{[\ ]} \approx$ [ ]([ ])^t, where t is the time in months

Decade decrease:

$f(t) = $ [ ]([ ])$^{[\ ]} \approx$ [ ]([ ])^t, where t is the time in decades

Learn the Math

EXAMPLE 2 Brad finds a population of flies in his barn. The initial population of flies is 50. The population of flies increases by a factor of 4 every week. Write a function to model the population. How long does it take for the population to double? When will the population equal 400?

Let x represent the time in weeks. Write a population function $f(x)$ for the flies.

$$f(x) = 50(4)^x$$

To find the time it takes for the population to double, rewrite the function with a base of 2.

$$f(x) = 50(4)^x = 50(2)^{2x}$$

The population doubles when $2^{2x} = 2$, or when $x = \frac{1}{2}$. So the population doubles after $\frac{1}{2}$ week.

Use a graph to find when the population equals 400.

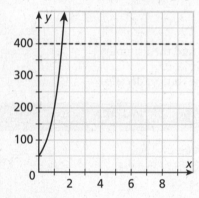

The population equals 400 after 1.5 weeks.

Do the Math

A different barn has an initial population of 200 flies. The population of flies increases by a factor of 4 every week. Write a function to model the population. When will the population equal 1000?

$$f(x) = \boxed{}\left(\boxed{}\right)^{\boxed{}}$$

The population will equal 1000 after about $\boxed{}$ weeks.

Determine the monthly interest rate for each given annual interest rate.

1. 4% annually

_____

_____

2. 9% annually

_____

_____

Each function shows the amount that an initial investment increases or decreases annually. Write a function for each change per month and per decade.

3. $A(t) = 400(1.2)^t$

_____

_____

_____

4. $A(t) = 700(0.97)^t$

_____

_____

_____

5. $A(t) = 250(0.91)^t$

_____

_____

_____

6. $A(t) = 600(1.08)^t$

_____

_____

_____

7. The function $f(x) = 90(16)^x$ describes an exponential growth function, where x is the time in years. How long does it take the initial value to double?

_____

_____

_____

_____

8. The function $f(x) = 150(0.8)^x$ describes an exponential decay function, where x is the time in years. Use a graph to find when the value of the function is equal to 60.

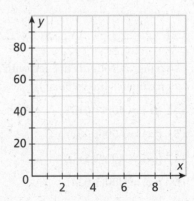

9. **Model with Mathematics** A car is purchased for $20,000. The value of the car decreases at a rate of 20% per year. Write an exponential function to describe the value of the car. Then write a function to describe the depreciation of the car at monthly intervals.

_____

_____

_____

_____

10. The population of fish in a pond is decreasing at a rate of 10% every year. The initial number of fish in the pond is 185. Write a function to describe the population of fish in the pond after x years. Use a graph to find when there will be 100 fish in the pond.

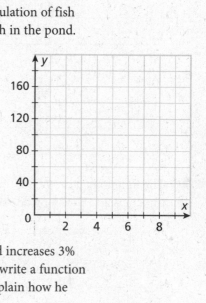

11. **Construct Arguments** Tristan knows that the value of a trading card increases 3% every year. The card is worth $12 when Tristan receives it. He wants to write a function to describe the value of the trading card after each quarter of a year. Explain how he can write this function. What is the function?

_____

_____

_____

_____

12. A savings account is opened with $400 and gains 1.5% annually. Which function best approximates the value of the account after x months?

Ⓐ $f(x) = 400(1.015)^x$

Ⓑ $f(x) = 400(1.001)^x$

Ⓒ $f(x) = 400(1.5)^x$

Ⓓ $f(x) = 400(1.034)^x$

Step It Out

Learn the Math

Exponential functions can be used to model growth or decay in many different situations, such as the growth of a population or the decay of a radioactive isotope over time.

The parent exponential growth function can be written as $f(x) = (1 + r)^x$. The values of this function increase by $100r\%$ from $x = 0$ to $x = 1$, by another $100r\%$ from $x = 1$ to $x = 2$, and so on. For instance, if $r = 0.2$, then the values of the function $f(x) = (1.2)^x$ increase by 20% each time x increases by 1.

Real-world models of exponential functions often include transformations of this parent function, in the form of $f(x) = a(1 + r)^x + k$, where a is the initial value of the function and $y = k$ replaces $y = 0$ as the asymptote of the function's graph.

The table below describes the effects of a and k on the parent exponential function.

Function	General Description	Specific Description
$f(x) = (1 + r)^x + 5$	Adding to the base results in a positive, vertical translation.	translation 5 units up
$f(x) = (1 + r)^x - 2$	Subtracting from the base results in a negative, vertical translation.	translation 2 units down
$f(x) = 12(1 + r)^x$	Multiplying the base by a number with an absolute value greater than 1 results in a vertical stretch.	stretch by a factor of 12
$f(x) = \frac{1}{2}(1 + r)^x$	Multiplying the base by a number with an absolute value between 0 and 1 results in a vertical compression.	compression by a factor of $\frac{1}{2}$
$f(x) = -3(1 + r)^x$	Multiplying the base by a negative number results in a reflection across the x-axis.	stretch by a factor of 3 and reflection across the x-axis

The statements above also apply to the parent exponential decay function $f(x) = (1 - r)^x$. The values of this function decrease by $100r\%$ for each increase of 1 in the x-value. For instance, if $r = 0.2$, then the values of the function $f(x) = (0.8)^x$ decrease by 20% each time x increases by 1.

Learn the Math

> **EXAMPLE 1** Write an exponential growth or decay function to model the following situation.

A scientist is studying how the cells in a petri dish change over time. She begins with a sample of c cells that increase at a rate of $100r\%$ each minute. Write an exponential function to model the situation.

The scientist is studying how the cells change over *time*, so the independent variable is time t, in minutes. Because the cells *increase* at a rate of $100r\%$ per minute, this is an exponential growth function. Use an addition sign in the base of the parent function.

$$f(t) = (1 + r)^t$$

However, there are c cells in the dish when the scientist starts to observe them. So, the initial amount, or a-value, is c. This will create a vertical stretch of the graph of the parent function.

$$f(t) = c(1 + r)^t$$

After t minutes, the petri dish will contain $f(t)$ cells.

Do the Math

Write an exponential growth or decay function to model the following situation.

There is a large population of ducks in Joe's town. Initially, there were d ducks in the town. The population is decreasing at a rate of $100r\%$ per year.

The population of ducks changes over time t, in _____. Because the ducks are _____ at a rate of $100r\%$ each year, this is an exponential _____ function. Use a _____ sign in the base of the parent function.

$$f\left(\boxed{}\right) = a\left(1 \,\boxed{}\, r\right)^{\boxed{}}$$

Initially, there are $\boxed{}$ ducks in the population.

So, the initial amount, or a-value, is $\boxed{}$. This will create a vertical stretch of the graph of the parent function.

$$f\left(\boxed{}\right) = \boxed{}\left(1 \,\boxed{}\, r\right)^{\boxed{}}$$

After t years, the population will contain $\boxed{}$ ducks.

© Houghton Mifflin Harcourt Publishing Company

Given each function $f(x)$, write the transformation of the function as $g(x)$.

1. $f(x) = 3^x$
transformation: up 3 units

$g(x) =$ _____

2. $f(x) = 8^x$
transformation: down 8 units

$g(x) =$ _____

3. $f(x) = (0.95)^x$
transformation: vertical stretch by a factor of 2

$g(x) =$ _____

4. $f(x) = (0.87)^x$
transformation: vertical compression by a factor of $\frac{1}{4}$ and reflection over the x-axis

$g(x) =$ _____

5. The graphs below show the function $f(x) = 5(3)^x$ and $g(x)$.

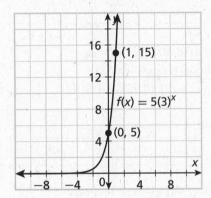

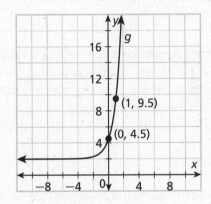

A. Describe the transformation from $f(x)$ to $g(x)$ in words. Then write a rule for $g(x)$.

_____

B. Write a rule for $h(x)$, a transformation of $g(x)$ involving a vertical stretch by a factor of 4 and a reflection across the x-axis.

_____

6. **Math on the Spot** Make a table of values for the function given. Then graph it on the same coordinate plane with the graph of $y = 0.7^x$. Describe the end behavior and find the y-intercept of each graph.

A. $f(x) = 0.3(0.7)^x$

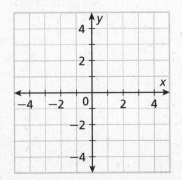

B. $f(x) = -2(0.7)^x$

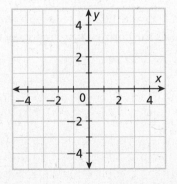

_____   _____

7. Erica's smoothie shop was selling 250 smoothies per day at the end of April. Beginning in May, her shop experienced an increase of 6% per day in the number of smoothies sold.

A. Write a function, $s(t)$, to represent the number of smoothies Erica's shop will sell on day t in May.

_____

B. How many smoothies will Erica's shop sell on day 8 in May?

_____

C. What function would model the situation if Erica had been selling 400 smoothies per day at the end of April?

_____

D. What kind of transformation occurs from the function in part A to the function in part C?

_____

8. Construct Arguments Saul writes the function $f(x) = 200(0.90)^x$ to model the decrease of an initial population of 200 organisms at a decay rate of 10% each hour. He says that if the initial population had been 100 more, the new function would be $g(x) = 200(0.90)^x + 100$. Is Saul correct? Explain why or why not.

_____

_____

9. Construct Arguments Nicole is given the function $f(x) = 3(4)^x - 5$. She says the function $g(x) = -\frac{1}{2}f(x) - 3$ has a horizontal asymptote of $y = 2$. Is Nicole correct? Explain why or why not.

_____

_____

10. The function $g(x)$ is a transformation of $f(x)$. Which equation describes $g(x)$?

Ⓐ $g(x) = -\frac{1}{2}f(x)$

Ⓑ $g(x) = -f(x)$

Ⓒ $g(x) = -f(x) + 6$

Ⓓ $g(x) = -f(x) - 2$

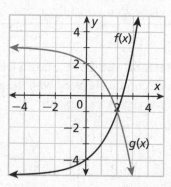

11. The function $k(x) = 6(1.02)^{x-12} - 4$ represents exponential growth. What is the horizontal asymptote of this function?

Ⓐ $y = 6$

Ⓑ $y = -4$

Ⓒ $y = 12$

Ⓓ $y = 0$

© Houghton Mifflin Harcourt Publishing Company

Step It Out

Learn the Math

EXAMPLE 1 A biologist observes two different samples of bacteria. The initial bacterial count for each sample is 100. The table shows the population at different times for Sample 1.

The population of Sample 2 can be represented by $g(x) = 100(1.5)^x$, where x is the time in hours. Which sample has the greatest rate of increase?

Sample 1

x	1	2	3	4	5	6
f(x)	160	256	410	655	1049	1678

From the form of the function, you can see that the rate of increase for Sample 2 is 1.5.

To find the rate of increase for Sample 1, divide consecutive items in the table.

rate of increase $= \frac{256}{160} = 1.6$

The rate of increase for Sample 1 is 1.6, which is greater than the rate of increase for Sample 2.

Do the Math

The biologist observes two other samples of bacteria. The initial bacterial count for each sample is 500. The population of Sample 3 can be represented by $f(x) = 500(1.8)^x$. The population of Sample 4 can be represented by the data in the table. Which sample has the greatest rate of increase?

Sample 4

x	1	2	3	4	5	6
g(x)	800	1280	2048	3277	5243	8389

The rate of increase for Sample 3 is $\boxed{}$.

To find the rate of increase for Sample 4, divide consecutive items in the table.

rate of increase $= \dfrac{\boxed{}}{\boxed{}} = \boxed{}$

The sample with the greatest rate of increase is Sample $\boxed{}$.

Learn the Math

EXAMPLE 2 Compare the initial values of the exponential functions. Which function has the greater initial value?

Function 1

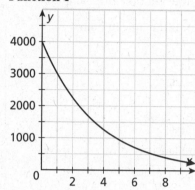

From the graph, the initial value of Function 1 is 4000.

Function 2

x	1	2	3	4
f(x)	3375	2531.25	1898.44	1423.83

To find the rate of decrease of Function 2, divide consecutive items in the table.

rate of decrease $= \dfrac{2531.25}{3375} = 0.75$

To find the initial value, substitute 1 for x, 3375 for $f(x)$, and 0.75 for b in $f(x) = ab^x$ and solve for a.

$f(x) = ab^x$

$3375 = a(0.75)^1$

$a = \dfrac{3375}{0.75} = 4500$

Function 2 has the greater initial value.

Do the Math

Which function has the greater initial value?

Function 3

x	1	2	3	4
f(x)	160	128	102.4	81.92

Function 4

x	1	2	3	4
f(x)	180	108	64.8	38.88

Learn the Math

EXAMPLE 3 A fish population is initially 200. After one year, the population is 320. Determine an exponential function to model these data. Estimate the population after 5 years. How does this compare to a second fish population with 2000 fish after 5 years?

First, find the rate of increase, b. Use this value to write a function to represent the population. Use the function to estimate the population after 5 years.

$b = \dfrac{320}{200} = 1.6, f(x) = 200(1.6)^x, f(5) = 200(1.6)^5 \approx 2097$

The first population is greater after 5 years than the second population.

Do the Math

A bee colony initially has 500 bees. After one month, the population is 700. Determine an exponential function to model this population. A second colony has a population of 6000 after 7 months. Which colony has the greater population after 7 months?

In each pair of exponential functions, determine which has the greater value at the indicated value of *x*.

1. $x = 4$: $f(x) = 5 \cdot 2^x$ and $g(x)$ contains points $(1, 6)$ and $(2, 18)$

_____

_____

_____

_____

_____

2. $x = 3$: $f(x) = 4 \cdot 3^x$ and $g(x)$ contains points $(1, 12)$ and $(2, 24)$

_____

_____

_____

_____

_____

3. The function $f(x)$ is shown in the graph, and the function $g(x)$ is shown in the table. Determine which function has the greater growth rate.

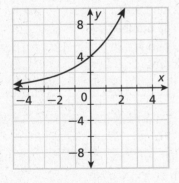

x	g(x)
1	16.8
2	23.52
3	32.928
4	46.0992

_____

_____

_____

_____

4. The function $f(x)$ is represented by the equation $f(x) = 75\left(\frac{1}{5}\right)^x$, and the function $g(x)$ is represented by the table. Which function has the greater initial value?

_____

_____

_____

_____

x	g(x)
1	64
2	51.2
3	40.96
4	32.768

5. The function $f(x) = 3000(1.1)^x$ represents the number of cells in Sample 1 after x hours. The function shown in the table represents the number of cells in Sample 2 after x hours. Which function has the greater growth rate? Which function has the greater number of cells after 5 hours?

x	1	2	3	4	5
$g(x)$	4200	4410	4631	4862	5105

_____

_____

_____

6. **Model with Mathematics** A function $f(x)$ is represented by the graph. Another function is represented by $g(x) = 8\left(\frac{1}{2}\right)^x$.

Use the graph to determine which function has a greater value when $x = 3$.

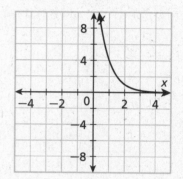

_____

_____

_____

7. The number of people attending Convention A can be modeled by $f(x) = 1200 \cdot 0.95^x$, where x is the number of years that the convention has been occurring. The number of people attending Convention B was 2200 in year 1 and 2100 in year 2. Which convention's attendance is decreasing at a greater rate? Explain your reasoning.

_____

_____

_____

8. The value of computer A after x years can be represented by $f(x) = 800 \cdot 0.7^x$. The value of computer B after x years is shown in the table. Which computer had the greatest initial value, and what was the initial value of that computer?

x	1	2	3	4
$g(x)$	510	306	183.60	110.16

Ⓐ Computer A; $560

Ⓑ Computer A; $800

Ⓒ Computer B; $510

Ⓓ Computer B; $850

Step It Out

Learn the Math

EXAMPLE 1 The data show the population for Granitetown for several years since its founding. Model the data with a piecewise-defined function. Then predict the population after 20 years.

Number of Years	0	1	2	3	4	5	6	7	8	9
Population	10	20	40	80	160	176	194	213	234	257

Look for patterns in the table. Granitetown was founded by a group of 10 people. Over the next 4 years, the population doubled each year. Although the population continues to increase after the fourth year, it is no longer doubling.

Write a function that models the population from year 0 to year 4.

The growth factor is $\frac{20}{10} = \frac{40}{20} = \frac{80}{40} = \frac{160}{80} = 2$. The function is $f(x) = 10(2)^x$.

Write a function that models the population from year 4 to year 9.

The growth factor is $\frac{176}{160} \approx \frac{194}{176} \approx \frac{213}{194} \approx \frac{234}{213} \approx \frac{257}{234} \approx 1.1$.

The starting value is the population at 4 years, or 160. The function is $f(x) = 160(1.1)^x$.

Use the two functions and corresponding intervals to write a piecewise-defined model for the population for Granitetown.

$$f(x) = \begin{cases} 10(2)^x, & 0 \leq x \leq 4 \\ 160(1.1)^x, & 4 < x \leq 9 \end{cases}$$

Predict the population after 20 years.

Although $20 > 9$, it is more likely that the population will continue the growth trend documented between year 4 and year 9 than it is that the population will begin doubling again. So, use the function defined for $4 < x \leq 9$.

$f(20) = 160(1.1)^{20} \approx 1076.4$

After 20 years, the population is expected to be about 1076 people.

The data show the population for deer in a rural area. Model the data with a piecewise-defined function. Then predict the deer population after 12 years.

Number of Years	0	1	2	3	4	5	6	7	8
Population	80	120	180	270	297	327	359	395	435

There seems to be one pattern between years 0 and ☐ and a different pattern between years ☐ and ☐.

The growth factor from 0 to ☐ years is ☐. The initial value for this interval is ☐.

The function is $f(x) = \boxed{}\left(\boxed{}\right)^x$.

The growth factor from ☐ to 8 years is ☐. The initial value for this interval is ☐.

The function is $f(x) = \boxed{}\left(\boxed{}\right)^x$.

Write a piecewise-defined exponential model for the deer population.

$$f(x) = \begin{cases} \boxed{}\left(\boxed{}\right)^x, & \boxed{} \le x \le \boxed{} \\ \boxed{}\left(\boxed{}\right)^x, & \boxed{} < x \le \boxed{} \end{cases}$$

Predict the population after 12 years.

The trend between ☐ $< x \le$ ☐ is likely to continue.

$$f\left(\boxed{}\right) = \boxed{}\left(\boxed{}\right)^x = \boxed{}$$

The population after 12 years is expected to be about ☐ deer.

© Houghton Mifflin Harcourt Publishing Company

**For each pair of points given, write an exponential model.
State whether your model is exponential growth or decay. Explain
your reasoning.**

1. $(0, 20)$ and $(1, 28)$

2. $(0, 60)$ and $(1, 48)$

3. Use the table at the right.

   A. Create an exponential model for the data.

   _____

   B. Calculate the squared residuals of your model. What does the sum of the
squared residuals indicate about your model?

x	y
0	200
1	340
2	580
3	1025
4	1735
5	3000
6	5280

x	y (actual)	y (predicted)	Residual	Square of Residual
0	200			
1	340			
2	580			
3	1025			
4	1735			
5	3000			
6	5280			

   _____

   C. Find an exponential regression function of the data. Then use residuals analysis to
determine whether the regression model or the model from Part A better fits the data.

   _____

   D. Use the better model to predict the value of the function when $x = 18$.

   _____

4. **Math on the Spot** The table gives the approximate values of diamonds of the same quality. Find an exponential model for the data. Use the model to estimate the weight of a diamond worth $6000.

Weight (carats)	Value ($)
0.5	1150
1.0	1430
2.0	2140
3.0	3210
4.0	4980

5. The table shows the population of Long Valley over the course of 10 years from its founding. Write a piecewise-defined function to model the data. Then estimate the population after 14 years.

Year	0	1	2	3	4	5	6	7	8	9
Population	800	1200	1800	2700	2835	2977	3126	3282	3446	3618

6. **Open Ended** Describe a real-world situation that could be modeled by $f(x) = 5000(0.85)^x$.

7. **Open Ended** During the California gold rush of the 1800s, boomtowns were established that eventually turned into ghost towns. Write a piecewise-defined function that might model the population of one of these towns.

8. Students find the following squared residual sums for four exponential models. Which squared residual sum represents the exponential model with the best fit?

(A) 18,934

(C) 8465

(B) 14,837

(D) 5193

Name _____

Step It Out

Learn the Math

EXAMPLE 1 ▶ Show that the function in the table is a linear function.

x	1	2	3	4	5
f(x)	342	359	376	393	410

The differences in x-values are equal, so subtract consecutive values of the function.

$f(2) - f(1) = 359 - 342 = 17$ $f(3) - f(2) = 376 - 359 = 17$

$f(4) - f(3) = 393 - 376 = 17$ $f(5) - f(4) = 410 - 393 = 17$

The function grows by equal differences over equal intervals, so the function is linear.

Do the Math

Show that the function in the table is a linear function.

x	1	2	3	4	5
f(x)	77	119	161	203	245

$f(2) - f(1) = \boxed{} - \boxed{} = \boxed{}$ $f(3) - f(2) = \boxed{} - \boxed{} = \boxed{}$

$f(4) - f(3) = \boxed{} - \boxed{} = \boxed{}$ $f(5) - f(4) = \boxed{} - \boxed{} = \boxed{}$

The function grows by _____ differences over _____ intervals, so the function

is _____.

Learn the Math

EXAMPLE 2 ▶ Show that the function in the table is an exponential function.

x	1	2	3	4	5
f(x)	23	69	207	621	1863

The differences in x-values are equal, so divide consecutive values of the function.

$\dfrac{f(2)}{f(1)} = \dfrac{69}{23} = 3$ $\dfrac{f(3)}{f(2)} = \dfrac{207}{69} = 3$ $\dfrac{f(4)}{f(3)} = \dfrac{621}{207} = 3$ $\dfrac{f(5)}{f(4)} = \dfrac{1863}{621} = 3$

The function grows by equal ratios over equal intervals, so the function is exponential.

Do the Math

Show that the function in the table is an exponential function.

x	1	2	3	4	5
f(x)	74	148	296	592	1184

Learn the Math

EXAMPLE 3 ▸ Jason starts a bank account with $500. Each month, he deposits $30 in the account. Hillary starts a bank account with $200. Each month, the value of her account increases by 1%. Find a model for each account.

Jason's bank account increases by a fixed amount each month, so it can be modeled by a linear function. The initial value is $500, and the difference is $30.

The amount in Jason's bank account can be modeled by $f(x) = 30x + 500$.

Hillary's bank account increases by a fixed percent increase each month, so it can be modeled by an exponential function. The initial value is $200, and the rate of increase is 0.01.

The amount in Hillary's bank account can be modeled by $f(x) = 200(1 + 0.01)^x = 200(1.01)^x$.

Do the Math

Martin starts a bank account with $350, and the value of his account increases by 1.5% each month. Veronica starts a bank account with $600 and deposits $50 in her account each month. Find a model for each account.

Martin's account can be modeled by a(n) _____ function: $f(x) = $ ⬚.

Veronica's account can be modeled by a(n) _____ function: $f(x) = $ ⬚.

Learn the Math

EXAMPLE 4 ▸ The population of a city each year for 5 years is shown in the table. Determine whether the population is best modeled by a linear or an exponential function.

t	0	1	2	3
$f(t)$	28,000	26,320	24,740	23,250

Make a table of differences and ratios to determine whether the function is linear or exponential.

t	$f(t)$	Difference	Ratio
0	28,000	—	—
1	26,320	−1,680	= 0.94
2	24,740	−1,580	≈ 0.94
3	23,250	−1,490	≈ 0.94

The ratios are about equal, so the population is best modeled by an exponential function.

Do the Math

The population of fish in a pond was initially 200. It was 185 after the first year, 170 after the second year, 155 after the third year, and 140 after the fourth year. Determine whether the population is best modeled by a linear or an exponential function.

Name _____

LESSON 13.2
More Practice

ONLINE
Video Tutorials and
Interactive Examples

State whether each data set is best represented by a linear or an exponential function. Then write a function to model the data.

1.

x	f(x)	Difference	Ratio
0	800	—	—
1	720		
2	648		
3	583.2		
4	524.88		

_____

_____

2.

x	f(x)	Difference	Ratio
0	157.2	—	—
1	190.9		
2	224.6		
3	258.3		
4	292		

_____

_____

3.

x	f(x)	Difference	Ratio
0	570	—	—
1	488		
2	406		
3	324		
4	242		

_____

_____

4. Use Tools The data show the earnings, in millions of dollars, for a company during a five-year period. Use a graphing calculator to find a best-fit linear model and an exponential model for the data. Which model best fits the data? Explain your reasoning.

Year	Sales (millions of dollars)
1	57.3
2	43.9
3	27.8
4	21.2
5	15.3

_____

_____

_____

5. **Math on the Spot** Graph each data set. Which kind of model best describes the data?

A.

Time (h)	0	1	2	3
Bacteria	5	10	20	40

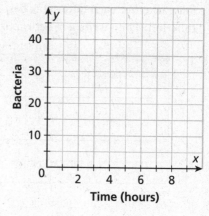

_____

_____

_____

B.

Time (min)	0	10	20	30	40
Distance (mi)	10	30	50	70	90

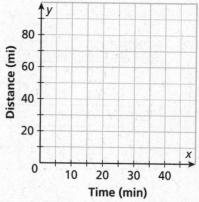

_____

_____

_____

6. An amusement park determines that its attendance for a season was 248,000 people. The park projects the attendance to increase by 5.4% each season over the next 5 seasons. Would a linear or exponential function best model the projected increase in attendance? Explain your reasoning. Write a function to model the attendance.

_____

_____

_____

7. The value of a collectible plate over a five-year period is shown in the table. Which function best represents the value of the plate each year?

Year	0	1	2	3	4
Value	$50	$58	$66	$74	$82

Ⓐ $f(x) = 8x + 50$

Ⓒ $f(x) = 50(1.16)^x$

Ⓑ $f(x) = 8x + 58$

Ⓓ $f(x) = 50(1.6)^x$

Step It Out

Learn the Math	Do the Math

Learn the Math

EXAMPLE 1 ► Graph the geometric sequence $f(1) = 4$, $f(n) = f(n-1) \cdot 3$ for $2 \leq n \leq 5$.

In this geometric sequence, n represents the position number, and $f(n)$ represents the term of the sequence. The first term, 4, is given in the rule of the sequence. To find the second term, multiply the first term by 3. To find the third term, multiply the second term by 3. Continue this pattern to complete the table.

n	1	2	3	4	5
$f(n)$	4	12	36	108	324

Plot the ordered pairs $(n, f(n))$ on the graph.

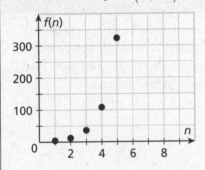

Do the Math

Graph the geometric sequence $f(1) = 2$, $f(n) = f(n-1) \cdot 5$ for $2 \leq n \leq 5$.

Complete the table.

n	1	2	3	4	5
$f(n)$	2				

Plot the ordered pairs $(n, f(n))$ on the graph.

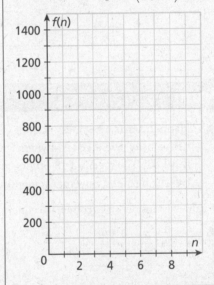

Learn the Math

EXAMPLE 2 ► You can use the graph of a geometric sequence to determine the rule for the sequence.

The point $(1, 80)$ indicates that $f(1) = 80$.

The common ratio is $\frac{40}{80} = \frac{1}{2}$.

The recursive rule is $f(1) = 80$, $f(n) = f(n-1) \cdot \frac{1}{2}$ for $2 \leq n \leq 5$.

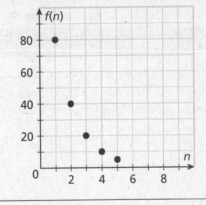

Do the Math

Write the recursive rule for the geometric sequence shown in the graph.

The point $\left(1,\boxed{}\right)$ indicates that $f(1)=\boxed{}$.

The common ratio is $\dfrac{1620}{\boxed{}}=\dfrac{\boxed{}}{\boxed{}}$.

The recursive rule is $f(1)=\boxed{}$, $f(n)=f(n-1)\cdot\dfrac{\boxed{}}{\boxed{}}$

for $\boxed{}\le n\le\boxed{}$.

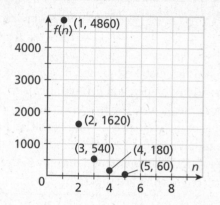

Learn the Math

EXAMPLE 3 Hannah starts a business making rings and selling them online. The day she launched her website, she received two orders. On the second day, she received six orders, on the third day, she received 18 orders, and on the fourth day, she received 54 orders. If this trend continues, how many ring orders will Hannah have on the ninth day?

Create a table of values to model the geometric sequence.

n	1	2	3	4
$f(n)$	2	6	18	54

The recursive rule for the sequence is $f(1)=2$, $f(n)=f(n-1)\cdot 3$ for $n\ge 2$.

Find the number of ring orders Hannah will have on the ninth day.

n	5	6	7	8	9
$f(n)$	162	486	1458	4374	13,122

Hannah will have 13,122 ring orders on the ninth day.

Do the Math

The first year Sam had a cell phone, he paid $50 per month for service. Every year since then, his monthly service fee has increased by 2%. Make a table and write the recursive rule for the geometric sequence. How much will Sam pay each month for service after he has had the cell phone for 7 years?

Determine whether each sequence is arithmetic or geometric. If it is geometric, find the common ratio, _r_.

1. 8, 13, 18, 23, . . .

2. $\frac{1}{2}$, 1, 2, 4, . . .

3. 4, 16, 64, 256, . . .

4. 17, 20, 23, 26, . . .

Write a recursive rule for each geometric sequence. Then, find the next three terms.

5. 3, 12, 48, 192, . . .

6. 600, 300, 150, 75, . . .

7. 6400, 4800, 3600, 2700, . . .

Find the indicated term of each geometric sequence.

8. $\frac{7}{3}$, 7, 21, . . .; 8th term

9. 4, 6, 9, . . .; 6th term

10. 270, 180, 120, . . .; 7th term

11. Math on the Spot Find the 9th term of the geometric sequence with $f(3) = 36$ and $f(5) = 324$. (If you watch the video for this problem, note that subscript notation is used instead of function notation. In particular, a_n is used in place of $f(n)$, a_3 in place of $f(3)$, and a_5 in place of $f(5)$.)

© Houghton Mifflin Harcourt Publishing Company

12. Andre wants to drink more water each day. He sets a goal to increase his cups of water per day according to the sequence 1, 2.5, 6.25, 15.63, . . .

   A. Is the sequence Andre plans to use geometric? Explain.

   _____

   B. What are the next two terms in the sequence?

   _____

   C. Is it practical for Andre to use this sequence to increase his water intake over a long period of time? Explain.

   _____

13. What happens to successive terms of a geometric sequence as the position number increases when the common ratio is less than 1?

   _____

14. **Construct Arguments** To write a sequence of numbers, Marcuss finds the next number in the sequence by doubling the previous number and adding the doubled number to the previous number. He claims that this sequence is a geometric sequence. Is Marcus correct? Explain why or why not. If it is a geometric sequence, what is the common ratio?

   _____

   _____

   _____

15. **Reason** The 9th term of a sequence is 1000. The 12th term of the sequence is 125. What is the 15th term of the sequence? Explain how you know.

   _____

   _____

   _____

16. Which situations could be modeled by a geometric sequence with a common ratio greater than one? Select all that apply.

   Ⓐ tracking a population that is decreasing over time

   Ⓑ analyzing bacterial growth

   Ⓒ increasing minutes of exercise per day

   Ⓓ measuring the speed of a car as it slows down

   Ⓔ measuring the height of a bouncy ball after each bounce

Name _____

Step It Out

Learn the Math

EXAMPLE 1 Graph the geometric sequence $f(n) = 100 \cdot 1.5^{(n-1)}$.

Create a table of values that shows $(n, f(n))$ pairs that can be plotted on a graph.

Position number, n	1	2	3	4	5	...
Term of the sequence, $f(n)$	100	150	225	337.5	506.25	...

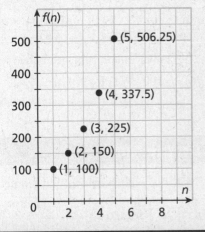

Plot the points.
The domain is $\{1, 2, 3, 4, 5, \ldots\}$ and the range is $\{100, 150, 225, 337.5, 506.25, \ldots\}$.

Do the Math

Graph the geometric sequence $f(n) = 2 \cdot \left(\dfrac{1}{2}\right)^{(n-1)}$.

Complete the table of values that shows $(n, f(n))$ pairs that can be plotted on a graph.

Position number, n	1	2	3	4	5	...
Term of the sequence, $f(n)$	2	☐	☐	☐	☐	...

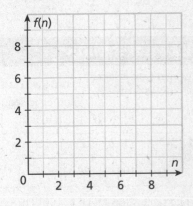

The domain is $\Big\{$ ☐ $\Big\}$.

The range is $\Big\{$ ☐ $\Big\}$.

Learn the Math

EXAMPLE 2 Write the explicit rule for the geometric sequence shown on the graph.

The point $(1, 200)$ on the graph shows that $f(1) = 200$.

To find the common ratio r, divide any $\frac{f(n)}{f(n-1)}$.

$$\frac{50}{200} = \frac{12.5}{50} = \frac{3.125}{12.5} = \frac{0.78125}{3.125} = \frac{1}{4}$$

The explicit rule for the geometric sequence for the graph is

$$f(n) = 200\left(\frac{1}{4}\right)^{n-1} \text{ for } 1 \leq n \leq 5.$$

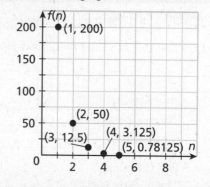

Do the Math

Write the explicit rule for the geometric sequence shown on the graph.

$f(1) = \boxed{}$ and $r = \dfrac{2}{\boxed{}} = \boxed{}$

Substitute these values into the general rule for a geometric sequence.

The explicit rule is $f(n) = \boxed{} \cdot \boxed{}^{n-1}$ for $n \geq \boxed{}$.

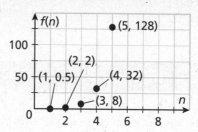

Learn the Math

EXAMPLE 3 Write the recursive rule for the geometric sequence shown in the table.

n	1	2	3	4	5
$f(n)$	100	20	4	$\frac{4}{5}$	$\frac{4}{25}$

The table shows $f(1) = 100$. The common ratio is $\frac{20}{100} = \frac{1}{5}$. The recursive rule is $f(1) = 100$, $f(n) = f(n-1) \cdot \frac{1}{5}$ for $n \geq 2$.

Do the Math

Write the recursive rule for the geometric sequence shown in the table.

n	1	2	3	4	5
$f(n)$	6	30	150	750	3750

The table shows $f(1) = \boxed{}$. The common ratio is $\frac{30}{\boxed{}} = \boxed{}$. The recursive rule is $f(1) = \boxed{}$, $f(n) = f(n-1) \cdot \boxed{}$ for $n \geq \boxed{}$.

Learn the Math

EXAMPLE 4 ▶ Eli drops a basketball from the bleachers onto the gym floor. The heights of the first three bounces are 15 feet, 12 feet, and 9.6 feet, respectively. The heights of the bounces form a geometric sequence. First write the recursive rule, and then write the explicit rule for the sequence.

The first term of the sequence is the height of the first bounce, 15.

The common ratio is $\frac{12}{15} = \frac{4}{5}$.

The recursive rule for the sequence is $f(1) = 15, f(n) = f(n-1) \cdot \frac{4}{5}$ for $n \geq 2$.

Use the recursive rule to write the explicit rule for the sequence.

Substitute $f(1)$ and r from the recursive rule into the general explicit rule $f(n) = f(1) \cdot r^{n-1}$.

The explicit rule is $f(n) = 15 \cdot \left(\frac{4}{5}\right)^{n-1}$ for $n \geq 2$.

Do the Math

Eli walks farther up the bleachers and drops a golf ball. The heights of the first four bounces of the golf ball, in feet, are 35, 14, 5.6, and 2.24. First write the recursive rule, and then write the explicit rule for the sequence.

The first term of the sequence is the height of the _____ bounce, $\boxed{}$.

The common ratio is $\dfrac{\boxed{}}{35} = \dfrac{\boxed{}}{\boxed{}}$.

The recursive rule for the sequence is $f(1) = \boxed{}, f(n) = f(n-1) \cdot \boxed{}$ for $n \geq \boxed{}$.

Substitute $f(1)$ and r from the recursive rule into the general explicit rule $f(n) = f(1) \cdot r^{n-1}$.

The explicit rule is $f(n) = \boxed{} \cdot \left(\boxed{}\right)^{n-1}$ for $n \geq \boxed{}$.

Learn the Math

Maia and a friend are discussing whether the "10-second rule," which implies that food dropped on the floor is safe from germs for 10 seconds, is true or not. Maia claims that she had seen the following data on the number of bacteria that accumulates on food after a piece of food had been dropped onto a dirty floor.

Number of seconds, n	1	2	3
Number of bacteria, $f(n)$	4	24	144

Maia uses a geometric sequence to represent the data. How many bacteria will be on the piece of food after 10 seconds?

The common ratio is $\frac{24}{4} = 6$, and $f(1) = 4$.

The explicit rule for the geometric sequence is $f(n) = 4 \cdot (6)^{n-1}$, where n represents the number of seconds and $f(n)$ represents the number of bacteria on the piece of food. Find $f(10)$ to determine the number of bacteria on the candy after 10 seconds.

$f(10) = 4 \cdot (6)^{10-1} = 40{,}310{,}784$

After 10 seconds, there would be over 40 million bacteria on the piece of food. The "10-second rule" would not be a good a rule if the data were correct.

Do the Math

Maia's friend does not believe the data that Maia claims to have seen is true. Maia says that the she has other data showing similar accumulation of bacteria on a piece of food and draws a graph of the other data.

Write the explicit rule for the geometric sequence shown in the graph. Then, use the rule to find the number of bacteria on the piece of food after 10 seconds.

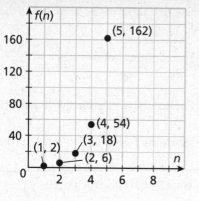

The common ratio is $\dfrac{6}{\boxed{}} = \boxed{}$, and $f(1) = \boxed{}$.

The explicit rule for the geometric sequence is $f(n) = \boxed{} \cdot \left(\boxed{}\right)^{n-1}$.

$f(10) = \boxed{} \cdot \left(\boxed{}\right)^{\boxed{}-1} = \boxed{}$

After 10 seconds, there will be about $\boxed{}$ bacteria on the piece of food.

Write an explicit rule for each sequence.

1. 3200, 1600, 800, 400, . . . _____

2. 12, 84, 588, 4116, . . . _____

3. 1395, 465, 155, 51.67, . . . _____

Write an explicit rule for the sequence shown on each graph.

4.

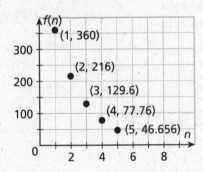

5.

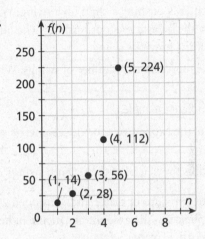

_____   _____

Write a recursive rule for each sequence.

6. $f(n) = 1990 \cdot \left(\frac{1}{2}\right)^{n-1}$

7. $f(n) = 3 \cdot (10)^{n-1}$

_____   _____

Write an explicit rule for each geometric sequence.

8. $f(1) = 2.5, f(n) = f(n-1) \cdot 10$ for $n \geq 2$

_____

9. $f(1) = 1498, f(n) = f(n-1) \cdot \frac{1}{8}$ for $n \geq 2$

_____

10. A geometric sequence is shown in the table.

    A. What is the first term of the sequence? _____

    B. What is the common ratio? _____

    C. What is an explicit rule for the geometric sequence? _____

    _____

    D. What is $f(12)$? _____

n	$f(n)$
1	300
2	375
3	468.75
4	585.9375

11. Math on the Spot For taking out the garbage each week, Charlotte earns 1 cent the first week, 2 cents the second week, 4 cents the third week, and so on, where she makes twice as much each week as she made the week before. If Charlotte will take out the garbage for 15 weeks, how much will she earn on the 15th week?

12. A babysitter is pushing a child on a swing. When the swing reaches a height of 5 feet, the babysitter stops pushing. The height of each swing is 80% of the height of the previous swing.

n	$f(n)$
1	5
2	
3	
4	

   A. Let n represent the number of swings. What does $f(n)$ represent?

   B. Complete the table.

   C. Write the explicit rule for the geometric sequence.

   D. What is the height of the seventh swing? _____

13. Ellen had two cups of coffee and consumed 200 mg of caffeine. The graph shows the amount of caffeine in her system n hours after she drinks the coffee.

   A. What is the common ratio, r, for this geometric sequence?

   B. Write an explicit rule to represent the amount of caffeine in Ellen's system after n hours.

   C. How much caffeine will be in Ellen's system after 8 hours?

(Graph showing points: (1, 200), (2, 170), (3, 144.5), (4, 122.825), (5, 104.401) with axes $f(n)$ vs n)

14. Given the geometric sequence, $f(n) = 5450 \left(\frac{1}{2}\right)^{n-1}$, which value represents $f(1)$?

   Ⓐ $\frac{1}{2}$

   Ⓑ 1

   Ⓒ 2725

   Ⓓ 5450

15. If $f(n)$ represents a geometric sequence, $f(3) = 5$, and $f(5) = 20$, which equation is an explicit rule for the sequence? Assume that the common ratio is positive.

   Ⓐ $f(n) = 5 \cdot 2^{n-1}$ Ⓒ $f(n) = \frac{5}{4} \cdot 2^{n-1}$

   Ⓑ $f(n) = \frac{5}{2} \cdot 2^{n-1}$ Ⓓ $f(n) = \frac{5}{8} \cdot 2^{n-1}$

Name _____

Step It Out

Learn the Math

> **EXAMPLE 1** Find the area of the triangle.

The formula for the area of a triangle is $A = \frac{1}{2}bh$.

Substitute $4x$ for b and $3x$ for h and multiply to find an expression for the area.

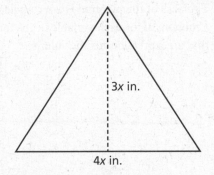

$$A = \frac{1}{2}bh$$
$$= \frac{1}{2}(4x)(3x)$$
$$= \frac{1}{2}(12x^2)$$
$$= 6x^2$$

The dimensions of the triangle are given in inches, so the units for the area are square inches, or in^2.

The area is $6x^2$ square inches.

Do the Math

A. Find the area of the rectangle.

The formula for the area of a rectangle is $A = lw$.

Substitute ☐ for l and ☐ for w and multiply to find an expression for the area.

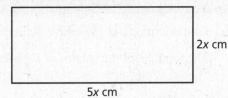

$$A = lw$$
$$= ☐ \cdot ☐$$
$$= ☐$$

The dimensions of the rectangle are given in _____, so the units for the area are _____, or _____.

The area is ☐ square centimeters.

B. Find the volume of the right rectangular prism.

The formula for the volume of a right rectangular prism is $V = Bh$, where B is the area of the base and h is the height.

Substitute ☐ for B and ☐ for h. Then multiply to find an expression for the volume.

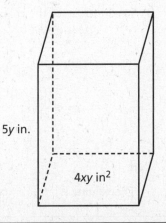

$$V = Bh$$
$$V = ☐ \cdot ☐$$
$$= ☐$$

The volume is ☐ cubic _____.

Learn the Math

EXAMPLE 2 Find the volume of the pyramid.

The formula for the volume of a pyramid is $V = \frac{1}{3}Bh$.

The base of the pyramid is a rectangle, so $B = lw$. Substitute a monomial for each variable in the formula and multiply to find an expression for the volume.

$$V = \frac{1}{3}Bh$$

$$= \frac{1}{3}lwh$$

$$= \frac{1}{3}(x)\left(\frac{1}{2}x\right)(3x)$$

$$= \frac{1}{3}\left(\frac{3}{2}x^3\right)$$

$$= \frac{1}{2}x^3$$

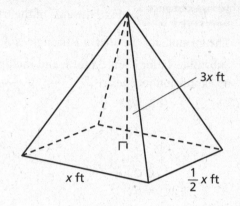

3x ft

x ft

$\frac{1}{2}$ x ft

The dimensions of the pyramid are given in feet, so the units for the volume are cubic feet, or ft³.

The volume is $\frac{1}{2}x^3$ cubic feet.

Do the Math

A. Find the volume of the sphere. Round to the nearest hundredth.

The formula for the volume of a sphere is $V = \frac{4}{3}\pi r^3$.

$$V = \frac{4}{3}\pi r^3$$

$$= \frac{4}{3}\pi \boxed{}^3$$

$$= \frac{4}{3}\pi \cdot \boxed{}^3 \cdot \boxed{}^3$$

$$\approx \boxed{} \cdot \boxed{}^3$$

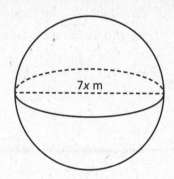

7x m

The units for the volume are _____. The volume is approximately $\boxed{}$ cubic meters.

B. Find the volume of the right rectangular prism.

The formula for the volume of a cylinder is $V = \pi r^2 h$.

$$V = \pi r^2 h$$

$$= \pi \boxed{}^2 \cdot \boxed{}$$

$$= \pi \cdot \boxed{}^2 \cdot \boxed{}^2 \cdot \boxed{}$$

$$= \boxed{}\pi \cdot \boxed{}^3$$

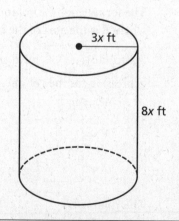

3x ft

8x ft

The volume is $\boxed{}$ cubic feet.

1. Circle the expressions that are monomials.

56 $\dfrac{3}{6}$ $7x$ $0.2 - x$ $x + 1$ $3x^2y$ x^5 $3x^2 + 2$

Find the product.

2. $(2x)(3x)$

_____

3. $(4xy)(7y)$

_____

4. $(9x^2)(y^2)$

_____

5. $(x^2y)(8y)$

_____

6. $(ab)(2ab)$

_____

7. $(3ab)(9a)$

_____

8. $(7ab^2)(ab^2)$

_____

9. $(5ab)(4ab^3)$

_____

10. $(2xy)(2xy)$

_____

11. $(4x^2y)(3xy)$

_____

12. $(8xy^2)(7xy)$

_____

13. $(5x^3y^2)(2xy^2)$

_____

14. $(6xy)(9xy^3)$

_____

15. $(x^3y)(x^2y^2)$

_____

16. Math on the Spot Multiply $(7x^2y)(-3x^4yz^8)$.

_____

17. The volume of a sphere is $\frac{4}{3}\pi(6x)^3$ cubic centimeters. What is the diameter?

_____

18. The radius of a sphere is $3x$ meters. What is the volume? _____

Find the area of each figure.

19.

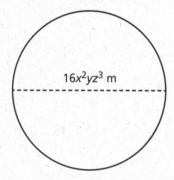

$16x^2yz^3$ m

_____

20.

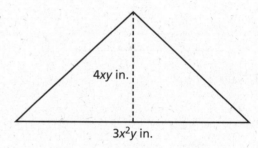

$4xy$ in.

$3x^2y$ in.

_____

Find the volume of each figure.

21.

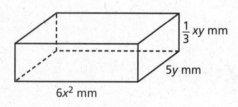

$\frac{1}{3}xy$ mm

$5y$ mm

$6x^2$ mm

_____

22.

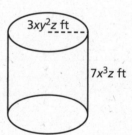

$3xy^2z$ ft

$7x^3z$ ft

_____

23. Open Ended Write a third-degree monomial with a coefficient of 4 and one variable.

_____

24. Which expression is a fourth-degree monomial with a coefficient of -2 and two variables?

Ⓐ $4x^{-1}y^{-1}$

Ⓑ $-2x^4$

Ⓒ $-2x^3y$

Ⓓ $\frac{1}{2}x^2y^2$

Name _____

Step It Out

Learn the Math

> **EXAMPLE 1** A rectangular tarp used to cover a pool has the dimensions shown. Write a simplified expression for the area of the tarp. Find the area of the tarp when $x = 5$ feet.

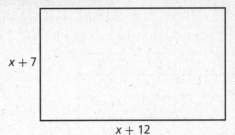

$x + 7$

$x + 12$

Use the Distributive Property.

$(x + 12)(x + 7) = x(x + 7) + 12(x + 7)$

$\qquad = x^2 + 7x + 12x + 84$

$\qquad = x^2 + 19x + 84$

The area of the tarp is $5^2 + 19(5) + 84 = 25 + 95 + 84 = 204$ square feet.

Use a multiplication matrix.

•	x	7
x	x^2	$7x$
12	$12x$	84

Do the Math

The newly designed rectangular athletic field has a length of $x + 16$ and a width of $x + 8$. Write a simplified expression for the area of the athletic field. Find the area of the field when $x = 40$ yards.

$x + 8$

$x + 16$

Use the Distributive Property.

$(x + 16)(x + 8) = \boxed{}(x + 8) + \boxed{}(x + 8)$

$= \boxed{}$

$= \boxed{}$

Use a multiplication matrix.

•	x	8
x		
16		

The area of the field is $\boxed{}$ square yards.

© Houghton Mifflin Harcourt Publishing Company

Learn the Math

EXAMPLE 2 A rectangular box is shown. Write a simplified expression for the volume of the box. Find the volume of the box when $x = 8$ inches.

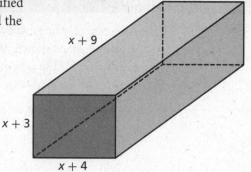

Find the area of the base. Use $B = lw$.

•	x	4
x	x^2	$4x$
3	$3x$	12

The area of the base is $x^2 + 7x + 12$.

Find the volume of the box. Use $V = Bh$.

$$\left(x^2 + 7x + 12\right)(x + 9) = x^2(x + 9) + 7x(x + 9) + 12(x + 9)$$
$$= x^3 + 9x^2 + 7x^2 + 63x + 12x + 108$$
$$V = x^3 + 16x^2 + 75x + 108$$

The volume of the box when $x = 8$ inches is $8^3 + 16(8)^2 + 75(8) + 108 = 2244$ cubic inches.

Do the Math

A rectangular chest is shown. Write a simplified expression for the volume of the chest. Find the volume of the chest when $x = 2$ feet.

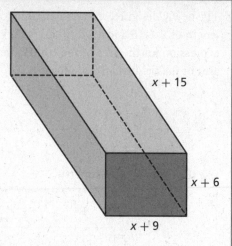

Find the area of the base. Use $B = lw$.

•	x	6
x		
9		

The area of the base is [   ].

Find the volume of the chest. Use $V = Bh$.

$$\left([\ ] + [\ ]x + [\ ]\right)(x + 15) = [\ ](x + 15) + [\ ](x + 15) + [\ ](x + 15)$$

$$= [\qquad\qquad]$$

$$V = [\qquad\qquad]$$

The volume of the chest when $x = 2$ feet is [   ] cubic feet.

Find the product. Express the product in standard form.

1. $4(x + 8)$

2. $3x(2y - 14)$

_____

_____

3. $(x + 11)(x + 16)$

4. $(x + 9)(x - 7)$

_____

_____

5. $(2x - 5)(x + 10)$

6. $(3x - 2)(2x - 14)$

_____

_____

7. $(x^2 + 4x + 3)(x + 6)$

8. $(x^2 - 6x + 9)(x - 7)$

_____

_____

177

9. **Math on the Spot** A board foot is 1 ft by 1 ft by 1 in. of lumber. The amount of lumber that can be harvested from a tree with a diameter of d is approximately $20 + 0.005(d^3 - 30d^2 + 300d - 1000)$ board feet. Use the Distributive Property to write an equivalent expression.

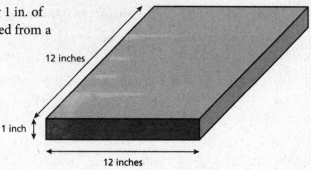

12 inches

1 inch

12 inches

_____

10. **Use Structure** A triangle has a base of $4x + 12$ and a height of $x + 6$. Write a simplified expression for the area of the triangle using the formula $A = \frac{1}{2}bh$. Then find the area of the triangle when $x = 7$ millimeters.

_____

11. Find an expression for the volume of a triangular prism where the base of the prism is a right triangle with base $4x + 6$ and height $x + 5$ and the height of the triangular prism is $x + 5$. Use the expression to find the volume when $x = 3$.

_____

12. Find the product. $(x^2 - 3x + 4)(2x + 8)$

Ⓐ $2x^3 + 14x^2 + 32x + 32$

Ⓑ $2x^3 + 2x^2 - 16x + 32$

Ⓒ $2x^3 - 2x^2 + 16x + 32$

Ⓓ $2x^3 - 2x^2 - 16x - 32$

© Houghton Mifflin Harcourt Publishing Company

15.3

Step It Out

Learn the Math	Do the Math
EXAMPLE 1 Multiply.	Multiply.

Learn the Math side:

$(x + 5)(x - 5)$

$(a + b)(a - b) = a^2 - b^2$

$(x + 5)(x - 5) = (x)^2 - (5)^2$

$\qquad\qquad\quad = x^2 - 25$

Do the Math side:

$(x + 7)(x - 7)$

$(a + b)(a - b) = a^2 - b^2$

$(x + 7)(x - 7) = (\boxed{})^2 - (\boxed{})^2$

$\qquad\qquad\quad = \boxed{} - \boxed{}$

Learn the Math side:

$(-2x + 1)(-2x - 1)$

$(a + b)(a - b) = a^2 - b^2$

$(-2x + 1)(-2x - 1) = (-2x)^2 - (1)^2$

$\qquad\qquad\qquad\quad = 4x^2 - 1$

Do the Math side:

$(3x + 5)(3x - 5)$

$(a + b)(a - b) = a^2 - b^2$

$(3x + 5)(3x - 5) = (\boxed{})^2 - (\boxed{})^2$

$\qquad\qquad\qquad = \boxed{} - \boxed{}$

Learn the Math	Do the Math
EXAMPLE 2 Multiply.	Multiply.

Learn the Math side:

$(x + 3)^2$

$(a + b)^2 = a^2 + 2ab + b^2$

$(x + 3)^2 = (x)^2 + 2(x)(3) + (3)^2$

$\qquad\quad = x^2 + 6x + 9$

Do the Math side:

$(x + 8)^2$

$(a + b)^2 = a^2 + 2ab + b^2$

$(x + 8)^2 - (\boxed{})^2 + 2(\boxed{})(\boxed{}) + (\boxed{})^2$

$\qquad\quad = \boxed{} + \boxed{} + \boxed{}$

Learn the Math side:

$(4x + y)^2$

$(a + b)^2 = a^2 + 2ab + b^2$

$(4x + y)^2 = (4x)^2 + 2(4x)(y) + (y)^2$

$\qquad\qquad = 16x^2 + 8xy + y^2$

Do the Math side:

$(2x + 5)^2$

$(a + b)^2 = a^2 + 2ab + b^2$

$(2x + 5)^2 = (\boxed{})^2 + 2(\boxed{})(\boxed{}) + (\boxed{})^2$

$\qquad\qquad = \boxed{} + \boxed{} + \boxed{}$

Learn the Math

EXAMPLE 3 Multiply.

$(x - 6)^2$

$(a - b)^2 = a^2 - 2ab + b^2$

$(x - 6)^2 = (x)^2 - 2(x)(6) + (6)^2$

$\qquad = x^2 - 12x + 36$

$(3x - 7y)^2$

$(a - b)^2 = a^2 - 2ab + b^2$

$(3x - 7y)^2 = (3x)^2 - 2(3x)(7y) + (7y)^2$

$\qquad = 9x^2 - 42xy + 49y^2$

Do the Math

Multiply.

$(x - 1)^2$

$(a - b)^2 = a^2 - 2ab + b^2$

$(x - 1)^2 = \left(\boxed{}\right)^2 - 2\left(\boxed{}\right)\left(\boxed{}\right) + \left(\boxed{}\right)^2$

$\qquad = \boxed{} - \boxed{} + \boxed{}$

$(x^2 - 2)^2$

$(a - b)^2 = a^2 - 2ab + b^2$

$(x^2 - 2)^2 = \left(\boxed{}\right)^2 - 2\left(\boxed{}\right)\left(\boxed{}\right) + \left(\boxed{}\right)^2$

$\qquad = \boxed{} - \boxed{} + \boxed{}$

Learn the Math

EXAMPLE 4   A landscaper is redesigning a property. The property currently has a circular pond with a diameter of 12 feet. The landscaper plans to expand the pond so that the radius is x feet longer than before. The landscaper wants to know the area of the new pond. Write an equation for the area of the new pond.

The diameter of the old pond is 12 feet, so the radius of the old pond is 6 feet.

The radius of the new pond is $(6 + x)$ feet.

Find the area of a circle.

$A = \pi r^2$

$\quad = \pi(6 + x)^2$

$\quad = \pi\left(6^2 + 2(6)(x) + x^2\right)$

$\quad = \pi\left(36 + 12x + x^2\right) \text{ ft}^2$

Do the Math

The landscaper also decides to reduce the size of a square flower garden. The old garden has sides that are 15 feet long. The landscaper plans to reduce the length of each side by y feet. Write an equation for the area of the new garden.

$A = \boxed{} \text{ ft}^2$

Name _____

LESSON 15.3
More Practice

ONLINE
Video Tutorials and
Interactive Examples

Multiply.

1. $(x + 4)(x - 4)$

2. $(9 - 2x)(9 + 2x)$

_____

_____

3. $(x + 11)^2$

4. $(3x + y^2)^2$

_____

_____

5. $(x - 4)^2$

6. $(7x - 3y)^2$

_____

_____

7. **Use Precision** Emily says that when she multiplies $(3x + 2)^2$ the answer is $9x^2 + 6x + 4$. Explain and correct her error.

_____

_____

_____

8. Evan drew a picture that is 9 inches long and 9 inches wide. He wants to resize the picture so it is $2x$ inches longer and $2x$ inches wider. What are the dimensions of the new picture? What is the area of the new picture?

_____

_____

_____

9. **Critique Reasoning** Chelsea has a circular mirror with a diameter of 8 inches. She decides to buy a new mirror with a diameter that is x inches less. Chelsea says that an expression for the area of her new mirror is $\pi(64 - 16x - x^2)$ square inches. Is she correct? If not, explain her error, and write an expression for the area of her new mirror.

_____

_____

_____

10. A school created a public recreation space. The length of the recreation space is $(2x + 7)$ feet, and the width is $(2x - 7)$ feet. Write an expression for the area of the space.

_____

_____

_____

11. Multiply $(5x - 4y)^2$.

Ⓐ $5x^2 - 40xy - 4y^2$

Ⓑ $25x^2 - 20xy + 16y^2$

Ⓒ $25x^2 - 40xy - 16y^2$

Ⓓ $25x^2 - 40xy + 16y^2$

12. Which expression is the square of a binomial?

Ⓐ $9x^2y + 30xy - 25y^2$

Ⓑ $9x^2y^2 - 30xy + 25y^2$

Ⓒ $25x^2 + 30xy - 9y^2$

Ⓓ $25x^2y^2 - 30xy + 9$

Step It Out

Learn the Math

EXAMPLE 1 ▶ Two residents from the town of Wrightsville donate their adjoining rectangular gardens in order to make a large community garden. In order to fence in the community garden, the residents need to calculate the perimeter of three sides of each garden. The adjoining side of the gardens will not be fenced. What is the perimeter of the entire community garden?

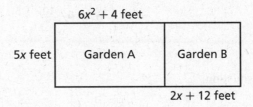

Identify the sum.

Use polynomials to model the situation.

Garden A: $(6x^2 + 4) + (6x^2 + 4) + 5x$ feet

Garden B: $5x + (2x + 12) + (2x + 12)$ feet

Use the horizontal format to simplify the expressions.

Garden A: $(6x^2 + 4) + (6x^2 + 4) + 5x = (6x^2 + 6x^2) + 5x + (4 + 4) = 12x^2 + 5x + 8$

Garden B: $5x + (2x + 12) + (2x + 12) = (5x + 2x + 2x) + (12 + 12) = 9x + 24$

Write an expression to solve the problem.

$(12x^2 + 5x + 8) + (9x + 24)$

Add the polynomials using a vertical format.

$$\begin{array}{r} 12x^2 + 5x + \ 8 \\ 9x + 24 \\ \hline 12x^2 + 14x + 32 \end{array}$$

The solution is $12x^2 + 14x + 32$ feet.

Do the Math

Kenny wraps four sides of boxes with ribbon. He would like to know how much more ribbon box A uses than box B. What is the difference in the amounts of ribbon he uses between the two boxes?

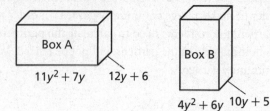

Box A

Box B

$11y^2 + 7y$ $12y + 6$

$4y^2 + 6y$ $10y + 5$

Identify the difference.

Use polynomials to model the situation.

Box A: $(11y^2 + 7y) + \left(\boxed{}\right) + (12y + 6) + \left(\boxed{}\right)$ or $2\left(\boxed{} + 7y\right) + 2\left(\boxed{} + 6\right)$ cm

Box B: $(4y^2 + 6y) + \left(\boxed{}\right) + (10y + 5) + \left(\boxed{}\right)$ or $2\left(\boxed{} + 6y\right) + 2\left(\boxed{} + 5\right)$ cm

Use the horizontal format to simplify the expressions.

Box A: $2\left(\boxed{} + 7y\right) + 2\left(\boxed{} + 6\right)$

$\quad = \left(\boxed{} + 14y\right) + \left(\boxed{} + 12\right)$

$\quad = \boxed{} + \left(14y + \boxed{}\right) + 12$

$\quad = \boxed{}y^2 + \boxed{}y + 12$

Box B: $2\left(\boxed{} + 6y\right) + 2\left(\boxed{} + 5\right)$

$\quad = \left(\boxed{} + 12y\right) + \left(\boxed{} + 10\right)$

$\quad = \boxed{} + \left(12y + \boxed{}\right) + 10$

$\quad = \boxed{}y^2 + \boxed{}y + 10$

Write an expression to solve the problem.

$\left(\boxed{}y^2 + \boxed{}y + 12\right) + \left(-\boxed{}y^2 - \boxed{}y - 10\right)$

Subtract the polynomials using a vertical format.

$\boxed{}y^2 + \boxed{}y + 12$

$- \boxed{}y^2 - \boxed{}y - 10$

$\overline{\boxed{}y^2 + \boxed{}y + 2}$

The difference is $\boxed{}y^2 + \boxed{}y + 2$ centimeters.

© Houghton Mifflin Harcourt Publishing Company

Find each sum or difference. Show your work.

1. $\left(4x^2 + 3x + 1\right) + \left(9x^2 + 7x + 10\right)$

2. $\left(3y^3 + 8x + 9\right) - \left(y^3 + 6x\right)$

_____

_____

3. $\left(24ab^4 + 16a + 9b + 12\right) + \left(15ab^4 + 7a + 11\right)$

4. $\left(-4m^2 + 5n + 6\right) - \left(6m^2 + 2n + 9\right)$

_____

_____

5. $\left(-9x^2y + 9xy + 5\right) - \left(-2x^2y + xy - 3\right)$

6. $\left(19mn - 13n + 7\right) + \left(16mn + 6m - 7\right)$

_____

_____

7. $\left(4a^3 + 7a + 10\right) + \left(-a^3 + 3a^2\right)$

8. $\left(12xy + x + 23y\right) + \left(16xy + 5x - 20y\right)$

_____

_____

9. $\left(y^2 + 15y\right) - \left(y^2 + 12y\right)$

10. $\left(13mn^2 - mn + 8\right) - \left(6mn - 5m\right)$

_____

_____

11. Open Ended When subtracting two polynomials, how does subtraction impact each monomial in the second polynomial?

_____

_____

12. Math on the Spot Libby puts a mat of width m and a frame of width f around an 8-inch by 10-inch picture. Find an expression for the perimeter of the entire frame.

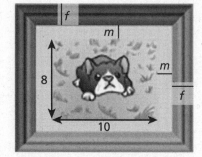

_____

_____

13. Reason Taryn wants to put pavers around the outside of her yard. The area of her yard is $6m^2 + 9m + 8$ square feet, and the area of the space that she wants to keep as grass is $4m^2 + 2m + 3$ square feet. Taryn says that the pavers will cover $10m^2 + 11m + 11$ square feet. How did Taryn find the area of the pavers? Do you agree or disagree with Taryn's calculations? If you disagree, what is the area of the pavers? Explain your reasoning.

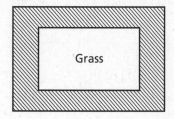

Grass

_____

_____

_____

_____

14. Some friends plan to repaint the front and one side of a house. They need to know the area of the sides of the house before they buy the paint. The area of the front of the rectangular house is $8b^2 + 7b$. The area of the side of the house is $4b^2 + 5$. Select all the expressions that represent the area that will be repainted.

Ⓐ $8b^2 + 4b^2 + 7b + 5$

Ⓑ $12b^2 + 12$

Ⓒ $12b^2 + 7b + 5$

Ⓓ $(8b^2 + 7b) + (4b^2 + 5)$

Ⓔ $12b^2 + 12b$

Step It Out

Learn the Math

EXAMPLE 1 A company that produces sleds has a revenue (in dollars) defined by the polynomial $28x - 0.001x^2$, where x is the number of sleds produced. The cost (in dollars) of producing x sleds is $15{,}000 + 3x + 0.001x^2$. Find the polynomial representing the profit from producing and selling x sleds and use it to calculate the profit from producing and selling 1000 sleds.

Use a verbal model.

Profit ?	=	Revenue $28x - 0.001x^2$	−	Cost $15{,}000 + 3x + 0.001x^2$

Calculate the profit by subtracting the cost from the revenue.

$$P = \left(28x - 0.001x^2\right) - \left(15{,}000 + 3x + 0.001x^2\right)$$

Distribute the subtraction sign.

$$P = 28x - 0.001x^2 - 15{,}000 - 3x - 0.001x^2$$

Rewrite the order of the terms.

$$P = -0.001x^2 - 0.001x^2 + 28x - 3x - 15{,}000$$

Combine like terms.

$$P = (-0.001 - 0.001)x^2 + (28 - 3)x - 15{,}000$$
$$= -0.002x^2 + 25x - 15{,}000$$

The profit from producing and selling x sleds is $-0.002x^2 + 25x - 15{,}000$. The profit from producing and selling 1000 sleds is $-0.002(1000)^2 + 25(1000) - 15{,}000 = \$8000$.

Do the Math

A company that produces textbooks has a revenue (in dollars) defined by the polynomial $21x - 0.00004x^2$, where x is the number of textbooks produced. The cost (in dollars) of producing x textbooks is $1250 + 5x + 0.00002x^2$. Find the polynomial representing the profit from producing and selling x textbooks and use it to calculate the profit from producing and selling 200,000 textbooks.

Use a verbal model.

$$\boxed{\begin{array}{c}\text{Profit}\\?\end{array}} = \boxed{\begin{array}{c}\text{Revenue}\\\square\,x - 0.00004x^2\end{array}} - \boxed{\begin{array}{c}\text{Cost}\\\square + \square\,x + 0.00002x^2\end{array}}$$

Calculate the profit by subtracting the cost from the revenue.

$$P = \left(\boxed{}\,x - 0.00004x^2\right) - \left(\boxed{} + \boxed{}\,x + 0.00002x^2\right)$$

Distribute the subtraction sign.

$$P = 21x \;\boxed{}\; 0.00004x^2 \;\boxed{}\; 1250 \;\boxed{}\; 5x \;\boxed{}\; 0.00002x^2$$

Rewrite the order of the terms.

$$P = \boxed{}\,0.00004x^2 - \boxed{}\,x^2 + \boxed{}\,x - 5x \;\boxed{}\; 1250$$

Combine like terms.

$$P = \left(\boxed{}\,0.00004 - \boxed{}\right)x^2 + \left(\boxed{} - 5\right)x \;\boxed{}\; 1250$$

$$= -\boxed{}\,x^2 + \boxed{}\,x \;\boxed{}\; 1250$$

The profit from producing and selling x textbooks is $-\boxed{}\,x^2 + \boxed{}\,x \;\boxed{}\; 1250$. The profit from producing and selling 200,000 textbooks is $-\boxed{}\,(200{,}000)^2 + \boxed{}\,(200{,}000)\;\boxed{}\;1250 = \$\boxed{}$.

Name _____

LESSON 16.2
More Practice

ONLINE
Video Tutorials and
Interactive Examples

Write the polynomial expression that gives the number of points in the *n*th figure in each sequence of figures shown.

1.

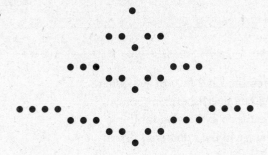

_____

2.

_____

3.

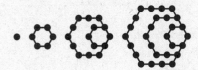

_____

4.

_____

Find a function that models each sequence of numbers for the *n*th number in the sequence.

5. 1, 8, 27, 64, 125, 216, 343

_____

6. 2, 6, 12, 20, 30, 42, 56

_____

7. 5, 17, 37, 65, 101, 145, 197

_____

8. 7, 9, 11, 13, 15, 17, 19

_____

9. The first terms of a sequence of figurate numbers are broken down as shown below.

$$5 = \frac{5(2)}{2} \qquad 5 + 10 = \frac{10(3)}{2} \qquad 5 + 10 + 15 = \frac{15(4)}{2} \qquad 5 + 10 + 15 + 20 = \frac{20(5)}{2}$$

What polynomial can model the *n*th term of this sequence?

_____

10. **Open Ended** Provide an example of a sequence of five figurate numbers whose nth term has four monomials in the polynomial function. What is the polynomial function that represents the sequence?

_____

_____

11. The rate that fish populate a lake per month can be represented as $2f^2 - 6f + 4$, where f represents the number of fish currently in the lake. The rate that fishermen remove fish from the lake can be represented as $f^2 + 9f + 2$. What is an expression for the change in the number of fish in the lake? What is the change in the number of fish in the lake per month if there are 100 fish currently in the lake?

_____

_____

_____

12. **Critique Reasoning** A company's revenue is defined by $8x^2 + 75x + 40$, and its cost is defined by $2x^2 + 500x + 10$. Lori thinks that the company's profit is $6x^2 + 575x + 50$. Her calculations are below. What was her mistake? Explain.

$P = 8x^2 + 75x + 40 - \left(2x^2 + 500x + 10\right)$

$= 8x^2 - 2x^2 + 75x + 500x + 40 + 10$

$= 6x^2 + 575x + 50$

_____

_____

_____

13. The first five terms of a sequence of figurate numbers are as follows:

$4(-6)$ $\qquad$ $8(-5)$ $\qquad$ $12(-4)$ $\qquad$ $16(-3)$ $\qquad$ $20(-2)$

Select all the polynomials that can model the nth term of this sequence.

Ⓐ $2n^2 - 14n$

Ⓑ $4n(n - 7)$

Ⓒ $n(4n - 14)$

Ⓓ $4n^2 - 28n$

Ⓔ $2n(n - 7)$

14. An analysis shows that the profit in thousands of dollars a company makes from manufacturing x thousand units of a product can be modeled by the polynomial $-0.32x^2 + 15x - 230$. The cost in thousands of dollars can be modeled by the polynomial $0.15x^2 + 5x + 230$. Which expression models the revenue in thousands of dollars?

Ⓐ $-0.17x^2 + 10x - 460$

Ⓒ $-0.47x^2 + 10x - 460$

Ⓑ $-0.17x^2 + 20x$

Ⓓ $-0.47x^2 + 20x$

Step It Out

Learn the Math

EXAMPLE 1 Solve $0 = 2x^2 + 4x - 16$ graphically.

Use a graphing calculator to graph the function $f(x) = 2x^2 + 4x - 16$.

Adjust the viewing window for the graph so that you have a clear view of the x-intercepts.

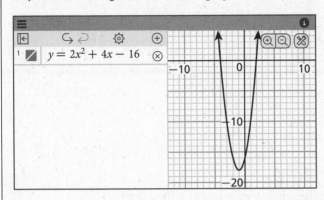

The x-intercepts appear to occur exactly on two whole units on the x-axis.

The x-intercepts appear to be -4 and 2.

Therefore, the solutions to the equation are -4 and 2.

Verify the solutions by substitution.

$f(-4) = 2(-4)^2 + 4(-4) - 16 = 32 - 16 - 16 = 0$

$f(2) = 2(2)^2 + 4(2) - 16 = 8 + 8 - 16 = 0$

Do the Math

Solve $0 = 3x^2 - 6x - 9$ graphically.

Use a graphing calculator and sketch the graph of the function $f(x) = 3x^2 - 6x - 9$.

The x-intercepts appear to be $\boxed{}$ and $\boxed{}$.

The solutions to the equation are $\boxed{}$ and $\boxed{}$.

Verify the solutions by substitution.

$f\left(\boxed{}\right) = 3\left(\boxed{}\right)^2 - 6\left(\boxed{}\right) - 9 = \boxed{} - \boxed{} - 9 = \boxed{}$

$f\left(\boxed{}\right) = 3\left(\boxed{}\right)^2 - 6\left(\boxed{}\right) - 9 = \boxed{} - \boxed{} - 9 = \boxed{}$

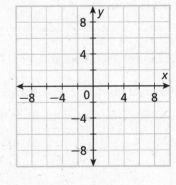

Learn the Math

EXAMPLE 2 Brayden drops a rock from a bridge into the water below at a height of 144 feet. The function $d(t) = 16t^2$ models the distance from the rock to the bridge after t seconds. Use a graph to determine how long it takes for the rock to hit the water.

Determine the values of t for which $16t^2 = 144$. Use a graphing calculator to solve $0 = 16t^2 - 144$.

Choose a viewing window that shows both x-intercepts.

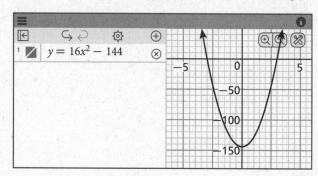

The x-intercepts appear to be -3 and 3. They occur on whole values on the x-axis.

The solutions to the equation are $t = -3$ and $t = 3$. However, since time cannot be negative, the solution $t = -3$ is not valid.

Verify that $t = 3$ is a solution.

$d(3) = 16(3)^2 = 16(9) = 144$

The rock will hit the water in 3 seconds.

Do the Math

Fritz is crossing a pedestrian bridge over a canyon that is 784 feet deep. He drops a stone into the canyon from the bridge. The function $d(t) = 16t^2$ models the distance from the stone to the bridge after t seconds. Use a graph to determine how long it takes for the stone to reach the canyon's floor.

Determine the values of t for which $16t^2 = \boxed{}$. Use a graphing

calculator to solve $\boxed{}$.

Choose a viewing window that shows both x-intercepts.

The x-intercepts appear to be $\boxed{}$ and $\boxed{}$.

The solutions to the equation are $\boxed{}$ and $\boxed{}$. Only use the

[positive / negative] solution to determine the time.

Verify that $t = \boxed{}$ is a solution.

$d\left(\boxed{}\right) = 16\left(\boxed{}\right)^2 = 16\left(\boxed{}\right) = \boxed{}$

The stone will reach the canyon's floor in $\boxed{}$ seconds.

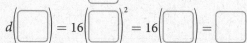

© Houghton Mifflin Harcourt Publishing Company

Graph each function to determine the zeros and locations of the x-intercepts.

1. $f(x) = x^2 + x - 12$

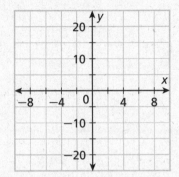

The x-intercepts of the graph are _____ and _____.

The zeros of the function are _____ and _____.

2. $f(x) = 5x^2 - 10x$

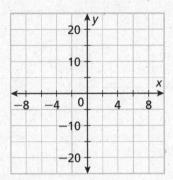

The x-intercepts of the graph are _____ and _____.

The zeros of the function are _____ and _____.

3. $f(x) = 2x^2 - 10x - 12$

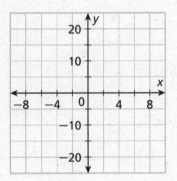

The x-intercepts of the graph are _____ and _____.

The zeros of the function are _____ and _____.

4. $f(x) = 3x^2 - 21x + 18$

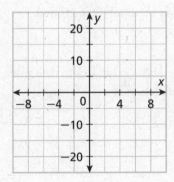

The x-intercepts of the graph are _____ and _____.

The zeros of the function are _____ and _____.

5. **Model with Mathematics** The function $f(x) = -3x^2 + 15x - 12$ models the area of a rectangle. Sketch a graph of the function to determine the values of x for which a rectangle exists. Explain your reasoning.

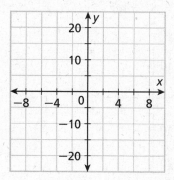

_____

_____

6. A sunflower seed falls from the edge of a balcony 150 feet above the ground. The function $d(t) = 16t^2$ models the distance from the sunflower seed to the balcony at t seconds. Determine the time, rounded to the nearest tenth of a second, it takes for the sunflower seed to hit the ground.

_____

7. **A.** Use a graphing calculator to determine the number of zeros for each of the following functions:

$f(x) = x^2 + 12x + 9, g(x) = x^2 + 9x + 9, h(x) = x^2 + 6x + 9, j(x) = x^2 + 9$
$r(x) = x^2 - 12x + 9, s(x) = x^2 - 9x + 9, t(x) = x^2 - 6x + 9$

_____

_____

_____

B. Consider the function $f(x) = x^2 + bx + 9$. For what values of b does the function have no zeros, one zero, and two zeros?

_____

8. **Reason** Explain how you can use a graph to solve the equation $x^2 - 4x - 18 = -3x - 6$.

_____

_____

9. What are the solutions to the equation $0 = x^2 - 7x - 18$?

Ⓐ −2 and −9   Ⓒ 2 and 9

Ⓑ 9 and −2   Ⓓ −9 and 2

Name _____

Step It Out

Learn the Math

EXAMPLE 1 ▶ Solve the equation $x^2 - x - 12 = 0$.

Factor the equation. $x^2 - x - 12 = (x + 3)(x - 4)$

Let $a = x + 3$ and $b = x - 4$. Then the equation $x^2 - x - 12 = 0$ becomes $ab = 0$.

Based on the Zero Product Property, $a = 0$ or $b = 0$.

$\quad\quad a = 0 \quad\quad\quad$ or $\quad\quad\quad\quad b = 0$

$\quad\quad x + 3 = 0 \quad$ or $\quad\quad\quad x - 4 = 0$

Solve each equation for x.

$\quad\quad x + 3 = 0 \quad$ or $\quad\quad\quad x - 4 = 0$

$\quad\quad x = -3 \quad\quad$ or $\quad\quad\quad\quad x = 4$

So, the solutions of the equation $x^2 - x - 12 = 0$ are $x = -3$ and $x = 4$.

The solutions $x = -3$ and $x = 4$ are the zeros of the corresponding function $f(x) = x^2 - x - 12$.

Do the Math

Solve the equation $x^2 - 12x + 35 = 0$.

Factor the equation. $x^2 - 12x + 35 = \left(x - \boxed{}\right)\left(x - \boxed{}\right)$

Let $a = x - \boxed{}$ and $b = x - \boxed{}$. Then the equation $x^2 - 12x + 35 = 0$ becomes $ab = 0$.

Based on the Zero Product Property, $a = 0$ or $b = 0$.

$\quad\quad a = 0 \quad\quad\quad$ or $\quad\quad\quad\quad b = 0$

$\quad\quad x - \boxed{} = 0 \quad$ or $\quad x - \boxed{} = 0$

Solve each equation for x.

$\quad\quad x - \boxed{} = 0 \quad$ or $\quad x - \boxed{} = 0$

$\quad\quad x = \boxed{} \quad\quad$ or $\quad\quad x = \boxed{}$

So, the solutions of the equation $x^2 - 12x + 35 = 0$ are $x = \boxed{}$ and $x = \boxed{}$.

The solutions $x = \boxed{}$ and $x = \boxed{}$ are the zeros of the corresponding function $f(x) = x^2 - 12x + 35$.

Learn the Math

EXAMPLE 2 Sandy has a box that measures 4 inches by 4 inches. She needs to find a box that increases the length and width of the original box by the same amount in order to fit a square platter with area 49 square inches. By how much does she need to increase the length and width to fit the platter?

Use a verbal model.

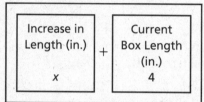 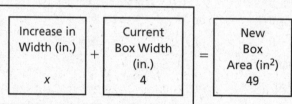

New Box Length (in.)　　　New Box Width (in.)

| Increase in Length (in.) x | + | Current Box Length (in.) 4 | • | Increase in Width (in.) x | + | Current Box Width (in.) 4 | = | New Box Area (in²) 49 |

Write an equation. $(x + 4)(x + 4) = 49$

Solve. $(x + 4)(x + 4) = 49 \rightarrow x^2 + 8x + 16 = 49 \rightarrow x^2 + 8x - 33 = 0$

$(x + 11)(x - 3) = 0 \rightarrow x = -11 \text{ or } x = 3$

Answer the question. The increase cannot be negative, so the only solution is $x = 3$. Sandy should find a box with a length and width increased by 3 inches so that the new dimensions are 7 inches by 7 inches.

Do the Math

Colby is getting a new refrigerator. He knows the ceiling is high enough to accommodate the new refrigerator. However, the floor space of 24 inches by 24 inches is not enough for it to fit. The new refrigerator has a square base of 1296 square inches. By how much does he need to increase the length and width of the empty space to fit the new refrigerator?

Use a verbal model.

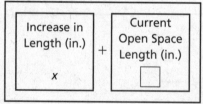 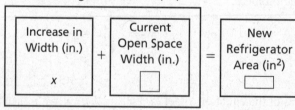

New Refrigerator Length (in.)　　　New Refrigerator Width (in.)

| Increase in Length (in.) x | + | Current Open Space Length (in.) ☐ | • | Increase in Width (in.) x | + | Current Open Space Width (in.) ☐ | = | New Refrigerator Area (in²) ☐ |

Write an equation. $\left(x + \boxed{}\right)\left(x + \boxed{}\right) = 1296$

Solve. $\left(x + \boxed{}\right)\left(x + \boxed{}\right) = 1296 \rightarrow x^2 + \boxed{}x + \boxed{} = 1296 \rightarrow x^2 + \boxed{}x - \boxed{} = 0$

$\left(x + \boxed{}\right)\left(x - \boxed{}\right) = 0 \rightarrow x = \boxed{} \text{ or } x = \boxed{}$

Answer the question. The increase cannot be negative, so the only solution is $x = \boxed{}$. Colby should increase the space for the refrigerator by a length and width of $\boxed{}$ inches. The new dimensions are $\boxed{}$ inches by $\boxed{}$ inches.

Name

LESSON 17.2
More Practice

ONLINE
Video Tutorials and
Interactive Examples

Find the zeros of each function. Solve the corresponding quadratic equations by factoring and using the Zero Product Property. Show your work.

1. $f(x) = x^2 + 4x - 5$

2. $f(x) = x^2 - 12x + 20$

3. $f(x) = x^2 + 4x - 21$

4. $f(x) = x^2 + 9x + 20$

5. $f(x) = x^2 + 15x + 36$

6. $f(x) = x^2 - 3x - 54$

7. $f(x) = x^2 - 15x + 44$

8. $f(x) = x^2 - 7x - 8$

9. $f(x) = x^2 - 9x - 36$

10. $f(x) = x^2 + 11x + 18$

11. Math on the Spot Solve the equation $x^2 + 8x + 12 = 0$.

12. Open Ended How does the Zero Product Property help you solve trinomial equations?

_____

_____

13. The area of a playground is $x^2 + 16x + 48$ square feet. What are the length and width of the playground? There is enough land to expand the playground by 6 feet in both directions. What could be the new area of the playground? Explain your answers.

_____

_____

14. Park rangers plan to expand the area of a park to 506 square miles. Currently, the length of the park is 18 miles and the width is 17 miles. They want to extend the length and the width by the same number of miles. If they are successful, what will the new dimensions of the park be? Explain.

_____

_____

_____

_____

15. A pool has the following shape. What is the area of the entire pool? How do you know?

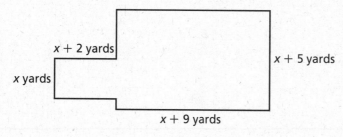

_____

_____

_____

_____

16. A painting is 16 inches by 20 inches. The painting along with its frame cannot be larger than 388 square inches to fit on the wall. The width of the frame is x inches. Select all the equations that represent the maximum size of the painting with its frame.

(A) $(2x + 16)(2x + 20) = 0$

(B) $(2x + 16)(2x + 20) = 388$

(C) $4x^2 + 72x - 68 = 0$

(D) $4x^2 + 72x + 320 = 0$

(E) $4x^2 + 320 = 388$

Step It Out

Learn the Math

EXAMPLE 1 ▶ The height of a ball launched in the air from a 12-foot platform is modeled by the equation $y = -16x^2 + 8x + 12$. To find the time x, in seconds, that the ball takes to reach a height of 4 feet, use the equation $-16x^2 + 8x + 12 = 4$.

Use the steps to solve the equation

The equation is given.

$$-16x^2 + 8x + 12 = 4$$

$$-16x^2 + 8x + 12 = 4$$

Write the equation in standard form.

$$-16x^2 + 8x + 8 = 0$$

Divide both sides by -8.

$$2x^2 - x - 1 = 0$$

Factor to rewrite the equation as a product.

$$(2x + 1)(x - 1) = 0$$

Use the Zero Product Property to solve.

$$(2x + 1) = 0 \text{ or } x - 1 = 0$$

Solve each equation for x.

$$x = -\frac{1}{2} \text{ or } x = 1$$

The answer cannot be negative seconds. The ball reaches a height of 4 feet in 1 second.

Do the Math

The height of another ball launched in the air from a 16-foot platform is modeled by the equation $y = -16x^2 + 4x + 16$. To find the time x, in seconds, that the ball takes to reach a height of 10 feet, use the equation $-16x^2 + 4x + 16 = 10$.

Use the steps to solve the equation $-16x^2 + 4x + 16 = 10$.

The equation is given.

$$-16x^2 + 4x + 16 = 10$$

Write the equation in standard form.

$$-16x^2 + 4x + \boxed{} = 0$$

Divide both sides by $\boxed{}$.

$$\boxed{}x^2 - \boxed{}x - \boxed{} = 0$$

Factor to rewrite the equation as a product.

$$\left(4x - \boxed{}\right)\left(\boxed{}x + 1\right) = 0$$

Use the Zero Product Property to solve.

$$4x - \boxed{} = 0 \text{ or } \boxed{}x + 1 = 0$$

Solve each equation for x.

$$x = \frac{\boxed{}}{\boxed{}} \text{ or } x = -\frac{\boxed{}}{\boxed{}}$$

The answer cannot be negative seconds. The ball reaches a height of 10 feet in $\dfrac{\boxed{}}{\boxed{}}$ second.

Learn the Math

EXAMPLE 2 A rectangular cake that measures 30 centimeters by 20 centimeters is centered on a cake stand. The stand has a total area of 1419 square centimeters. Let x represent the width of the cake stand around the cake that is visible. What is the width of the cake stand that is visible?

Use a verbal model.

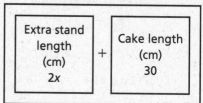
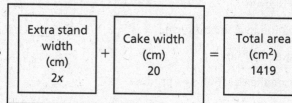

Total length (cm)

| Extra stand length (cm) $2x$ | + | Cake length (cm) 30 |

Total width (cm)

| Extra stand width (cm) $2x$ | + | Cake width (cm) 20 | = | Total area (cm^2) 1419 |

Write an equation. $(2x + 30)(2x + 20) = 1419$

Solve the equation. $4x^2 + 100x + 600 = 1419 \rightarrow 4x^2 + 100x - 819 = 0$

$(2x + 63)(2x - 13) = 0 \rightarrow x = -\dfrac{63}{2} = -31\dfrac{1}{2}$ or $x = \dfrac{13}{2} = 6\dfrac{1}{2}$

Answer the question. The width around the cake cannot be negative, so the only solution is $x = 6\dfrac{1}{2}$. The width of the cake stand that is visible is $6\dfrac{1}{2}$ centimeters.

Do the Math

Volunteers build a uniform wooden border around a sandbox that is 5 feet by 8 feet. The sandbox and wooden border have a total area of 108 square feet. The width of the wooden border can be represented as x. What is the width of the wooden border?

Use a verbal model.

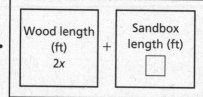

Total width (ft)

| Wood width (ft) $2x$ | + | Sandbox width (ft) ☐ |

Total length (ft)

| Wood length (ft) $2x$ | + | Sandbox length (ft) ☐ | = | Total area (ft^2) ☐ |

Write an equation. $\left(2x + \boxed{}\right)\left(\boxed{} + 8\right) = 108$

Solve. $\boxed{}x^2 + 26x + \boxed{} = 108 \rightarrow \boxed{}x^2 + 26x - \boxed{} = 0$

$\left(2x + \boxed{}\right)\left(\boxed{}x - \boxed{}\right) = 0 \rightarrow x = -\dfrac{\boxed{}}{\boxed{}} = -\boxed{}\dfrac{\boxed{}}{\boxed{}}$ or $x = \dfrac{\boxed{}}{\boxed{}} = \boxed{}$

Answer the question. The width of the wooden border cannot be negative, so the only solution is $x = \boxed{}$. The width of the wooden border is $\boxed{}$ feet.

Name _____

LESSON 17.3
More Practice

ONLINE
Ed Video Tutorials and
Interactive Examples

Factor each expression.

1. $12x^2 + 27x + 6$

_____

2. $8x^2 + 18x - 35$

_____

3. $18x^2 + 36x$

_____

4. $6x^2 + 13x + 6$

_____

5. $4x^2 - 35x + 24$

_____

6. $12x^2 + 34x - 56$

_____

Solve each quadratic equation by factoring.

7. $3x^2 + 10x + 3 = 0$

_____

8. $25x^2 - 45x = 0$

_____

9. $11x^2 - 26x + 8 = 0$

_____

10. $24x^2 + 14x - 5 = 0$

_____

11. $7x^2 - 15x + 8 = 0$

_____

12. $20x^2 + 22x - 70 = 0$

_____

13. $15x^2 - 19x - 56 = 0$

_____

14. $28x^2 - 79x + 36 = 0$

_____

15. Open Ended Explain how to factor $ax^2 + bx + c$ to someone who does not know how to factor.

_____

_____

16. Math on the Spot The diver's height above the water during a dive can be modeled by $h = -16t^2 + 8t + 8$, where h is height in feet and t is time in seconds. Find the time it takes the diver to reach the water.

_____

17. Reason Abstractly A ball is tossed from a platform. The height of the ball can be represented as $h = -16t^2 + 2t + 6$, where h is the height in feet and t is the time in seconds. A balloon is released into the air from the ground at a rate of $h = 6t$. When will the ball and balloon meet? Explain your reasoning.

_____

_____

_____

18. The area of the shaded figure is 208 square meters.

The triangle's base and height are both x.

What is the value of x? Show your work.

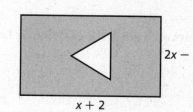

$2x - 4$

$x + 2$

_____

_____

_____

19. The area of a parallelogram is shown in the diagram, where x represents the height in inches. If the area is 95 square inches, what is the height?

Ⓐ 8 inches

Ⓒ 2 inches

Ⓑ $1\frac{1}{2}$ inches

Ⓓ $1\frac{3}{4}$ inches

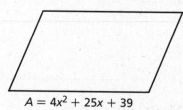

$A = 4x^2 + 25x + 39$

20. Select all the points of intersection of the functions $f(x) = 5x^2 + 2x - 20$ and $g(x) = x^2 - 6x + 25$.

Ⓐ $\left(-\dfrac{5}{2}, \dfrac{25}{4}\right)$

Ⓑ $\left(\dfrac{5}{2}, \dfrac{65}{4}\right)$

Ⓒ $\left(\dfrac{9}{2}, \dfrac{79}{4}\right)$

Ⓓ $\left(-\dfrac{9}{2}, \dfrac{289}{4}\right)$

Ⓔ $\left(-\dfrac{5}{2}, \dfrac{185}{4}\right)$

Step It Out

Learn the Math	**Do the Math**
EXAMPLE 1 Factor $x^2 + 8x + 16$ and $9x^2 + 12x + 4$.	Factor.

Learn the Math

$a^2 + 2ab + b^2 = (a + b)(a + b)$
$\qquad\qquad\quad = (a + b)^2$

$x^2 + 8x + 16 = x^2 + 2(x)(4) + 4^2$
$\qquad\qquad\quad = (x + 4)(x + 4)$
$\qquad\qquad\quad = (x + 4)^2$

$9x^2 + 12x + 4 = (3x)^2 + 2(3x)(2) + 2^2$
$\qquad\qquad\qquad = (3x + 2)(3x + 2)$
$\qquad\qquad\qquad = (3x + 2)^2$

Do the Math

Factor.

$x^2 + 16x + 64$

$= \left(\boxed{}\right)^2 + 2\left(\boxed{}\right)\left(\boxed{}\right) + \left(\boxed{}\right)^2$

$= \left(\boxed{} + \boxed{}\right)\left(\boxed{} + \boxed{}\right)$

$= \left(\boxed{} + \boxed{}\right)^2$

$25x^2 + 30x + 9$

$= \left(\boxed{}\right)^2 + 2\left(\boxed{}\right)\left(\boxed{}\right) + \left(\boxed{}\right)^2$

$= \left(\boxed{} + \boxed{}\right)\left(\boxed{} + \boxed{}\right)$

$= \left(\boxed{} + \boxed{}\right)^2$

Learn the Math	**Do the Math**
EXAMPLE 2 Factor $x^2 - 14x + 49$ and $36x^2 - 36x + 1$.	Factor.

Learn the Math

$a^2 - 2ab + b^2 = (a - b)(a - b)$
$\qquad\qquad\quad = (a - b)^2$

$x^2 - 14x + 49 = x^2 - 2(x)(7) + 7^2$
$\qquad\qquad\qquad = (x - 7)(x - 7)$
$\qquad\qquad\qquad = (x - 7)^2$

$36x^2 - 12x + 1 = (6x)^2 - 2(6x)(1) + 1^2$
$\qquad\qquad\qquad = (6x - 1)(6x - 1)$
$\qquad\qquad\qquad = (6x - 1)^2$

Do the Math

Factor.

$x^2 - 10x + 25$

$= \left(\boxed{}\right)^2 - 2\left(\boxed{}\right)\left(\boxed{}\right) + \left(\boxed{}\right)^2$

$= \left(\boxed{} - \boxed{}\right)\left(\boxed{} - \boxed{}\right)$

$= \left(\boxed{} - \boxed{}\right)^2$

$4x^2 - 12xy + 9y^2$

$= \left(\boxed{}\right)^2 - 2\left(\boxed{}\right)\left(\boxed{}\right) + \left(\boxed{}\right)^2$

$= \left(\boxed{} - \boxed{}\right)\left(\boxed{} - \boxed{}\right)$

$= \left(\boxed{} - \boxed{}\right)^2$

Learn the Math

EXAMPLE 3 ▶ The area of a doormat can be found using the equation $A = x^2 - 48x + 1536$, where x is the length of the doormat. If the area of the doormat is 960 square inches, find the dimensions of the doormat.

Write an equation.

$x^2 - 48x + 1536 = 960$

Solve the equation.

$x^2 - 48x + 1536 = 960$	Given equation
$x^2 - 48x + 576 = 0$	Rearrange terms to set equal to zero.
$(x - 24)^2 = 0$	Factor the quadratic.
$x = 24$	Find the solution.

Divide the area by the dimension to find the other dimension.

$960 \div 24 = 40$

The dimensions of the doormat are 24 inches by 40 inches.

Do the Math

The area of a rectangular garden can be found using the equation $A = x^2 - 64x + 1600$, where x is the length of the garden. If the area of the garden is 576 square feet, what are the dimensions of the garden?

Learn the Math

EXAMPLE 4 ▶ A hummingbird drops a seed from 400 feet above the ground. How long will it take for the seed to reach the ground?

Use the equation $h(t) = -16t^2 + v_0 t + h_0$ to model this situation. In this case, $v_0 = 0$ because the seed is dropped, and $h_0 = 400$.

$0 = -16t^2 + 400$

$0 = t^2 - 25$

$0 = (t - 5)(t + 5)$

$t = 5$ or $t = -5$

The negative value is not valid in this situation because time cannot be negative. The seed reaches the ground in 5 seconds.

Do the Math

Jesse dropped a pebble over the edge of a cliff that is 144 feet high. How long will it take for the pebble to hit the ground?

Factor each expression.

1. $x^2 - 81$

_____

2. $x^2 + 12x + 36$

_____

3. $4x^2 - 28x + 49$

_____

4. $25x^2 - 64y^2$

_____

Solve each equation by factoring.

5. $x^2 - 100 = 0$

6. $4x^2 + 12x + 9 = 0$

7. $3x^2 - 30x + 75 = 0$

8. $25x^2 - 60x + 36 = 0$

9. **Model with Mathematics** Mike dropped a pair of binoculars off a bridge that is 324 feet above a creek. Use the function $h(t) = -16t^2 + h_0$, where h is in feet and t is in seconds. How long did it take for the binoculars to hit the creek?

_____

_____

_____

10. **Math on the Spot** The garden in Annie's yard is in the shape of a square. The area of the garden is $36x^2 + 60x + 25$ ft^2. The dimensions of the garden are approximately $cx + d$, where c and d are whole numbers. Find an expression for the perimeter of the garden. Find the perimeter when $x = 10$ ft.

_____

_____

11. **Critique Reasoning** Sally designs a rectangular poster to hang in her bedroom. She wants the area of her poster to be 216 square inches. The area of her poster can be found using the equation $A = x^2 - 24x + 360$ where x is the poster's width. Sally says that she can find the width of her poster by substituting 0 for A and solving the equation. Explain her error. Then solve the equation to find the dimensions of the poster.

_____

_____

_____

12. The side length in feet of a square helicopter landing pad can be found by solving the equation $x^2 - 40x + 400 = 0$ for x. What is the perimeter of the landing pad?

_____

_____

_____

13. Solve $9x^2 - 42x + 49 = 0$.

Ⓐ $x = -\dfrac{7}{3}$

Ⓑ $x = \dfrac{7}{3}$

Ⓒ $x = \dfrac{3}{7}$

Ⓓ $x = \dfrac{7}{3}$ and $x = -\dfrac{7}{3}$

14. Which expression is a factor of $16x^4 - 112x^3 + 196x^2$?

Ⓐ $2x^2 - 7$

Ⓑ $4x^2 - 7$

Ⓒ $2x - 7$

Ⓓ $4x - 7$

Step It Out

Learn the Math

EXAMPLE 1 Anna is entering a poster in an art contest. The contest rules specify that all poster entries have the same area. Anna is trying to decide whether she wants to create a square poster or a circular poster.

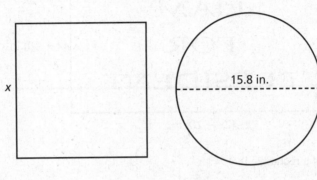

If Anna chooses the square poster, what length, to the nearest inch, must she make the side?

Area of square = Area of circle

$s^2 = \pi r^2$	Use the formulas for the area of a square and for the area of a circle.
$s^2 = \pi(7.9)^2$	Divide the diameter of the circle by 2 and substitute for the radius.
$s^2 = 62.41\pi$	Square 7.9.
$s \approx \pm 14$	Take the square root of both sides.

A side length cannot be negative. So, for the areas of the square and the circle to be equal, the side length of the square must be 14 inches.

What area must all posters entered into the art contest have? Check your work.

Area of square   Area of circle

$A = s^2$ $A = \pi r^2$

$\quad = 14^2$ $\quad = \pi(7.9)^2$

$\quad = 196 \text{ in}^2$ $\quad \approx 196 \text{ in}^2$

All posters entered into the art contest must have an area of 196 square inches.

Do the Math

Liam is creating a poster to advertise his candidacy for student council president. The school regulates that posters can have a maximum area of 1050 square centimeters. What dimensions should Liam make his poster so it can cover the maximum area?

LIAM
FOR
PRESIDENT

$(x + 10)$ in.

$(2x - 20)$ in.

The formula for the area of a rectangle is $A = \boxed{} \cdot \boxed{}$.

Substitute the expressions for the length and width of Liam's poster in the formula for length and width and set equal to $\boxed{}$. Then solve for x.

$$\left(2x - \boxed{}\right)\left(x + \boxed{}\right) = \boxed{}$$

$$2x^{\boxed{}} + \boxed{}x - \boxed{}x - \boxed{} = \boxed{}$$

$$2x^{\boxed{}} - \boxed{} = \boxed{}$$

$$2x^{\boxed{}} = \boxed{}$$

$$x^{\boxed{}} = \boxed{}$$

$$x = \pm\boxed{}$$

An x-value of $\boxed{}$ would cause the dimensions of the rectangle to be negative, so only use the

_____ root. To have the maximum area, Liam's poster should be $2 \cdot \boxed{} - 20$, or $\boxed{}$ inches

by $\boxed{} + 10$, or $\boxed{}$ inches.

Name _____

LESSON 18.1
More Practice

⊙Ed **ONLINE**
Video Tutorials and
Interactive Examples

Solve each equation by finding square roots. If the equation has no real
number solutions, write *no solution*.

1. $w^2 = 81$

_____

2. $a^2 = 49$

_____

3. $l^2 - 36 = 0$

_____

4. $\frac{1}{2}x^2 - 32 = 0$

_____

5. $b^2 = -121$

_____

6. $-6r^2 = -24$

_____

7. $-6y^2 + 6 = -48$

_____

8. $2z^2 - 3 = 197$

_____

Solve each equation. Give the answer in simplest radical form. Then use a calculator to approximate the
solution to two decimal places, if necessary.

9. $3y^2 - 36 = 0$

_____

10. $\frac{1}{3}h^2 = 49$

_____

11. $3s^2 + 1 = 7$

_____

12. $2a^2 + 7 = 29$

_____

13. $-\frac{1}{2}w^2 + 75 = 0$

_____

14. $v^2 - 5 = 5$

_____

Write a quadratic equation to model each problem. Then solve the equation. Round your answer to the nearest tenth if necessary.

15. Find the radius of a circle if the area is 372 square centimeters. _____

16. Find the side length of a square if the area is 58 square inches. _____

17. Find the side length of an equilateral triangle if the area is 63 square meters given $A = \dfrac{\sqrt{3}}{4}s^2$.

    _____

18. **Math on the Spot** A nursery manager is buying fencing to enclose three sides of a garden, with two short sides and one long side. The garden is a rectangle with sides $2x$ and $3x$, where x is feet. The area of the garden is 3000 square feet. The manager can buy fencing in whole feet only. How many feet of fencing should he buy?

19. Two different sizes of circular plates are sold at a home goods store. The radius of the smaller plate is 1 centimeter less than the radius of the larger plate. The area of the smaller plate is 500 square centimeters.

    A. What is the radius of the smaller plate to the nearest hundredth of a centimeter?

    _____

    B. What is the area of the larger plate to the nearest square centimeter?

    _____

20. **Critique Reasoning** Two students try to solve $s^2 + 64 = 0$ as shown. Which student made an error? Describe the error.

    Patrick

    $s^2 + 64 = 0$

    $s^2 = -64$

    $s = \pm \sqrt{64}$

    $s = \pm 8$

    Juan

    $s^2 + 64 = 0$

    $s^2 = -64$

    no solution

    _____

    _____

21. What are the solutions of the equation $8c^2 - 72 = -40$?

    Ⓐ no solution

    Ⓑ -2

    Ⓒ ± 4

    Ⓓ ± 2

Step It Out

Learn the Math

EXAMPLE 1 ▶ Solve $3x^2 - 4x = 4$ by completing the square.

Method 1: Use the coefficient a^2

$$3x^2 - 4x = 4$$
$$3(3x^2 - 4x) = 3(4)$$
$$9x^2 - 12x = 12$$
$$9x^2 - 12x + 4 = 12 + 4$$
$$9x^2 - 12x + 4 = 16$$
$$(3x - 2)^2 = 16$$
$$3x - 2 = \pm\sqrt{16}$$
$$3x - 2 = \pm 4$$
$$3x = 2 \pm 4$$
$$x = 2 \text{ or } x = -\frac{2}{3}$$

Method 2: Use the coefficient 1

$$3x^2 - 4x = 4$$
$$\frac{1}{3}(3x^2 - 4x) = \frac{1}{3}(4)$$
$$x^2 - \frac{4}{3}x = \frac{4}{3}$$
$$x^2 - \frac{4}{3}x + \frac{4}{9} = \frac{4}{3} + \frac{4}{9}$$
$$\left(x - \frac{2}{3}\right)^2 = \frac{16}{9}$$
$$x - \frac{2}{3} = \pm\frac{4}{3}$$
$$x = \frac{2}{3} \pm \frac{4}{3}$$
$$x = 2 \text{ or } x = -\frac{2}{3}$$

Do the Math

Solve $5x^2 + 4x = 1$ by completing the square.

Method 1: Use the coefficient a^2

$$\boxed{}(5x^2 + 4x) = \boxed{}(1)$$

$$\boxed{}x^2 + \boxed{}x = \boxed{}$$

$$\boxed{}x^2 + \boxed{}x + \boxed{} = \boxed{} + \boxed{}$$

$$\left(\boxed{}x + \boxed{}\right)^2 = \boxed{}$$

$$\boxed{}x + \boxed{} = \pm\boxed{}$$

$$x = \boxed{} \text{ or } x = \boxed{}$$

Method 2: Use the coefficient 1

$$\boxed{}(5x^2 + 4x) = \boxed{}(1)$$

$$\boxed{}x^2 + \boxed{}x = \boxed{}$$

$$\boxed{}x^2 + \boxed{}x + \boxed{} = \boxed{} + \boxed{}$$

$$\left(\boxed{}x + \boxed{}\right)^2 = \boxed{}$$

$$\boxed{}x + \boxed{} = \pm\boxed{}$$

$$x = \boxed{} \text{ or } x = \boxed{}$$

Learn the Math

EXAMPLE 2 A baseball player hits a ball from a height of 4 feet. If the initial vertical velocity of the ball is 80 feet per second, how long will it take the ball to hit the ground? Use the formula $h(t) = -16t^2 + v_0 t + h_0$. Find an exact answer and an approximate answer.

Substitute 4 for h_0 and 80 for v_0 into the formula and set equal to 0.

$$-16t^2 + 80t + 4 = 0$$
$$16t^2 - 80t = 4$$
$$16t^2 - 80t + 100 = 4 + 100$$
$$(4t - 10)^2 = 104$$
$$4t - 10 = \pm\sqrt{104}$$
$$4t - 10 = \pm 2\sqrt{26}$$
$$4t = 10 \pm 2\sqrt{26}$$
$$t = \frac{5 \pm \sqrt{26}}{2}$$

Time is not negative, so the solution is $t = \dfrac{5 + \sqrt{26}}{2} \approx 5.0$.

Using a calculator for an approximate answer, the ball will hit the ground in approximately 5.0 seconds.

Do the Math

A toy rocket is launched from a height of 6 feet. If the initial vertical velocity of the rocket is 50 feet per second, how long will it take the rocket to hit the ground? Find an exact answer and an approximate answer to the nearest tenth.

Substitute the initial vertical velocity and starting height into the formula.

$$\boxed{} = -16t^2 + \boxed{}t + \boxed{}$$

Rewrite the equation as an equivalent equation with a perfect square trinomial: _____

Write the equation in factored form: _____

The exact solutions are _____ and _____. Omit the _____ solution.

The rocket will hit the ground in approximately $\boxed{}$ seconds.

Solve each equation by completing the square. When necessary, express your final answer in simplest radical form.

1. $x^2 + 4x = 5$

2. $x^2 - 5x = 8$

_____

_____

3. $x^2 - 6x = 9$

4. $3x^2 + 10x = -3$

_____

_____

5. $2x^2 + 5x = 10$

6. $5x^2 + 12x = -\dfrac{27}{5}$

_____

_____

7. **Math on the Spot** The height h of a flying disc thrown into the air from a starting height of 4 meters with an initial velocity of 4 meters per second can be modeled using the equation $h = -5t^2 + 4t + 4$, where t represents time in seconds. How long will the flying disc remain in the air?

_____

8. The area of a rectangle is 200 square meters. If the length is 14 more than the width, what is the width of the rectangle, rounded to the nearest tenth? Show your work.

_____

9. A model rocket is launched from the ground. If the initial vertical velocity of the rocket is 104 feet per second, how long will it take the rocket to return to the ground? Use the formula $h(t) = -16t^2 + v_0t + h_0$. Show your work.

_____

10. What is the solution to the equation $6x^2 = 8x + 3$?

(A) $x = \dfrac{4 \pm \sqrt{34}}{6}$

(B) $x = \dfrac{6 \pm \sqrt{34}}{4}$

(C) $x = \dfrac{-4 \pm \sqrt{34}}{6}$

(D) $x = \dfrac{-6 \pm \sqrt{34}}{4}$

11. Which equation is equivalent to $2x^2 - 16x - 43 = -3$?

(A) $(x + 16)^2 = 40$

(B) $(x - 16)^2 = 36$

(C) $(x - 4)^2 = 40$

(D) $(x - 4)^2 = 36$

Step It Out

Learn the Math

EXAMPLE 1 ▶ Use the Quadratic Formula to solve $x^2 - 7x = 18$.

$x^2 - 7x - 18 = 0$ Rewrite the equation in standard form.

$a = 1, b = -7, c = -18$ Identify the values of a, b, and c.

$x = \dfrac{-(-7) \pm \sqrt{(-7)^2 - 4(1)(-18)}}{2(1)}$ Substitute the values of a, b, and c into the Quadratic Formula.

$x = \dfrac{7 \pm \sqrt{121}}{2}$ Simplify inside all parentheses and simplify the radicand.

$x = \dfrac{7 \pm 11}{2}$ Evaluate the square root.

$x = \dfrac{7 + 11}{2}$ or $x = \dfrac{7 - 11}{2}$ Separate the $\pm$ into two separate equations.

$x = 9$ or $x = -2$ Simplify both equations.

Do the Math

Use the Quadratic Formula to solve $x^2 - 15 = -2x$.

$\boxed{} = 0$ Rewrite the equation in standard form.

$x = \dfrac{-\left(\boxed{}\right) \pm \sqrt{\left(\boxed{}\right)^2 - 4\left(\boxed{}\right)\left(\boxed{}\right)}}{2\left(\boxed{}\right)}$ Substitute the values of a, b, and c into the Quadratic Formula.

$x = \dfrac{\boxed{} \pm \sqrt{\boxed{}}}{\boxed{}}$ Simplify inside all parentheses and simplify the radicand.

$x = \boxed{}$ or $x = \boxed{}$ Evaluate the square root, separate into two equations, and simplify both equations.

Learn the Math

EXAMPLE 2 A baseball player hits a home run from a pitch that reaches the plate with a height of 1.5 meters and an initial vertical velocity of 45 meters per second. About how long is the ball at least 12 meters above the ground? Round your answer to the nearest hundredth of a second.

$h(t) = -4.9t^2 + v_0 t + h_0$	Use the formula for the height of a projectile.
$12 = -4.9t^2 + 45t + 1.5$	Substitute values for h_0, v_0, and $h(t)$.
$t = \dfrac{-(45) \pm \sqrt{(45)^2 - 4(-4.9)(-10.5)}}{2(-4.9)}$	Use the standard form for the previous equation and substitute a, b, and c into the Quadratic Formula.
$t = \dfrac{-45 \pm 42.65}{-9.8}$	Simplify inside all parentheses and simplify the radicand. Evaluate the square root.
$t = 0.24$ or $t = 8.94$	Separate into two equations and simplify each equation.
$8.94 - 0.24 = 8.7$	Subtract.

The ball is above 12 meters for about 8.7 seconds.

Do the Math

A golfer hits a ball from a height of 0.03 meter off the ground with an initial vertical velocity of 30 meters per second. For how long is the ball at least 3 meters above the ground? Round your answer to the nearest hundredth of a second. Use the formula $h(t) = -4.9t^2 + v_0 t + h_0$.

$\boxed{} = -4.9t^2 + \boxed{}t + \boxed{}$	Substitute values for h_0, v_0, and $h(t)$.
$t = \dfrac{-\left(\boxed{}\right) \pm \sqrt{\left(\boxed{}\right)^2 - 4\left(\boxed{}\right)\left(\boxed{}\right)}}{2\left(\boxed{}\right)}$	Use the standard form for the previous equation and substitute a, b, and c into the Quadratic Formula.
$t = \boxed{}$ or $t = \boxed{}$	Simplify inside all parentheses and simplify the radicand. Evaluate the square root. Separate into two equations and simplify each equation.

The ball is above 3 meters for about $\boxed{}$ seconds.

Name _____

Solve each equation using the Quadratic Formula. Where necessary, express your final answer in simplest radical form.

1. $x^2 - 8x - 20 = 0$

2. $x^2 + 6x = 8$

_____

3. $2x^2 + 7x - 15 = 0$

4. $3x^2 - 10x = -4$

_____

5. $4x^2 - 2 = x$

6. $6x^2 + 18x = 5$

_____

© Houghton Mifflin Harcourt Publishing Company

7. **Math on the Spot** A weight 2 feet above the ground on a carnival strength test shoots straight up with an initial velocity of 30 feet per second. Will the weight ring the bell at the top of the 25 ft pole? Use the discriminant to explain your answer.

_____

_____

_____

8. The volume of a closet is given by the formula $V(x) = 6(x^2 - 10x + 14)$, where x is the length of the closet in feet.

   A. If the volume of the closet is 144 cubic feet, find the length of the closet, rounded to the nearest tenth of a foot.

   _____

   B. If the height of the closet is 6 feet, what is the width of the closet, rounded to the nearest tenth of a foot?

   _____

9. A football player kicks a ball in the air to the returner from an initial height of 0.1 meter. The initial vertical velocity of the ball is 38 meters per second. If the returner catches the ball at a height of 1.5 meters, how long after the kick does he catch the ball? Show your work.

   _____

10. What is the solution to the equation $4x^2 = 2x + 3$?

    Ⓐ no real solution

    Ⓑ $x = \dfrac{1 + \sqrt{13}}{4}$ or $x = \dfrac{1 - \sqrt{13}}{4}$

    Ⓒ $x = \dfrac{-1 + \sqrt{13}}{4}$ or $x = \dfrac{-1 - \sqrt{13}}{4}$

    Ⓓ $x = \dfrac{1 + 2\sqrt{3}}{4}$ or $x = \dfrac{1 - 2\sqrt{3}}{4}$

11. Which equation has no real solutions?

    Ⓐ $4x^2 - 12x + 8 = 0$

    Ⓑ $8x^2 - 8x + 10 = 0$

    Ⓒ $8x^2 + 10x - 8 = 0$

    Ⓓ $8x^2 + 8x - 10 = 0$

Name _____

Step It Out

Learn the Math	Do the Math

Learn the Math

> **EXAMPLE 1** ▶ Solve the quadratic equation $2x^2 - 5 = 43$ using different methods, or explain why a method is not applicable.

Factoring: The equation written in standard form $ax^2 + bx + c = 0$ is $2x^2 - 48 = 0$. There is no sum of the product of the outer factors and the product of inner factors that is equal to b, or 0, so the equation is not factorable.

Square roots: Use this method because the equation does not have a bx term.

$$2x^2 - 5 = 43$$
$$2x^2 = 48$$
$$x^2 = 24$$
$$x = \pm\sqrt{24}$$
$$x = 2\sqrt{6} \text{ or } x = -2\sqrt{6}$$

Completing the square: This method can be used on any solvable quadratic equation. However, when the equation is in the form $ax^2 + bx + c = 0$ and a and c are not perfect squares, this method can be time consuming.

Quadratic Formula:

$$x = \frac{-b \pm \sqrt{b^2 - 4ac}}{2a}$$
$$x = \frac{0 \pm \sqrt{0^2 - 4(2)(-48)}}{2(2)}$$
$$x = \frac{0 \pm \sqrt{384}}{4}$$
$$x = \frac{\pm\sqrt{384}}{4}$$
$$x = 2\sqrt{6} \text{ or } x = -2\sqrt{6}$$

Do the Math

Solve the quadratic equation $(x + 4)^2 - 18 = 0$ using different methods, or explain why a method is not applicable.

Factoring: The equation written in standard form $ax^2 + \boxed{} + c = 0$ is $x^2 + \boxed{}x - 2 = 0$. There is no sum of the product of the outer factors and the product of the inner factors that is equal to b,

or $\boxed{}$, so the equation is not factorable.

Square roots: Use this method because the

equation does not have a $\boxed{}$ term.

$$(x + 4)^2 - 18 = 0$$
$$(x + 4)^2 = \boxed{}$$
$$x + 4 = \pm\sqrt{\boxed{}}$$
$$x = \boxed{} \pm \boxed{}\sqrt{\boxed{}}$$
$$x = \boxed{} \text{ or } x = \boxed{}$$

Completing the square: The equation is in the form $ax^2 + bx + c = 0$, and a and c are not _____. This method can be time consuming.

Quadratic Formula:

$$x = \frac{-b \pm \sqrt{b^2 - 4ac}}{2a}$$
$$x = \frac{-\boxed{} \pm \sqrt{\boxed{}^2 - 4\left(\boxed{}\right)\left(\boxed{}\right)}}{2\boxed{}}$$
$$x = \frac{-\boxed{} \pm \sqrt{\boxed{}}}{\boxed{}}$$
$$x = \boxed{} \text{ or } x = \boxed{}$$

Learn the Math

EXAMPLE 2 ▶ The owner of a local coffee shop is thinking about changing the prices for their coffee drinks. The lattes currently cost $4.50, and customers have requested a decrease in price. The model $P(x) = -0.2x^2 + 1.8x + 12$ represents the profits made from selling lattes, where x represents the price of a latte and P represents the profit in hundreds of dollars. Solve the related quadratic equation to find the price the coffee shop should charge for a latte if the coffee shop wants to earn a profit of $1600.

Choose a method. Factoring will be difficult because the coefficients are not whole numbers. The square root method cannot be used because the quadratic model has a bx term. Completing the square will also be difficult because of the decimal values in the model.

Solve the related quadratic equation using the Quadratic Formula. Write the equation for the desired profit, $16 = -0.2x^2 + 1.8x + 12$. Rewrite the equation in standard form. Then solve.

$$x = \frac{-1.8 \pm \sqrt{1.8^2 - 4(-0.2)(-4)}}{2(-0.2)}$$

$$x = \frac{-1.8 \pm \sqrt{3.24 - 3.2}}{-0.4}$$

$$x = \frac{-1.8 \pm \sqrt{0.04}}{-0.4}$$

$$x = \frac{-1.8 \pm 0.2}{-0.4}$$

$$x = 4 \text{ or } x = 5$$

If the coffee shop would like to decrease the price of their lattes and earn a profit of $1600, they should charge $4.00 per latte.

Do the Math

The owner of the coffee shop plans to sell baked goods. The equation $P(x) = -0.4x^2 + 0.6x + 14$ represents the profit the shop will make selling baked goods, where x represents the price of a baked good and P represents the profit in hundreds of dollars.

How much should the coffee shop charge for baked goods to earn a profit of $1220? Solve the quadratic equation using the Quadratic Formula.

Write the equation for the desired profit, $\boxed{} = -0.4x^2 + 0.6x + 14$.

Rewrite the equation in standard form. Then solve.

$$x = \frac{-0.6 \pm \sqrt{0.6^2 - 4(-0.4)\left(\boxed{}\right)}}{2(-0.4)}$$

$$x = \frac{-0.6 \pm \sqrt{3.6 + \boxed{}}}{-0.8}$$

$$x = \frac{-0.6 \pm \sqrt{\boxed{}}}{-0.8}$$

$$x \approx \boxed{} \text{ or } x \approx \boxed{}$$

A negative x-value is not appropriate for this situation, so the coffee shop should charge approximately $\boxed{}$ for a baked good.

© Houghton Mifflin Harcourt Publishing Company

For each equation, state the method of solving that requires the fewest steps: factoring, square roots, Quadratic Formula, graphing, or completing the square.

1. $25x^2 = 14$

_____

2. $x^2 + 9x + 18 = 0$

_____

3. $9x^2 + x = 10$

_____

4. $2x^2 + 3x - 3 = 0$

_____

5. Complete the table. Determine all methods you can use to solve each equation.

Equation	Factoring	Square roots	Completing the square	Quadratic Formula
$2(x - 1)^2 = 8$				
$4x^2 + 12x = 4$				
$x^2 + 4x - 21 = 0$				
$16x^2 = 10$				

Speculate which solution method is the most appropriate to solve each equation. Explain your reasoning and solve. If necessary, leave answers in radical form.

6. $x^2 - 2x - 8 = 0$

7. $4(x - 1)^2 = 5$

8. $2x^2 + 20x - 100 = 0$

9. $x^2 + 7x + 1 = 0$

10. **Math on the Spot** Rayna rebuilt her model rocket hoping to make it go higher. She wants it to reach a height of 50 feet. Her rebuilt rocket has an initial velocity of 54 feet per second upward. She launches her rocket from a launching pad 2 feet off the ground. Will her new rocket reach 50 feet? If not, how fast would her rocket need to go to meet her goal?

11. At what x-values does the graph of $f(x) = (x + 3)^2 - 7$ intersect the x-axis?

12. The equation $h(t) = -16t^2 + 19t + 3$ models the path of a projectile where h is the height of the object in feet and t is the time in seconds.

 A. What method is the most appropriate for solving the equation when $0 = -16t^2 + 19t + 3$?

 B. What will the value of t represent when the equation $0 = -16t^2 + 19t + 3$ is solved?

 C. Solve the equation. Which solution(s) make sense in the context of the model? Round to the nearest hundredth.

13. The equation $x^2 + 12x + 2 = 6$ can be solved by completing the square.

 A. What is the first step to solve the equation by completing the square?

 B. Solve the equation.

14. Which quadratic equation has solutions $x = -6$ and $x = 5$?

 (A) $x^2 + x = 30$ (C) $x^2 - x = 30$

 (B) $x^2 + x = -30$ (D) $x^2 - x = -30$

15. Which quadratic equation can be most easily solved using square roots?

 (A) $10x^2 + 25x + 5 = 0$ (C) $100x^2 + 25x + 50 = 0$

 (B) $10x^2 - 3 = 0$ (D) $100x^2 - 9 = 0$

Step It Out

Learn the Math

EXAMPLE 1 ▶ A bridge manufacturer is experimenting with paraboloid-shaped suspension lines. The design of a new suspension line is shown in the figure. Units are measured in meters. What is the distance between the top edges of the suspension line?

To find the distance between the two top edges of the suspension line, first write the equation of the parabola in vertex form.

To write the equation of the parabola in vertex form, locate the vertex and another point on the graph.

The vertex is at $(6, 5)$, and another point on the graph is $(4, 6)$.

The vertex form of a quadratic function is given by $y = a(x - h)^2 + k$. Substitute the values of the vertex and the other point into this equation and solve for a.

$$6 = a(4 - 6)^2 + 5$$
$$1 = a(-2)^2$$
$$\frac{1}{4} = a$$

So, the suspension line is modeled by $f(x) = \frac{1}{4}(x - 6)^2 + 5$.

The top edges of the suspension line have a y-value of 10.

By setting $f(x)$ equal to 10 and solving for x, you can determine the x-values of the endpoints of the suspension line. Then, you can subtract those values to determine the distance between the top edges.

$$10 = \frac{1}{4}(x - 6)^2 + 5$$
$$5 = \frac{1}{4}(x - 6)^2$$
$$20 = (x - 6)^2$$
$$\pm\sqrt{20} = x - 6$$
$$6 \pm 2\sqrt{5} = x$$

The x-values of the endpoints are $x = 6 + 2\sqrt{5} \approx 10.47$ and $x = 6 - 2\sqrt{5} \approx 1.53$.

Finally, $10.47 - 1.53 = 8.94$. So, the top edges of the suspension line are approximately 9 meters apart.

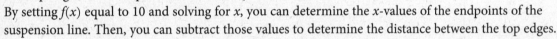

Do the Math

An umbrella manufacturer is experimenting with paraboloid-shaped umbrellas. The design of a new umbrella is shown in the figure. Units are measured in feet. What is the distance between the bottom edges of the umbrella?

Write the equation of the parabola in vertex form.

To write the equation of the parabola in vertex form, locate the vertex and another point on the graph.

The vertex is at $\left(\boxed{}, \boxed{}\right)$ and another point on the

graph is $\left(3, \boxed{}\right)$.

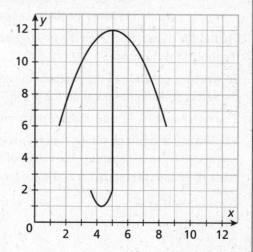

Substitute the values of the vertex and the other point into the equation for the vertex form of a quadratic function and solve for a.

$$y = a(x - h)^2 + k$$

$$\boxed{} = a\left(3 - \boxed{}\right)^2 + \boxed{}$$

$$\boxed{} = a\left(\boxed{}\right)^2$$

$$-\frac{\boxed{}}{\boxed{}} = a$$

So, the umbrella is modeled by $f(x) = -\dfrac{\boxed{}}{\boxed{}}\left(x - \boxed{}\right)^2 + \boxed{}$.

The bottom edges of the umbrella have a y-value of $\boxed{}$. By setting $f(x)$ equal to $\boxed{}$

and solving for x, you can determine the x-values of the endpoints of the umbrella. Then, you can subtract those values to determine the distance between the bottom edges.

$$\boxed{} = -\frac{\boxed{}}{\boxed{}}\left(x - \boxed{}\right)^2 + \boxed{}$$

$$x = \boxed{} \pm \boxed{}$$

Finally, $\boxed{} - \boxed{} = \boxed{}$. So, the bottom edges of the umbrella are approximately $\boxed{}$ feet apart.

Name

LESSON 19.1
More Practice

ONLINE
Video Tutorials and
Interactive Examples

1. What is the axis of symmetry of $f(x) = -2x^2$? Why is the vertex the highest point on the graph?

_____

2. For what x-values does the function $f(x) = 6x^2$ decrease? Why is the vertex the lowest point on the graph?

_____

Graph each quadratic function. Identify how the graph is related to the graph of the parent function. State the axis of symmetry and the vertex.

3. $f(x) = 3(x + 7)^2 + 1$

4. $f(x) = -4(x + 1)^2$

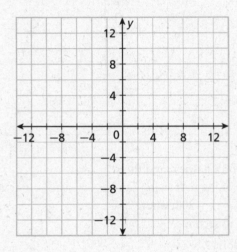

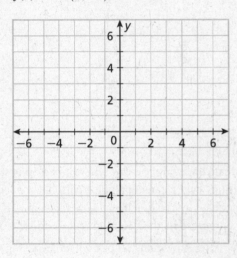

State the values for a, h, and k and how they transform the graph of the parent function $f(x) = x^2$.

5. $f(x) = -\frac{1}{3}(x - 2)^2 + 6$

6. $f(x) = -8x^2 - 5$

7. $f(x) = \frac{3}{5}(x + 3)^2 - \frac{2}{5}$

8. $f(x) = -\frac{9}{4}(x + 11)^2$

Write the equation in vertex form $g(x) = a(x - h)^2 + k$ **for each graph of a quadratic function.**

9.

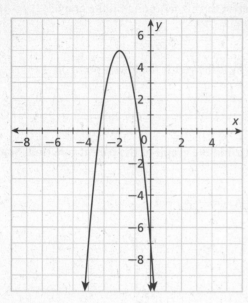

10.

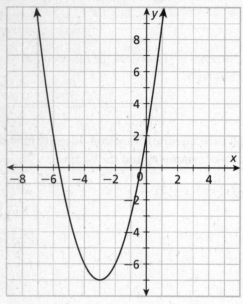

_____

_____

11. A canyon swing is a ride where a person is strapped in a seat by a harness and then swings over a canyon along a path like a pendulum. The path of the first swing can be modeled by the function $f(x) = 0.006(x - 100)^2 + 1240$ for $0 \leq x \leq 200$, where $f(x)$ represents the height in meters and x represents the time in seconds.

A. After how many seconds does the swing reach its lowest point?

_____

B. How far above the canyon does the swing ascend?

_____

12. Use Structure Troy kicks a football from the ground. After 2 seconds, the football reaches its maximum height. The graph shows the height $h(t)$ of the ball (in feet) at time t (in seconds). Write the function $h(t)$ in vertex form. Devon catches the ball when it is 3.5 feet above the ground. How long is the football in the air before it is caught?

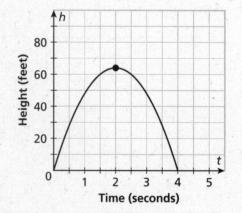

_____

13. What is the vertex of $f(x) = 2(x + 4)^2 - 1$?

Ⓐ $(4, 1)$ Ⓒ $(-4, 1)$

Ⓑ $(4, -1)$ Ⓓ $(-4, -1)$

Step It Out

Learn the Math

EXAMPLE 1 You can approximate the shape of a hammock using a parabola. Graph the function $f(x) = 0.08x^2 - 0.8x + 4$ representing the shape of the hammock.

Write $f(x)$ in vertex form.

$$f(x) = 0.08x^2 - 0.8x + 4$$
$$= 0.08(x^2 - 10x) + 4$$
$$= 0.08(x^2 - 10x + 25 - 25) + 4$$
$$= 0.08(x^2 - 10x + 25) + 4 - (0.08)(25)$$
$$= 0.08(x^2 - 10x + 25) + 4 - 2$$
$$= 0.08(x - 5)^2 + 2$$

Identify the vertex, axis of symmetry, y-intercept, and another point on the graph.

vertex: $(5, 2)$, axis of symmetry: $x = 5$, y-intercept: $(0, 4)$, another point: $(10, 4)$

Sketch the graph.

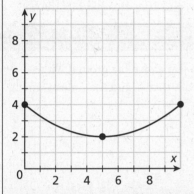

Do the Math

Carly wants to draw a hill in her picture. She will use the graph of the function $f(x) = -0.3125x^2 + 2.5x + 1$ as the shape of her hill. Write the function in vertex form. Identify the vertex, axis of symmetry, and y-intercept. Sketch a graph of the function.

vertex form: $f(x) = \boxed{}\left(x - \boxed{}\right)^2 + \boxed{}$

vertex: $\left(\boxed{}, \boxed{}\right)$, axis of symmetry: $x = \boxed{}$,

y-intercept: $\left(\boxed{}, \boxed{}\right)$

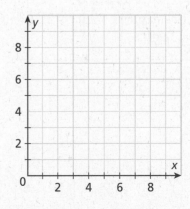

Learn the Math

EXAMPLE 2 Heather practices hitting a volleyball straight up in the air. She hits the ball 6 feet above the ground with a speed of 24 feet per second. What is the maximum height that the volleyball reaches and the time at which that height is achieved?

Recall that projectile height can be modeled by $h(t) = -16t^2 + v_0 t + h_0$, where h is the height of the object in feet, t is the time in seconds, v_0 is the initial velocity in feet per second, and h_0 is the initial height in feet.

The height of the volleyball can be modeled by $h(t) = -16t^2 + 24t + 6$. To find the maximum height of the ball, rewrite the function in vertex form.

$$h(t) = -16t^2 + 24t + 6$$
$$= -16(t^2 - 1.5t) + 6$$
$$= -16(t^2 - 1.5t + 0.5625 - 0.5625) + 6$$
$$= -16(t^2 - 1.5t + 0.5625) + 6 - (-16)(0.5625)$$
$$= -16(t^2 - 1.5t + 0.5625) + 6 + 9$$
$$= -16(t - 0.75)^2 + 15$$

The vertex of the parabola is $(0.75, 15)$.

The maximum height of the volleyball is 15 feet. This height occurs 0.75 second after Heather hits the ball.

Do the Math

Lamar throws a tennis ball straight up in the air. He throws the ball from 6 feet above the ground with a speed of 64 feet per second. What is the maximum height that the tennis ball reaches and the time at which that height is achieved?

Write a function to model the height of the tennis ball.

$$h(t) = \boxed{}\, t^2 + \boxed{}\, t + \boxed{}$$

Write the function in vertex form.

$$h(t) = \boxed{}\left(t - \boxed{}\right)^2 + \boxed{}$$

The vertex of the parabola is $\left(\boxed{}, \boxed{}\right)$.

The maximum height of the tennis ball is $\boxed{}$ feet. This height occurs $\boxed{}$ seconds after Lamar throws the ball.

Convert each quadratic function from vertex form to standard form.

1. $f(x) = 2(x - 5)^2 - 7$

2. $f(x) = -(x + 6)^2 + 2$

_____

_____

3. Math on the Spot Write the equations in standard form.

A. $y = 2(x - 5)^2 + 4$

B. $y = -4(x + 1)^2 - 7$

_____

_____

Convert each quadratic function from standard form to vertex form.

4. $f(x) = 3x^2 - 24x + 59$

5. $f(x) = -2x^2 + 28x - 99$

_____

_____

Graph each quadratic function.

6. $f(x) = x^2 - 6x + 5$

7. $f(x) = -x^2 - 4x - 1$

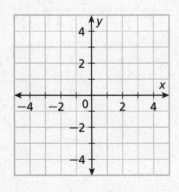

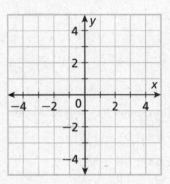

8. **Critique Reasoning** Carlos writes the function $h(t) = -16t^2 + 128t + 4$ in vertex form as $h(t) = -16(t - 4)^2 + 260$. Carlos states that the maximum value of the function is 4. Is Carlos correct? Explain your reasoning.

_____

_____

_____

9. **Model with Mathematics** Sophia practices catching a softball by throwing it straight up in the air and catching it. She throws the ball with a speed of 40 feet per second, and she releases the ball when it is 4 feet above the ground. Write a model to represent this situation. What is the maximum height of the softball?

_____

_____

_____

10. **Critique Reasoning** Kellen writes the function $f(x) = x^2 + 6x + 6$ in vertex form as $f(x) = (x + 3)^2 + 6$. Explain Kellen's error. Write the function in vertex form.

_____

_____

_____

11. The shape of a drainage ditch can be modeled by the equation $f(x) = 0.5x^2 - 2x - 2$. Graph the parabola representing the shape of the drainage ditch.

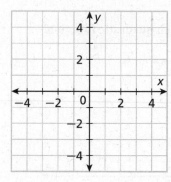

12. Which function shows $f(x) = -3x^2 + 30x - 73$ in vertex form?

Ⓐ $f(x) = -3(x - 5)^2 - 148$

Ⓑ $f(x) = -3(x - 5)^2 - 98$

Ⓒ $f(x) = -3(x - 5)^2 - 73$

Ⓓ $f(x) = -3(x - 5)^2 + 2$

Name _____

Step It Out

Learn the Math

EXAMPLE 1 ▶ Graph $f(x) = x^2 - 2x - 8$.

Factor to write $f(x)$ in intercept form.

$$f(x) = x^2 - 2x - 8 = (x - 4)(x + 2)$$

Identify the x-intercepts. The x-intercepts are 4 and -2.

Identify the vertex and axis of symmetry.

$$x = \frac{x_1 + x_2}{2} = \frac{4 + (-2)}{2} = 1, \ y = (1)^2 - 2(1) - 8 = -9$$

The vertex is $(1, -9)$. The axis of symmetry is $x = 1$.

Sketch the graph.

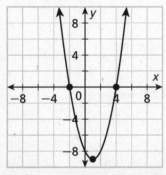

Do the Math

Graph $f(x) = x^2 + 8x + 15$.

intercept form: $f(x) = \left(x \ \boxed{} \ \boxed{}\right)\left(x \ \boxed{} \ \boxed{}\right)$

x-intercepts: $\boxed{}$ and $\boxed{}$

vertex: $\left(\boxed{}, \boxed{}\right)$

axis of symmetry: $x = \boxed{}$

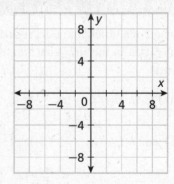

Learn the Math

EXAMPLE 2 The height of a model rocket can be modeled by the function $h(t) = -16t^2 + 200t$. Find and interpret the t-intercepts, h-intercept, and vertex in this situation.

You can use the intercept form to find the t-intercepts of the parabola. This will tell you how long the rocket was in the air.

$h(t) = -16t(t - 12.5)$

$t = 0$ or $t = 12.5$

The rocket was in the air for 12.5 seconds.

You can use the vertex form to find the vertex of the parabola. This will tell you the maximum height of the rocket and when it occurred.

$h(t) = -16(t - 6.25)^2 + 625$

vertex: $(6.25, 625)$

The maximum height of the rocket was 625 feet, which occurred 6.25 seconds after the launch.

You can use the standard form to find the h-intercept of the parabola. This will tell you the initial height of the rocket.

$h(t) = -16t^2 + 200t$

$h(0) = 0$

The initial height of the rocket is 0 feet. The rocket was launched from the ground.

Do the Math

The height of a different model rocket can be modeled by the function $h(t) = -16t^2 + 224t$. How long was the rocket in the air? What was the maximum height of the rocket? From what height was the rocket launched?

standard form: $h(t) = -16t^2 + 224t$

vertex form: $h(t) = \boxed{}\left(t - \boxed{}\right)^2 + \boxed{}$

intercept form: $h(t) = \boxed{}\left(t - \boxed{}\right)$

The rocket was in the air for $\boxed{}$ seconds.

The maximum height of the rocket was $\boxed{}$ feet.

The rocket was launched from a height of $\boxed{}$ feet.

Write each function in intercept form and identify the zeros
and *x*-intercepts.

1. $f(x) = -x^2 + 3x + 28$

_____

_____

_____

2. $f(x) = x^2 - 13x + 40$

_____

_____

_____

3. $f(x) = 4x^2 + 5x - 6$

_____

_____

_____

4. $f(x) = -6x^2 - 17x - 5$

_____

_____

_____

Graph each function.

5. $f(x) = (x - 6)(x - 2)$

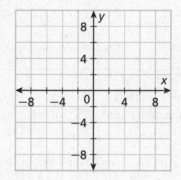

6. $f(x) = -(x + 3)(x - 3)$

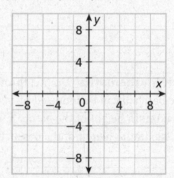

7. $f(x) = -2x^2 + 24x - 64$

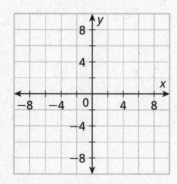

8. $f(x) = x^2 + 4x - 5$

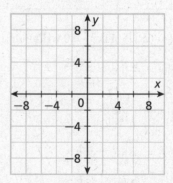

9. **Open Ended** Write a function in intercept form that has x-intercepts located at $(2, 0)$ and $(-4, 0)$. Graph the function.

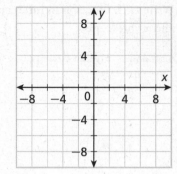

_____

_____

_____

10. **Model with Mathematics** The shape of a hill can be modeled by the function $f(x) = -0.01(x - 5)(x - 65)$ where the x-axis represents the base of the hill and the units are feet. What is the width of the hill? What is the height of the hill?

_____

_____

_____

11. **Critique Reasoning** Jalen writes the function $f(x) = 2x^2 + 9x + 4$ in intercept form. He incorrectly states that the zeros of the function are $x = \frac{1}{2}$ and $x = 4$. Describe Jalen's error. Find the correct zeros of the function.

_____

_____

_____

12. **Model with Mathematics** Donnie throws a baseball straight up in the air. The height of the baseball can be modeled by $h(t) = -16t^2 + 32t + 5$. Donnie wants to know the maximum height of the baseball. What form of the function should he use? What is the maximum height of the baseball?

_____

_____

_____

13. What is $f(x) = 6x^2 + 11x - 10$ written in intercept form?

Ⓐ $f(x) = 6\left(x - \frac{2}{3}\right)\left(x - \frac{5}{2}\right)$

Ⓑ $f(x) = 6\left(x - \frac{2}{3}\right)\left(x + \frac{5}{2}\right)$

Ⓒ $f(x) = 6\left(x + \frac{2}{3}\right)\left(x - \frac{5}{2}\right)$

Ⓓ $f(x) = 6\left(x + \frac{2}{3}\right)\left(x + \frac{5}{2}\right)$

Name _____

Step It Out

Learn the Math

EXAMPLE 1 ▶ The function $f(x)$ is defined by $f(x) = \frac{1}{2}(x-4)(x+8)$.

The graph of $g(x)$ is shown in the figure and $h(x)$ is a quadratic function expressed in the table.

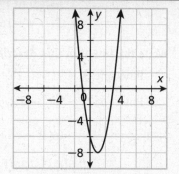

Find the minimum values.

$f(x)$: The axis of symmetry is $x = \frac{x_1 + x_2}{2} = \frac{4 + (-8)}{2} = -2$. The coordinates of the vertex are $(-2, -18)$. The minimum value is -18.

$g(x)$: The vertex is $(1, -8)$. The minimum value is -8.

$h(x)$: The vertex is $(-5, -25)$. The minimum value is -25.

Find the x-intercepts.

$f(x)$: The x-intercepts are 4 and -8.

$g(x)$: The x-intercepts are -1 and 3.

$h(x)$: The vertex form of the function is $h(x) = (x+5)^2 - 25$. When y is set equal to 0, the x-intercepts are -10 and 0.

x	h(x)
−8	−16
−6	−24
−5	−25
−4	−24
−2	−16

Compare the functions.

$h(x)$ has the least minimum value, -25, and $f(x)$ has the greatest x-intercept, 4.

Do the Math

The function $f(x)$ is defined by $f(x) = -2(x+3)(x+6)$.

The graph of $g(x)$ is shown in the figure and $h(x)$ is a quadratic function expressed in the table.

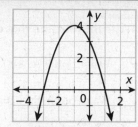

Find the maximum values.

$f(x)$: The axis of symmetry is $x = \frac{x_1 + x_2}{2} = -\dfrac{\boxed{}}{2} = -\boxed{}$.

The coordinates of the vertex are $\left(-\boxed{}, \boxed{}\right)$. The maximum value is $\boxed{}$.

$g(x)$: The vertex is $\left(\boxed{}, \boxed{}\right)$. The maximum value is $\boxed{}$.

$h(x)$: The vertex is $\left(\boxed{}, \boxed{}\right)$. The maximum value is $\boxed{}$.

x	h(x)
−8	5
−7	8
−6	9
−5	8
−4	5

Find the x-intercepts.

$f(x)$: The x-intercepts are $\boxed{}$ and $\boxed{}$. $g(x)$: The x-intercepts are $\boxed{}$ and $\boxed{}$.

$h(x)$: The vertex form is $h(x) = -\left(x + \boxed{}\right)^2 + \boxed{}$. The x-intercepts are $\boxed{}$ and $\boxed{}$.

Compare the functions.

$\boxed{}$ has the greatest maximum value, $\boxed{}$, and $\boxed{}$ has the greatest x-intercept, $\boxed{}$.

Learn the Math

EXAMPLE 2   Two pinecones detach from branches due to wind. Pinecone A reaches a maximum height of 12 feet after $\frac{1}{2}$ second. The height of pinecone B is represented by $B(t) = -16t^2 + 32t - 2$.

Write the function that describes the height of each pinecone in vertex form.

Pinecone A: $A(t) = -16\left(t - \frac{1}{2}\right)^2 + 12$

Pinecone B: $-16t^2 + 32t - 2 = 0 \rightarrow -16t^2 + 32t = 2$

$$-16\left(t^2 - 2t + 1\right) = 2 - 16(1) \rightarrow -16(t - 1)^2 = -14$$

$B(t) = -16(t - 1)^2 + 14$ The maximum height is 14 feet.

The maximum height of pinecone B is greater than the maximum height of pinecone A.

Compare the initial vertical velocities.

Convert the function for the height of pinecone A to standard form: $A(t) = -16t^2 + 16t + 8$.

Compare the linear coefficient of $A(t) = -16t^2 + 16t + 8$ with the linear coefficient of $B(t) = -16t^2 + 32t - 2$. Because $32 > 16$, pinecone B had the greater initial vertical velocity.

Do the Math

The heights of two falling water bottles are described by the functions. Water bottle A reaches a maximum height of 20 feet after 1 second. The height of water bottle B is represented by $B(t) = -16t^2 + 32t + 9$.

Write the function that describes the height of each water bottle in vertex form.

Water bottle A: $A(t) = -16\left(t - \boxed{}\right)^2 + \boxed{}$

Water bottle B: $-16t^2 + 32t + 9 = 0 \rightarrow -16t^2 + 32t = \boxed{}$

$$-16\left(t^2 - \boxed{}\,t + 1\right) = \boxed{} - 16(1) \rightarrow -16\left(t - \boxed{}\right)^2 = \boxed{}$$

$B(t) = -16\left(t - \boxed{}\right)^2 + \boxed{}$ The maximum height is $\boxed{}$ feet.

The maximum height of water bottle $\boxed{}$ is greater than the maximum height of water bottle $\boxed{}$.

Compare the initial vertical velocities.

Convert the function for the height of water bottle A to standard form: $A(t) = -16t^2 + \boxed{}\,t + \boxed{}$.

Compare the linear coefficient of $A(t) = -16t^2 + \boxed{}\,t + \boxed{}$ with the linear coefficient of $B(t) = -16t^2 + 32t + 9$. The initial vertical velocity of water bottle A is _____ the initial vertical velocity of water bottle B.

For each pair of functions, determine whether *f* or *g* has the greatest *x*-intercept among all the *x*-intercepts for both functions.

1. $f(x) = 2(x + 9)(x - 5)$

x	g(x)
−5	0
−3	−12
2	−24.5
7	−12
9	0

_____

2. $f(x) = -x^2 + 12x - 20$

x	g(x)
−2	0
0	6
2	8
4	6
6	0

_____

3. $f(x) = \frac{1}{3}(x - 2)^2$

x	g(x)
−10	−6
−8	0
−7.5	0.25
−7	0
−5	−6

_____

4. $f(x) = \frac{1}{4}(x - 3)(x + 6)$

x	g(x)
−2	0
0	5
4	9
8	5
10	0

_____

5. $f(x) = -x^2 - 2x + 3$

$g(x) = 4(x + 3)(x - 7)$

_____

6. $f(x) = (x + 8)^2 - 4$

$g(x) = \frac{1}{5}(x - 5)(x + 6)$

_____

7. **Open Ended** Write a function that has a maximum value of 18 in standard form, vertex form, and intercept form. Which form do you prefer to use with the given information? Why?

_____

_____

8. Two objects were thrown off different platforms. Object A's height is represented by $A(t) = -16t^2 + 24t + 9$, where t is time in seconds and $A(t)$ is the height of the object in feet. Object B's height is represented by the graph.

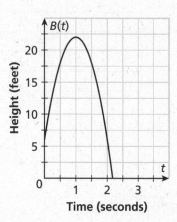

   A. What is the maximum height of each object? Which object has the greater maximum height?

   _____

   _____

   B. Which object hits the ground first? Explain.

   _____

   _____

9. Which statement is true about the function $f(x) = x^2$ and the function g represented by the graph?

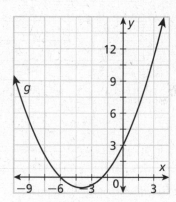

   Ⓐ f has both the greater minimum value and the greater y-intercept.

   Ⓑ g has both the greater minimum value and the greater y-intercept.

   Ⓒ f has the greater minimum value and g has the greater y-intercept.

   Ⓓ g has the greater minimum value and f has the greater y-intercept.

10. The function f is defined by $f(x) = -(x + 3)(x - 2)$. g is represented by the graph shown, and h is a quadratic function expressed in the table. Which of the following statements is true?

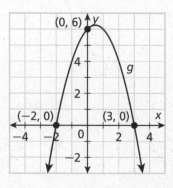

   Ⓐ f and g have the greatest maximum value.

   Ⓑ Only g has the greatest maximum value.

   Ⓒ f and h have the greatest maximum value.

   Ⓓ Only h has the greatest maximum value.

x	h(x)
−1	−12
0	−6
1	−2
2	0
3	0

19.5

Step It Out

Learn the Math

EXAMPLE 1 The scatter plot shows data that roughly follow a quadratic relationship. Find a quadratic function that models the data.

The vertex of the function appears to be at $(3, -4)$.

Substitute this value into the vertex form of a quadratic equation.

$f(x) = a(x - h)^2 + k$

$f(x) = a(x - 3)^2 - 4$

Use a second point, such as $(1, 0)$, to solve for a.

$f(x) = a(x - 3)^2 - 4$

$0 = a(1 - 3)^2 - 4$

$0 = 4a - 4$

$4 = 4a$

$1 = a$

The data can be modeled by $f(x) = (x - 3)^2 - 4$.

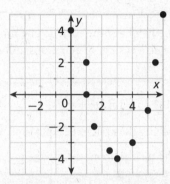

Do the Math

The scatter plot shows data that roughly follow a quadratic relationship. Find a quadratic function that models the data.

The vertex of the function appears to be at $\left(\boxed{}, \boxed{}\right)$.

Substitute this value into the vertex of a quadratic equation.

$f(x) = a\left(x \boxed{}\boxed{}\right)^2 + \boxed{}$

Use a second point to solve for a.

$a = \boxed{}$

The data can be modeled by $f(x) = \boxed{}\left(x \boxed{}\boxed{}\right)^2 + \boxed{}$.

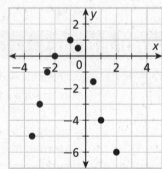

Learn the Math

EXAMPLE 2 A rock is thrown off a cliff. The height of the rock in feet after t seconds is shown in the table. Find a quadratic model for the given situation.

t	1	2	3	4
h	199	181	131	49

The height of the rock can be modeled by $h(t) = -16t^2 + v_0t + h_0$. Substitute two points from the data to create a system of equations and solve for v_0 and h_0.

$$\begin{cases} 199 = -16(1)^2 + v_0(1) + h_0 \\ 181 = -16(2)^2 + v_0(2) + h_0 \end{cases} \longrightarrow \begin{cases} 215 = v_0 + h_0 \\ 245 = 2v_0 + h_0 \end{cases}$$

Solving the system of equations, you find that $v_0 = 30$ and $h_0 = 185$.

The quadratic model for the given situation is $h(t) = -16t^2 + 30t + 185$.

Do the Math

Gregory throws a rock off a bridge. The height of the rock in feet after t seconds is shown in the table. Find a quadratic model for the situation.

t	1	2	3	4
h	167	167	135	71

Learn the Math

EXAMPLE 3 The table shows the height h in feet of a soccer ball when it is x feet from where it was kicked. Use regression to find a function that fits the data.

Distance	Height	Distance	Height
8	8	40	12
16	12	44	10
26	16	52	2

Using a graphing calculator, enter the data points from the table. Then use the graphing calculator to find the quadratic regression function.

A function that models the data is $h(x) \approx -0.022x^2 + 1.195x - 0.617$ with $r^2 = 0.9872$.

Do the Math

The number of visitors to a website after posting a news story is given in the table. Let v be the number of visitors, in thousands, t hours after the news story was posted.

Hours	Visitors	Hours	Visitors
0.5	10.2	7	64.1
2	29.2	9	49.3
4	55.5	12	11.1

Use a graphing calculator to find a quadratic function that models the data.

Name _____

LESSON 19.5
More Practice

ONLINE
Ed
Video Tutorials and
Interactive Examples

Determine if the data set can be modeled using a quadratic function by finding second differences.

1.

x	f(x)
−2	−14
−1	−4
0	2
1	4
2	2

_____

2.

x	f(x)
1	−3
2	−2
3	0
4	4
5	12

_____

Use the vertex form of a quadratic function to fit a quadratic curve to the data.

3.

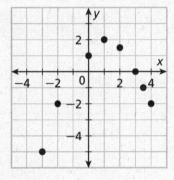

_____

_____

4.

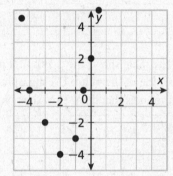

_____

_____

Use the projectile motion function to fit a quadratic curve to the projectile motion data.

5.

t	h
1	197
2	224
3	219
4	182
5	113

_____

_____

6.

t	h
1	68
2	44
3	−12
4	−100
5	−220

_____

_____

7. Math on the Spot Is the function represented by the table quadratic? Explain.

x	y
−4	−6
−2	6
0	10
2	6
4	−6

_____

_____

_____

8. Open Ended Plot points on a coordinate plane in the shape of a parabola, including the vertex. Use the vertex form of a quadratic function to fit a quadratic curve to the data.

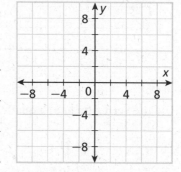

_____

_____

_____

_____

9. Use Tools The table shows the depth of a pond at different distances from the west side of the pond. Use a graphing calculator to find a quadratic regression function that models that data. How deep is the pond 8 feet from the west side?

Distance from West Side	5.3	11.4	16.7	27.4	33.6	38.7
Depth	−5.1	−9.7	−12	−10	−6.5	−2.1

_____

_____

_____

10. Jenna tosses a marble off a cliff. The height of the marble in feet after t seconds relative to an observation platform is shown in the table. Find a quadratic model for the situation.

t	1	2	3	4	5
h	74	38	−30	−130	−262

Ⓐ $h(t) = -16t^2 + 36t + 38$

Ⓑ $h(t) = -16(t - 1)^2 + 74$

Ⓒ $h(t) = -16t^2 + 12t + 78$

Ⓓ $h(t) = -16t^2 + 78t + 12$

© Houghton Mifflin Harcourt Publishing Company

Name _____

Step It Out

Learn the Math

EXAMPLE 1 The table shows the population of a city over 50 years from its inception.

Time	0	5	10	15	20	25	30	35	40	45	50
Population	200	355	575	670	1130	1925	2000	3350	4920	7920	11,300

Identify the best model by comparing the graphs of the models to the scatter plot and by looking for residual plots with no visible pattern. Use the best model to predict the city's population after 60 years, rounded to the nearest whole number.

	Equation	r^2
Linear	$y = 192.04545x - 1624.31818$	0.79536
Quadratic	$y = 6.51352x^2 - 133.63054x + 818.25175$	0.97377
Exponential	$y = 231.14933 \cdot 1.081484^x$	0.99724

From the table, the exponential regression equation has the best fit because $r^2 = 0.99724$ is closer to 1 than r^2 for the quadratic or linear model. The graphs of each regression equation and plots of the residuals are shown.

Linear   **Quadratic**   **Exponential**

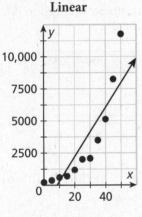
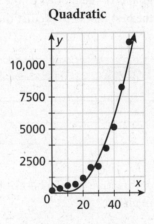
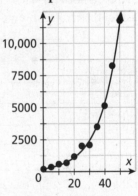

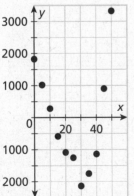
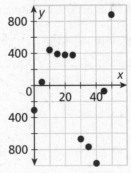
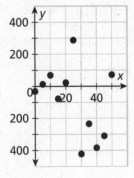

The quadratic and exponential residual plots have no visible patterns.

In 60 years, the population is expected to be about $y \approx 231.14934 \cdot 1.08148^{60}$, or about 25,410 people.

Do the Math

The table shows the height of a drone (in feet) in the air over two hours.

Time (min)	Height (ft)
10	4
20	49
30	63
40	78
50	93
60	106
70	124
80	132
90	113
100	101
110	89
120	81

Identify the best model by comparing the graphs of the models to the scatter plot and by looking for residual plots with no visible pattern. Use the best model to predict the height of the drone, rounded to the nearest foot, after 135 minutes.

	Equation	r^2
Linear		
Quadratic		
Exponential		

From the table, the _____ regression equation has the best fit because $r^2 = $ ☐ is closer to 1 than r^2 for the _____ or _____ model.

The residual plot for the _____ model has no visible pattern.

After 135 minutes, the expected height of the drone is about ☐ feet.

© Houghton Mifflin Harcourt Publishing Company

Name _____

LESSON 20.1
More Practice

ONLINE
Ed   Video Tutorials and
Interactive Examples

Use a graphing calculator to plot each set of data points. Describe the observed shape and end behavior. Does a linear, quadratic, or exponential function best model the data? Use the coefficient of determination and residual plots to support your answer. State the equation for the line or curve of best fit.

1.

x	−4	−3	−2	−1	0	1	2	3
$f(x)$	0.3	0.76	1.7	3.77	6.5	14.8	32.8	123.4

_____

_____

_____

2.

x	−4	−3	−2	−1	0	1	2	3
$f(x)$	5.3	2.1	−1.4	−3.15	−1.01	2.7	6.3	14.8

_____

_____

_____

3.

x	−4	−3	−2	−1	0	1	2	3
$f(x)$	−12.4	−7.5	−1.9	3.98	9.23	15.3	19.78	25.04

_____

_____

_____

4.

x	−4	−3	−2	−1	0	1	2	3
$f(x)$	85.1	63.4	35.8	24.6	10.8	9.7	12.1	16.6

_____

_____

_____

5. Use the data to determine a regression model and which function is the best fit.

Years since 2005	Portable MP3 player sales (millions)
0	4.229
1	5.559
2	5.968
3	5.844
4	5.207
5	4.728

A. What is the coefficient of determination for linear regression, quadratic regression, and exponential regression?

_____

B. What is the equation for the model of best fit?

_____

C. Based on your model, what would you expect the total portable MP3 player sales to be in the year 2011? What would you expect sales to be in the year 2012?

_____

6. For which of the following data is an exponential model the best fit?

Ⓐ

x	−4	−1	3	5	9
y	3.2	14.1	31.3	40.7	64.2

Ⓒ

x	−4	−1	3	5	9
y	16.3	3.4	1.1	0.76	0.045

Ⓑ

x	−4	−1	3	5	9
y	3.4	6.8	8.7	7.3	3.7

Ⓓ

x	−4	−1	3	5	9
y	7.5	3.2	−1.3	4.6	13.2

7. Which model best fits the data in the table?

x	−3	−2	−1	0	1	2
f(x)	0.27	0.89	2.13	4.86	12.71	30.64

Ⓐ $f(x) = 5.4297x + 11.2982$

Ⓑ $f(x) = 5.0014 \cdot 2.5280^x$

Ⓒ $f(x) = 2.0177x^2 + 7.4474x + 5.9177$

Ⓓ $f(x) = 5.2156x + 5$

Step It Out

Learn the Math

EXAMPLE 1 A doughnut shop bases its price per doughnut on how many flavors they have available. Their sales model is $p(x) = 3 + 1.2x$, where $p(x)$ is the price per doughnut in dollars and x is the number of flavors available.

The number of doughnuts sold, $d(x)$, is a function of the number of flavors available: $d(x) = 6x + 48$. The shop's daily revenue is equal to the price per doughnut times the number of doughnuts sold. A function that models the doughnut shop's daily revenue, $R(x)$, is:

$$R(x) = p(x) \cdot d(x)$$
$$= (3 + 1.2x)(6x + 48)$$
$$= 18x + 144 + 7.2x^2 + 57.6x$$
$$= 7.2x^2 + 75.6x + 144$$

Use the function to determine the doughnut shop's revenue on a day they offer 10 doughnut flavors.

$$R(10) = 7.2(10)^2 + 75.6(10) + 144$$
$$= 1620$$

The daily revenue when the doughnut shop offers 10 flavors is $1620.

Do the Math

Cindy grows a variety of flowers to sell to florists each day. The price she charges depends on the number of varieties she grows. The price per flower in dollars is modeled by $f(x) = 0.75x + 1.5$, where x is the number of varieties of flowers she grows.

Cindy has discovered that the number of flowers she sells, $n(x)$, is also a function of the number of

varieties of flowers she grows, $n(x) = 20 - 0.5x$. Her revenue is equal to the _____ times the

number of _____. A function that models Cindy's revenue, $R(x)$, is:

$$R(x) = f(x) \cdot \boxed{}$$

$$= \left(\boxed{} + \boxed{} \right)\left(\boxed{} - \boxed{} \right)$$

$$= \boxed{}\,x - \boxed{}\,x^2 + \boxed{} - \boxed{}\,x$$

$$= \boxed{}$$

Use the function to determine Cindy's revenue if she grows 15 varieties of flowers.

$$R(15) = \boxed{}$$

$$= \boxed{}$$

If Cindy grows 15 varieties of flowers, her daily revenue will be $\boxed{}$.

Learn the Math

EXAMPLE 2 Henry wants to design a rectangular swimming pool with the volume (in cubic yards) and base area (in square yards) given below.

$$\text{Volume of pool: } V(x) = x^2 + 8x + 12$$

$$\text{Area of base of pool: } A(x) = x + 6$$

Write an expression for the height of the pool.

Recall the formula for volume of a rectangular prism: $V = Bh$. Using function notation, the volume is given by $V(x) = A(x) \cdot h(x)$.

Substitute expressions for $V(x)$ and $A(x)$ and solve to find the height:

$$x^2 + 8x + 12 = (x + 6) \cdot h(x)$$

$$\frac{x^2 + 8x + 12}{x + 6} = h(x)$$

$$\frac{(x + 2)(x + 6)}{x + 6} = h(x)$$

$$x + 2 = h(x)$$

An expression for the height of the swimming pool is $x + 2$ yards.

Do the Math

A library with a rectangular perimeter has the area (in square feet) and width (in feet) listed below.

$$\text{Area of library: } A(x) = x^2 + 7x + 12$$

$$\text{Width of library: } w(x) = x + 3$$

Anna wants to build a wall-to-wall bookshelf that spans the entire length of the library.

Write an expression for the length of the library. Recall the formula for area of a rectangle: $A = lw$. Using function notation, the area is given by

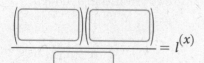

$A(x) = \boxed{} \cdot \boxed{}$. Substitute expressions for $A(x)$ and $w(x)$ and solve to find the length:

$$\boxed{} = l(x) \cdot \boxed{}$$

$$\frac{\boxed{}}{\boxed{}} = l(x)$$

$$\frac{\boxed{}\boxed{}}{\boxed{}} = l(x)$$

$$\boxed{} = l(x)$$

An expression for the length of the library is $\boxed{}$ feet.

Given $f(x) = x - 2$, $g(x) = x^3 - 8$, and $h(x) = 5x$, perform the indicated operations. State any restrictions.

1. $g(x) \cdot h(x)$

2. $g(x) \div f(x)$

_____

3. $f(x) + g(x)$

4. $f(x) \cdot h(x)$

_____

Given $f(x) = 4x$, $g(x) = 9x^2 - 16$, $h(x) = 3x + 4$, and $a(x) = 2 \cdot \left(\frac{1}{2}\right)^x$, perform the indicated operations. State any restrictions.

5. $(f + h)(x)$

6. $\left(\dfrac{g}{h}\right)(x)$

_____

7. $(f \cdot g)(x)$

8. $(a - g)(x)$

_____

9. The price of sweet corn per dozen drops $0.45 from $3.98. Write an equation in simplified form to model the price for x dozens of sweet corn.

_____

10. The area of a gymnasium is $x^2 + 9x + 20$ square feet, and the length is $x + 4$ feet. Find the width of the gym. Show your work.

_____

_____

_____

11. The length of a rectangular deck is $x + 7$ feet, and the width is $3x + 4$ feet.

A. What is an expression for the perimeter of the deck?

B. Nathan plans to install a railing around the entire deck. If $x = 2$, how many feet of railing will Nathan need? Show your work.

_____

_____

_____

12. Open Ended If the volume of a rectangular baking dish is $x^3 + 9x^2 + 18x$, what is a possible length of the dish? Explain.

_____

13. Expand $x(2x - 4)(x^3 + 2)$.

Ⓐ $-2x^5 + 4x^4 - 4x^2 + 8x$

Ⓑ $2x^5 - 4x^4 + 4x^2 - 8x$

Ⓒ $4x^5 - 4x^4 + 4x^2 - 8x$

Ⓓ $2x^4 - 4x^3 + 4x - 8$

14. The area of a rectangle is represented by $2x^2 + 5x - 12$, and the width is represented by $x + 4$. Which expression represents the length of the rectangle?

Ⓐ $x + 3$

Ⓑ $2x + 3$

Ⓒ $2x - 3$

Ⓓ $x - 3$

Step It Out

Learn the Math

EXAMPLE 1 The population of bacteria, in hundreds, of two different samples after x hours can be modeled by the equations shown below.

Sample A: $f(x) = 30(0.7)^x$

Sample B: $g(x) = -0.25(x - 9)^2 + 25$

When will the populations of bacteria in the two samples be the same?

To determine when the two populations are equal, graph both functions in the same coordinate plane and find the points of intersection on the graph.

Solutions appear to be approximately $(2, 13.5)$ and $(19, 0)$.

Use a graphing calculator to find better approximations to the hundredths.

The solutions of the system are approximately $(2.23, 13.54)$ and $(18.99, 0.03)$.

Samples A and B will have the same population of 1354 after 2.2 hours and the same population of 3 after 19 hours.

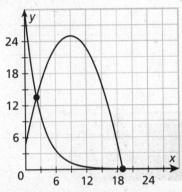

Do the Math

The population of a third sample of bacteria can be modeled by the following equation.

Sample C: $h(x) = 25 - 1.2x$

When will the populations of Sample B and Sample C be the same?

Graph the functions g and h.

Use a graphing calculator to find solutions to the hundredths.

The solutions of the system are approximately

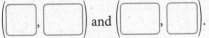 and ⬚⬚.

Samples B and C will have the same population of ⬚ after ⬚ hours and the same population of ⬚ after ⬚ hours.

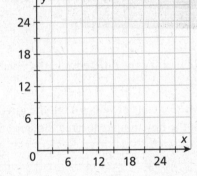

Learn the Math

EXAMPLE 2 ▶ Use a table of values to find the solutions of the system of equations.

$$\begin{cases} y = (x+2)^2 - 1 \\ y = 2x + 3 \end{cases}$$

x	$y = (x+2)^2 - 1$	$y = 2x + 3$
−3	0	−3
−2	−1	−1
−1	0	1
0	3	3
1	8	5
2	15	7

The equations have the same values when $x = -2$ and $x = 0$.

The solutions are $(-2, -1)$ and $(0, 3)$.

Do the Math

Use a table of values to find the solution of the system of equations.

$$\begin{cases} y = 0.5(x+1)^2 + 3 \\ y = -0.5x + 2.5 \end{cases}$$

x	$y = 0.5(x+1)^2 + 3$	$y = -0.5x + 2.5$
−3		
−2		
−1		
0		
1		
2		

The solutions of the system are $\left(\boxed{}, \boxed{}\right)$ and $\left(\boxed{}, \boxed{}\right)$.

Learn the Math

EXAMPLE 3 ▶ Solve the system to the nearest tenth using successive approximations.

$$\begin{cases} y = x^2 - 3x + 3 \\ y = 4 - x \end{cases}$$

Let $f(x)$ be the difference in the y-values of the two equations.

$f(x) = x^2 - 3x + 3 - (4 - x) = x^2 - 2x - 1$

Make a table of values. Find the intervals where the sign of the function changes. These are where the zeros of the function are located. Because the function is quadratic there are at most two zeros.

x	−3	−2	−1	0	1	2	3	4
$f(x)$	14	7	2	−1	−2	−1	2	7

The zeros occur between −1 and 0 and between 2 and 3. Use smaller increments to find a better approximation of the zeros.

x	−0.6	−0.5	−0.4	−0.3	2.3	2.4	2.5	2.6
$f(x)$	0.56	0.25	−0.04	−0.31	−0.31	−0.04	0.25	0.56

Substitute the values of x into one of the original equations to find the solutions of the system of equations. The solutions of the system are approximately $(-0.4, 4.4)$ and $(2.4, 1.6)$.

Do the Math

Solve the system to the nearest tenth using successive approximations. $\begin{cases} y = x^2 - 4x + 2 \\ y = x - 1 \end{cases}$

© Houghton Mifflin Harcourt Publishing Company

Name

LESSON 20.3
More Practice

ONLINE
Video Tutorials and
Interactive Examples

Determine the number of solutions for each system.

1.

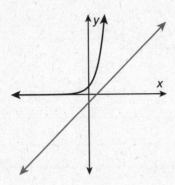

_____

2.

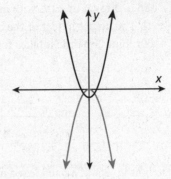

_____

3.

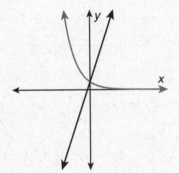

_____

4.

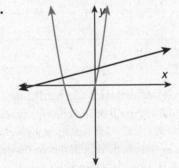

_____

Solve the system to the nearest tenth using successive approximations.

5. $\begin{cases} y = x^2 + 6x - 3 \\ y = -0.5x - 4 \end{cases}$

6. $\begin{cases} y = 2^x \\ y = -3x + 6 \end{cases}$

7. **Math on the Spot** An elevator rises at a constant rate of 10 feet per second. Its height in feet after t seconds is given by $h = 10t$. At the instant the elevator is at ground level, a ball is thrown upward with an initial velocity of 60 feet per second from ground level. The height in feet of the ball after t seconds is given by $h(t) = -16t^2 + 60t$. Find the time it takes for the ball and the elevator to reach the same height.

    _____

    _____

    _____

8. **Reason** The height in feet of a ball kicked in the air after t seconds can be represented by $h(t) = -16t^2 + 40t$. Another ball is kicked at the same time, and its height in feet is represented by $g(t) = -16t^2 + 40t + 1$. Molly says that both balls will reach the same height at the same time. Is Molly correct? Explain.

    _____

    _____

    _____

9. **Model with Mathematics** A chairlift takes people to the top of a hill. The path of the chairlift is represented by $y = \frac{8}{7}x$, where x and y are distances in feet. The hill appears to be in the shape of a parabola modeled by $y = -0.01x^2 + 1.4x + 31$. Graph the equations on the same coordinate plane. Find the point of intersection. What is the height of the hill?

    _____

    _____

    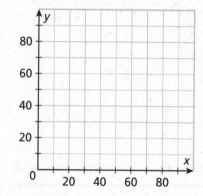

10. Two baseballs are thrown at the same time. The height of one baseball in feet after x seconds is represented by $f(x) = -16x^2 + 45x + 4$, and the height of the other in feet after x seconds is represented by $g(x) = -16x^2 + 50x + 3$. When will the two baseballs be at the same height?

    Ⓐ 0.2 second

    Ⓑ 5 seconds

    Ⓒ 7 seconds

    Ⓓ 12.36 seconds

Name _____

Step It Out

Learn the Math

EXAMPLE 1 Identify the zeros of the cubic functions $f(x) = 3x^3 + 15x^2 - 150x$ and $g(x) = (x + 2)(4x^2 - 4x - 24)$.

Write the functions in intercept form.

$$f(x) = 3x^3 + 15x^2 - 150x$$
$$= 3x(x^2 + 5x - 50)$$
$$= 3x(x - 5)(x + 10)$$

$$g(x) = (x + 2)(4x^2 - 4x - 24)$$
$$= (x + 2)(4(x^2 - x - 6))$$
$$= 4(x + 2)(x - 3)(x + 2)$$
$$= 4(x + 2)^2(x - 3)$$

Identify the zeros.

The factors $3x$, $x - 5$, and $x + 10$ indicate that 0, 5, and −10 are zeros of $f(x)$.

The factors $x + 2$ and $x - 3$ indicate that −2 and 3 are zeros of $g(x)$.

Do the Math

Identify the zeros of the cubic functions $f(x) = 2x^3 - 18x^2 + 36x$ and $g(x) = (x - 1)(-2x^2 - 12x + 14)$.

Write the functions in intercept form.

$$f(x) = 2x^3 - 18x^2 + 36x$$
$$= 2x\left(x^2 - \boxed{}x + \boxed{}\right)$$
$$= 2x\left(x - \boxed{}\right)\left(x - \boxed{}\right)$$

$$g(x) = (x - 1)\left(-2x^2 - 12x + 14\right)$$
$$= (x - 1)\left(-2\left(x^2 + \boxed{}x - \boxed{}\right)\right)$$
$$= -2(x - 1)\left(x - \boxed{}\right)\left(x + \boxed{}\right)$$
$$= -2\left(x - \boxed{}\right)^2\left(x + \boxed{}\right)$$

Identify the zeros.

The factors $2x$, $x - \boxed{}$, and $x - \boxed{}$ indicate that $\boxed{}$, $\boxed{}$, and $\boxed{}$ are zeros of $f(x)$.

The factors $x - \boxed{}$ and $x + \boxed{}$ indicate that $\boxed{}$ and $\boxed{}$ are zeros of $g(x)$.

Learn the Math

EXAMPLE 2 Create a rough sketch of the graph of $f(x) = -x^3 - 6x^2 - 9x$.

End behavior: As $x \to -\infty$, $f(x) \to +\infty$, and as $x \to +\infty$, $f(x) \to -\infty$.

Zeros: Factor the cubic expression to write the function in intercept form.

$f(x) = -x^3 - 6x^2 - 9x \to -x(x^2 + 6x + 9) \to -x(x + 3)^2$

The factors x and $x + 3$ indicate that 0 and -3 are zeros of the function.

Sketch.

Based on the end behavior, the left side of the graph should go up and the right side of the graph should go down.

The graph must cross the x-axis at 0. Because the factor $x + 3$ is raised to the second power in the intercept form of the function, the graph is tangent to the x-axis at -3.

Using these facts, the graph starts at the upper left, comes down to touch the x-axis at -3, goes back up and has a turning point between -3 and 0, then crosses the x-axis at 0, and continues to the lower right.

Do the Math

Create a rough sketch of the graph of $f(x) = x^3 - 8x^2 + 16x$.

Learn the Math

EXAMPLE 3 A piece of cardboard measures 22 centimeters by 14 centimeters. Squares of side length x centimeters are cut from all four corners so the cardboard can be folded into a box. What should the side length of the squares be to get a box with the maximum volume?

Write a function.

The volume is $V(x) = (22 - 2x)(14 - 2x)(x)$, which simplifies to $V(x) = 4x^3 - 72x^2 + 308x$.

Define the domain.

If no squares are cut, then $x = 0$. The largest squares that can be cut have a side length of 7 centimeters because that is half the length of the shortest side. Since a side length cannot be 0, the domain is $0 < x < 7$.

Find the maximum.

Use a graphing calculator to graph the function $V(x) = 4x^3 - 72x^2 + 308x$. The graph has a maximum on the domain $0 < x < 7$ at approximately $(2.79, 385.74)$.

Answer the question.

The maximum volume of the box is approximately 385.74 cubic centimeters. To create a box with this volume, squares should be cut with a side length of approximately 2.79 centimeters.

Do the Math

A piece of cardboard measures 26 centimeters by 16 centimeters. Squares of side length x centimeters are cut from all four corners so the cardboard can be folded into a box. What should the side length of the squares be to get a box with the maximum volume?

Use a graph of each function to find the *x*-intercepts, end behavior, number
of turning points, and intervals over which the function is positive and negative.

1. $f(x) = -4x^3 - 16x^2 - 16x$

_____

_____

_____

_____

_____

_____

_____

2. $f(x) = -x^3 + 2x^2$

_____

_____

_____

_____

_____

_____

3. $f(x) = x^3 - 9x$

_____

_____

_____

_____

_____

_____

4. $f(x) = 2x^3 - 2x^2 - 24x$

_____

_____

_____

_____

_____

_____

_____

Sketch a rough graph of the functions.

5. $f(x) = (x + 5)^2(-x - 1)$

6. $f(x) = (x + 1)(x^2 - 5x + 7)$

7. What is a possible function for the graph? Explain your reasoning.

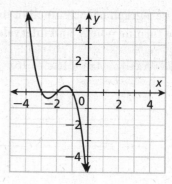

_____

_____

_____

_____

8. **Open Ended** What are two possible functions that have zeros of -7, 0, and 7? Explain.

_____

_____

_____

9. **Model with Mathematics** A building is shaped like a cylinder with a hemisphere as the roof. The height of the cylinder is $(x + 6)$ feet and the radius of the hemisphere is x feet. What is a function that represents the volume of the building?

_____

10. **Critique Reasoning** McKayla analyzed the function $f(x) = 2x^3 - 5x^2 + 12$. She said that when $x < 0$ and $x > 1.67$, $f(x)$ is positive and when $0 < x < 1.67$, $f(x)$ is negative. Do you agree with McKayla? Why or why not?

_____

_____

11. What is the function $f(x) = x^3 + x^2 - 30x$ in intercept form?

Ⓐ $f(x) = x(x - 6)(x + 5)$

Ⓑ $f(x) = x(x - 5)^2$

Ⓒ $f(x) = x(x + 6)(x - 5)$

Ⓓ $f(x) = x(x - 6)^2$

12. Which best describes the graph of $f(x) = x^3 + x^2 - 2x$?

Ⓐ x-intercepts: at -2, 0, and 1; end behavior: As $x \to -\infty$, $f(x) \to -\infty$, and as $x \to +\infty$, $f(x) \to +\infty$.

Ⓑ x-intercepts: at -1, 0, and 2; end behavior: As $x \to -\infty$, $f(x) \to -\infty$, and as $x \to +\infty$, $f(x) \to +\infty$.

Ⓒ x-intercepts: at -2, 0, and 1; end behavior: As $x \to -\infty$, $f(x) \to \infty$, and as $x \to +\infty$, $f(x) \to -\infty$.

Ⓓ x-intercepts: at -1, 0, and 2; end behavior: As $x \to -\infty$, $f(x) \to \infty$, and as $x \to +\infty$, $f(x) \to -\infty$.

Step It Out

Learn the Math

EXAMPLE 1 A survey of 100 randomly selected students was conducted asking whether they prefer to study in the library, at home, or outside. The results are shown in the frequency table.

		Study Location			
		Library	Home	Outside	Total
Age	Under 16	35	10	5	50
	16 and older	21	22	7	50
	Total	56	32	12	100

Create a *relative* frequency table. Because the total number of people surveyed is 100, divide each entry in the frequency table by 100.

> The value 0.35 represents the *joint* relative frequency of students who are under 16 and prefer to study in the library.

		Study Location			
		Library	Home	Outside	Total
Age	Under 16	0.35	0.10	0.05	0.50
	16 and older	0.21	0.22	0.07	0.50
	Total	0.56	0.32	0.12	1.00

> The value 0.32 represents the *marginal* relative frequency of all students who prefer to study at home regardless of their age.

Do the Math

A survey of 100 randomly selected students was conducted asking their favorite sport out of basketball, football, and hockey. Some of the results are shown in the frequency table.

		Favorite Sport			
		Basketball	Football	Hockey	Total
Age	Under 14		15	8	50
	14 and older	18	13		
	Total	45		27	100

A. Complete the frequency table.

B. Use the frequency table to create a *relative* frequency table.

C. In the relative frequency table, the value 0.18 represents the _____ relative frequency of students who are _____ and prefer _____.

D. In the relative frequency table, the value 0.27 represents the _____ relative frequency of all students who prefer _____.

Learn the Math

EXAMPLE 2 The results of a survey about whether artists prefer painting, drawing, or sculpting are shown in the relative frequency table.

		Preferred Art			
		Drawing	Painting	Sculpting	Total
Age	Under 35	0.175	0.115	0.155	0.445
	35 to under 50	0.085	0.14	0.09	0.315
	50 and older	0.055	0.15	0.035	0.24
	Total	0.315	0.405	0.28	1.00

The table shows nine **joint** relative frequencies in **bold** and six *marginal* relative frequencies in *italics*. Looking for relationships between the relative frequencies can help you determine whether one characteristic can influence a distribution.

Notice that as age increases, preferences in drawing and sculpting both decrease while preference in painting increases. Vendors at an art event could use this information to alter their marketing strategies. For example, a vendor who sells clay might target her marketing to those under 35 while a vendor who sells canvases, paint, and brushes might target those 50 and older.

Do the Math

Some of the results of a survey conducted at a pet store about whether people prefer birds, reptiles, or fish as pets are shown in the relative frequency table.

		Preferred Pet			
		Birds	Reptiles	Fish	Total
Age	Under 16	0.10	0.20	0.03	
	16 to under 37	0.12	0.12		0.31
	37 and older		0.09	0.11	0.36
	Total	0.38		0.21	1.00

A. Complete the relative frequency table.

B. The values 0.38, _____, 0.21, _____, 0.31, and 0.36 are _____ relative frequencies.

C. The value _____ represents the number of people 37 and older who prefer reptiles. This is a _____ relative frequency.

D. It appears that as age increases, preference in _____ and _____ increases, while preference in _____ decreases.

E. The owner of the pet store should invest the most money in supplies for _____ and _____ because about double the number of people prefer them over _____.

Name ___

LESSON 21.1
More Practice

ONLINE
Video Tutorials and
Interactive Examples

1. Use the two-way frequency table to answer the questions. Round your answers to the nearest hundredth.

		Allergic Response		
		Cats	Dogs	Total
Allergic?	Yes	22	10	32
	No	33	35	68
	Total	55	45	100

A. Create a two-way relative frequency for the given data.

B. What percent of respondents say they are allergic to dogs? _____

C. What percent of respondents say they are not allergic to either cats or dogs? _____

D. Which values are joint relative frequencies? _____

E. Which values are marginal relative frequencies? _____

2. A geography student randomly surveyed people about their preferred method of travel: car, train, or plane. He presented the raw data in a two-way frequency table.

		Preferred Method of Travel			
		Car	Train	Plane	Total
Age	Under 25	2	13	35	50
	25 and older	14	8	28	50
	Total	16	21	63	100

A. Create a two-way relative frequency table. Round answers to the nearest hundredth.

B. What is the relative frequency of a person who is under 25 and prefers to travel by plane? What type of frequency is this? _____

C. What is the relative frequency of people age 25 and older for all three methods of travel? What type of frequency is this? _____

D. Which values are joint relative frequencies? _____

E. Which values are marginal relative frequencies? _____

3. A survey of 122 people was conducted about their favorite genre of music. Those younger than 21 responded: 28 hip hop, 17 rock, and 8 country. Those 21 and older responded: 17 hip hop, 25 rock, and 27 country. Answer the following questions about this survey. Round your answers to the nearest hundredth.

A. What is the probability that a randomly selected respondent in this survey is 21 or older and prefers rock music? _____

B. What is the probability that a randomly selected respondent in this survey is younger than 21 and prefers country music? _____

C. What is the probability that any randomly selected respondent in this survey prefers hip hop? _____

4. **Math on the Spot** One hundred fifty students were surveyed about which mode of transportation they take to and from school each day. The results are shown in the two-way frequency table. Fill in the missing information.

		Mode of School Transportation			
		Bus	Walk	Other	Total
Gender	Girl	35	22	23	80
	Boy	28		17	
	Total				

5. The owner of a pizzeria surveys 300 customers about their preference for three pizza toppings she offers. She plans to take one of the toppings off the menu.

		Preferred Pizza Type			
		Sardines	Pineapple	Pepperoni	Total
Age	Under 15	0.02	0.13	0.35	0.50
	15 and older	0.14	0.08	0.28	0.50
	Total	0.16	0.21	0.63	1.00

A. Which pizza topping is the least popular with those under 15 years of age? Explain how you know.

_____

B. Which pizza topping is the least popular with those of age 15 years or older? Explain how you know.

_____

C. Which topping would you recommend that the owner remove from the menu? Explain.

_____

6. A survey of 137 people was conducted about their favorite electronic devices. Those younger than 27 responded: 11 laptop, 27 tablet, and 36 phone. Those 27 and older responded: 21 laptop, 24 tablet, and 18 phone. What is the probability that a randomly selected respondent in this survey is younger than 27 and prefers a tablet? Round your answer to the nearest hundredth.

_____

7. Survey results report the preference for vegetables: 30 people selected broccoli, 67 people selected kale, and 12 people selected spinach. What number represents the denominator used to calculate the relative frequency?

   (A) 97   (C) 67

   (B) 109   (D) 79

Name _____

Step It Out

Learn the Math

EXAMPLE 1 ▶ The results of a survey of 300 high school student athletes about their favorite music genre are shown.

		Genre			
		Rap	**Rock**	**Other**	**Total**
Sport	**Football**	0.31	0.20	0.11	0.62
	Soccer	0.07	0.08	0.05	0.20
	Volleyball	0.09	0.02	0.07	0.18
	Total	0.47	0.30	0.23	1.00

Determine whether there is a likely association between the students of a certain sport and the genre of music they prefer. Examine the relationship between soccer and rap.

The percent of those who play soccer who like rap is $\frac{0.07}{0.20} = 35\%$.

The percent of all those surveyed who like rap is $\frac{0.47}{1.00} = 47\%$.

The percent of soccer players who like rap (35%) is considerably lower than the percent of total student athletes who like rap (47%). It is likely that soccer players prefer rap less than other student athletes.

Do the Math

The results of a survey of 500 students about their favorite genre of movie are shown.

		Genre			
		Action	**Romance**	**Other**	**Total**
Grade	**Grade 9**	0.14	0.09	0.23	0.46
	Grade 12	0.12	0.13	0.29	0.54
	Total	0.26	0.22	0.52	1.00

Determine whether there is a likely relationship between grade and the action movie genre. Examine the relationship between grade and action movies.

Percent of those in Grade 9 who prefer action movies: $\frac{\boxed{}}{0.46} \approx \boxed{}\%$

Percent of those in Grade 12 who prefer action movies: $\frac{0.12}{\boxed{}} \approx \boxed{}\%$

Percent of all of those surveyed who prefer action movies: $\frac{\boxed{}}{\boxed{}} = \boxed{}\%$

The percent of students in Grade 9 who prefer action movies is _____ than the percent of all surveyed who prefer action movies. The percent of students in Grade 12 who prefer action movies is _____ than the percent of all surveyed who prefer action movies. Therefore, it is likely that _____ are more likely to prefer action movies.

Learn the Math

EXAMPLE 2 The results of a survey of 300 people about whether they prefer reading on paper or on an electronic device are shown.

		Reading Preference		
		Electronic	Paper	Total
Age	10–30	0.30	0.36	0.66
	31–80	0.12	0.22	0.34
	Total	0.42	0.58	1.00

Determine whether there is an association between age and a preference for reading on an electronic device.

The joint relative frequency of younger people who prefer electronic reading is 30%.

The marginal relative frequency of people ages 10–30 is 66%.

The conditional relative frequency of those who prefer electronic reading, given they are ages 10–30, is $\frac{0.30}{0.66} \approx 45\%$.

The conditional relative frequency of those who prefer electronic reading, given they are ages 31–80, is $\frac{0.12}{0.34} \approx 35\%$.

The marginal relative frequency of people surveyed who prefer electronic reading is 42%.

Because 45% of those ages 10–30 prefer electronic reading and 35% of those ages 31–80 prefer electronic reading, there is likely an association between age and the preference for reading on an electronic device, though the association is not necessarily a strong one.

Do the Math

A group of 100 students in a chemistry class was surveyed about their study habits and their scores on a recent chemistry test. The results of the survey are shown.

		Earned an A		
		Yes	No	Total
Studied at Least One Hour	Yes	0.27	0.16	0.43
	No	0.05	0.52	0.57
	Total	0.32	0.68	1.00

Determine whether there is an association between earning an A and studying for at least one hour on the chemistry test.

Name _____

1. People were surveyed about their preference for phone calls or text messages.

		Communication		
		Text	**Phone**	**Total**
Age	**13–30**	0.48	0.10	0.58
	31–60	0.14	0.28	0.42
	Total	0.62	0.38	1.00

A. What is the joint relative frequency of those aged 13–30 who prefer phone calls? _____

B. What is the marginal relative frequency of those who prefer phone calls? _____

C. What is the conditional relative frequency of those who prefer phone calls, given they are aged 13–30? _____

D. What is the conditional relative frequency of those who are aged 13–30, given they prefer phone calls? _____

2. The two-way frequency table shows the results of a survey about the time students wake up on Saturdays.

		Wake Up Time				
		Before 7	**7–8**	**8–9**	**After 9**	**Total**
Grade	**7–8**	18	15	21	45	99
	9–10	6	18	18	54	96
	11–12	3	9	15	78	105
	Total	27	42	54	177	300

A. Create a two-way relative frequency table.

		Wake Up Time				
		Before 7	**7–8**	**8–9**	**After 9**	**Total**
Grade	**7–8**					
	9–10					
	11–12					
	Total					

B. What is the joint relative frequency of those who wake up after 9 and are in grades 11–12? _____

C. What is the marginal relative frequency of those in grades 11–12? _____

D. What is the conditional relative frequency of those waking up after 9, given they are in grades 11–12? _____

E. What is the conditional relative frequency of those in grades 11–12, given they wake up after 9? _____

3. **Math on the Spot** Steve took a survey in his school because he was interested in the question "Does age influence which snack a student prefers: popcorn or pretzels?" If there is no influence, then the distribution of ages within each subgroup of snack preference should roughly equal the distribution of ages within the whole group. Use the results of Steve's survey to investigate possible influences of age on snack preference.

		Snack Preference		
		Popcorn	Pretzels	Total
Age	**10–13**	20	37	57
	14–18	25	18	43
	Total	45	55	100

_____
_____
_____

4. **Reason** The results of a study involving SAT scores and annual salary are shown in the two-way frequency table.

		Salary (in thousands of dollars)			
		Under 50	50–100	Over 100	Total
Score	**Above 1400**	50	220	80	350
	1200–1400	350	760	90	1200
	Below 1200	300	100	50	450
	Total	700	1080	220	2000

A. Create a two-way relative frequency table. How is the relative frequency table helpful for finding associations?

_____

B. Is there an association between higher salaries and higher SAT scores? Use relative frequencies to explain your reasoning.

_____

_____

C. Is there an association between lower salaries and lower SAT scores? Use relative frequencies to explain your reasoning.

_____

_____

5. Comparing which two relative frequencies allows you to identify an association?

Ⓐ joint and marginal   Ⓒ marginal and conditional

Ⓑ joint and conditional   Ⓓ two marginal frequencies

© Houghton Mifflin Harcourt Publishing Company

Name _____

Step It Out

Learn the Math

EXAMPLE 1   Jose works part-time as a barber. Over the last seven days, he's had the following numbers of customers: 4, 5, 6, 3, 4, 2, 7.

A. Find the interquartile range of the data set.

First, put the data in order and find the middle number, which is the median, or Q_2:

2, 3, 4, **4**, 5, 6, 7. So, $Q_2 = 4$.

Next, find the first quartile, Q_1, by locating the middle number in the lower half of the data set:

2, **3**, 4, 4, 5, 6, 7. So, $Q_1 = 3$.

Finally, find the third quartile, Q_3, by locating the middle number in the upper half of the data set:

2, 3, 4, 4, 5, **6**, 7. So, $Q_3 = 6$.

The interquartile range is the difference between Q_3 and Q_1: IQR = $6 - 3 = 3$.

B. Find the mean and the standard deviation of the data set.

The mean is $\frac{2 + 3 + 4 + 4 + 5 + 6 + 7}{7}$, or approximately 4.4.

$$\sigma \approx \sqrt{\frac{(2 - 4.4)^2 + (3 - 4.4)^2 + (4 - 4.4)^2 + (4 - 4.4)^2 + (5 - 4.4)^2 + (6 - 4.4)^2 + (7 - 4.4)^2}{7}}$$

$$= \sqrt{\frac{(-2.4)^2 + (-1.4)^2 + (-0.4)^2 + (-0.4)^2 + (0.6)^2 + (1.6)^2 + (2.6)^2}{7}} = \sqrt{\frac{17.72}{7}} \approx 1.6$$

C. Find the outliers.

An outlier is a data value, x, such that $x < Q_1 - 1.5(\text{IQR})$ or $x > Q_3 + 1.5(\text{IQR})$.

For this data set, an outlier would be any x-value such that $x < 3 - 1.5(3) = -1.5$ or $x > 6 + 1.5(3) = 10.5$.

Jose did not have fewer than -1.5 customers or more than 10.5 customers, so there are no outliers.

Do the Math

Kennedy and her friends are packaging food for their local food bank. They put rice, soy, and veggies in a plastic bag and then seal it. They try to keep the weight of each bag (in grams) within a certain range. The last 10 bags weighed in at 383, 396, 398, 383, 393, 390, 391, 383, 390, and 398.

A. Find the interquartile range.

$Q_2 = \boxed{}$; $Q_1 = \boxed{}$; $Q_3 = \boxed{}$; $IQR = \boxed{} - \boxed{} = \boxed{}$

B. Find the standard deviation.

The number of data points is $\boxed{}$. The mean is $\boxed{}$ and $\sigma \approx \boxed{}$.

C. Find the outliers.

Outliers would be values of x such that $x < \boxed{} - 1.5\left(\boxed{}\right) = \boxed{}$

or $x > \boxed{} + 1.5\left(\boxed{}\right) = \boxed{}$. So, there are _____ outliers in this data set.

Learn the Math

EXAMPLE 2 Mr. Pearson records his students' scores on the last math test.

1st period	85	90	80	95	90	75	85	80	85
2nd period	75	100	80	90	95	90	50	95	90
3rd period	65	70	75	80	70	70	70	100	75

1st period

Mean = 85

Median = 85

IQR = 90 − 80 = 10

$\sigma \approx 5.8$

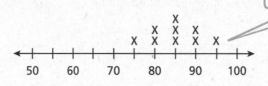

This distribution is symmetric.

2nd period

Mean = 85

Median = 90

IQR = 95 − 77.5 = 17.5

$\sigma \approx 14.3$

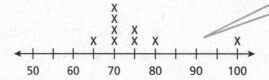

This distribution is skewed left.

3rd period

Mean = 75

Median = 70

IQR = 77.5 − 70 = 7.5

$\sigma \approx 9.7$

This distribution is skewed right.

If all three data sets were symmetrically distributed, it would be appropriate to compare them using their means. However, because two of the distributions are skewed, the medians are a better basis for comparison. The reason for this is that the outlier for 2nd period lowers the mean, making it appear that the entire class did not perform as well, whereas the outlier for 3rd period makes it appear that the entire class performed better than it actually did.

Do the Math

Raj, Kayla, and Penny are in a running club. The table below shows the number of miles they ran last week.

A. Create a dot plot of each runner's miles and identify the shape of the distribution.

B. Find the mean, median, IQR, and standard deviation for each.

C. What can you conclude about each of the runners? Justify your statements with data.

Raj	4	6	10	4	16	2	6
Kayla	8	6	10	4	12	2	14
Penny	6	10	8	2	8	10	8

Name _____

LESSON 22.1
More Practice

ONLINE
Video Tutorials and
Interactive Examples

Calculate the median and IQR for each data set.

1. {4, 5, 7, 8, 8, 9, 10, 12, 14}

median = _____

IQR = _____

2. {35, 40, 40, 50, 65, 70, 75, 75, 80, 90}

median = _____

IQR = _____

For each data set, determine if an outlier exists. Explain why or why not.

3. {10, 39, 12, 26, 22, 20, 18}

_____

_____

_____

4. {2, 42, 28, 26, 48, 32, 66}

_____

_____

_____

5. Ricardo recorded the number of miles he was able to drive between the times he filled his gas tank. The numbers he recorded are 321, 300, 312, 256, 299, 314, and 296.

A. Find the median and IQR for the data.

_____

_____

B. Does an outlier exist? Explain.

_____

_____

6. Lily and Ezra both take piano lessons and record their practice time, in minutes, each week for nine weeks:

Lily	125	105	120	135	120	125	115	120	130
Ezra	160	140	70	90	130	120	110	100	80

A. For each data set, create a dot plot and identify the shape of the distribution.

_____

B. Which data set has a greater standard deviation? A greater IQR?

_____

C. Does either set have an outlier?

_____

D. Who do you think is better at practicing piano? On what statistics do you base your answer?

_____

7. Reason Use the dot plot to answer the following questions.

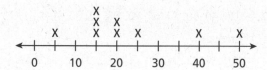

A. How could the data set be changed without changing the median?

_____

B. If one of the data points at 15 were moved to 10, how could you change another data point to keep the mean the same?

_____

C. If the two highest data points were removed, what changes would you expect to see in the mean, median, interquartile range, and standard deviation? Explain.

_____

_____

8. Open Ended Create a data set with the following characteristics: range = 10, IQR = 6, mean = 5, and symmetric distribution.

_____

_____

9. Math on the Spot The data table shows the number of miles walked for a charity by two fundraising teams. Make a dot plot and determine the type of distribution for each team. Explain what the distribution means for each.

Miles	1	2	3	4	5	6
Members of Team A	6	7	4	2	0	1
Members of Team B	3	4	6	4	3	0

_____

_____

_____

_____

10. What value does 5 represent for the data set {4, 3, 6, 8, 9, 8, 3}?

Ⓐ mean

Ⓑ median

Ⓒ range

Ⓓ interquartile range

11. Which data set has an IQR equal to 6?

Ⓐ {10, 14, 17, 26, 16, 10, 11, 16}

Ⓑ {10, 16, 15, 16, 13, 14, 10, 12}

Ⓒ {20, 10, 12, 18, 12, 17, 16, 15}

Ⓓ {16, 16, 11, 18, 21, 13, 14, 19}

Step It Out

Learn the Math

EXAMPLE 1 The table shows the time (in minutes) spent on homework by 15 students one night. Use the data to create a histogram.

30	18	12	17	20
10	23	15	24	17
20	25	17	20	25

First, create a frequency table. The data values range from 10 to 30, so use an interval width of 5.

Time (min)	Frequency
6–10	1
11–15	2
16–20	7
21–25	4
26–30	1

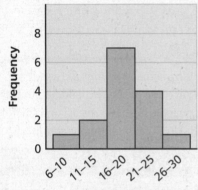

Do the Math

The table shows the height (in inches) of 20 athletes. Use the data to create a histogram.

60	50	54	56	67	71	77	58	72	63
69	64	65	61	64	67	66	69	58	53

The data values range from ☐ to ☐, so use an interval width of 5.

Height (inches)	50–54	55–☐	60–☐	☐–69	70–☐	☐–☐
Frequency	☐	3	☐	6	☐	1

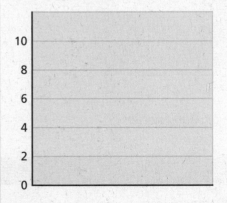

Learn the Math

EXAMPLE 2 ▷ The table shows the average number of minutes Denise spent on social media each day for about three weeks. Create a box plot for the data.

30	50	60	50	25	80	40	70	60	35
55	90	20	45	60	35	75	120	35	45

First, order the numbers from least to greatest.

20, 25, 30, 35, 35, 35, 40, 45, 45, 50,

50, 55, 60, 60, 60, 70, 75, 80, 90, 120

The minimum is 20, and the maximum is 120. The median is the average of the two middle numbers, $\frac{50 + 50}{2}$, or 50. The first quartile is $\frac{35 + 35}{2}$, or 35, and the third quartile is $\frac{60 + 70}{2}$, or 65. Use this five-number summary to create the box plot.

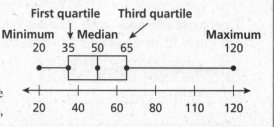

Do the Math

The table shows the average number of hours per week Ken engages in physical activities. Create a box plot for the data.

8	2	6	11	4	6
8	7	5	10	11	14

Learn the Math

EXAMPLE 3 ▷ Two baseball teams are about to play a game. The histograms display the number of runs scored for each team over the past 20 games.

The Wildcats have a relatively symmetric distribution with a peak at 6–8 runs. The Lions have a distribution that is slightly skewed right and has a peak at 0–2 runs. So, the Wildcats have a higher mean number of runs than the Lions.

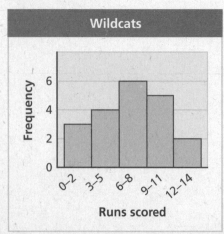

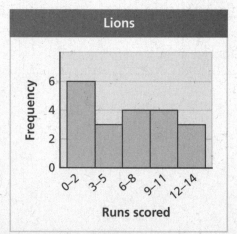

Do the Math

The Wildcats have a [higher / lower] median and a [larger / smaller] IQR than the Lions.

In terms of runs scored, the [Wildcats / Lions] are more consistent.

© Houghton Mifflin Harcourt Publishing Company

Name _____

LESSON 22.2
More Practice

ONLINE
Video Tutorials and
Interactive Examples

Create a histogram for each data set. Label the axes.

1.

12	11	14	14	4	9	3	6	7	19
8	1	6	8	7	7	13	5	15	20

2.

40	16	19	23	22	24	21	35	28	29
27	29	31	29	18	30	25	26	32	11

Create a box plot for each data set. Identify the range and interquartile range.

3. {3, 16, 34, 17, 24, 28, 20, 13, 45, 38, 24, 28, 10, 24, 28, 20}

4. {6, 9, 17, 8, 4, 12, 13, 0, 18, 15, 20, 16, 10, 16, 17, 4, 19, 13, 8, 18}

5. Math on the Spot These box plots compare the number of points scored during the first 9 years of Michael Jordan's and Hakeem Olajuwon's careers (1984–1993).

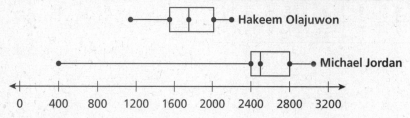

A. Compare the medians and the ranges.

_____

B. Compare the interquartile range of the data for each.

_____

6. Use Structure The table shows the fuel efficiency for a sample of 10 cars from each of two car dealers.

Fuel Efficiency (miles per gallon)									
1	**2**	**3**	**4**	**5**	**6**	**7**	**8**	**9**	**10**
Cruz's Cars									
8	24	16	14	26	36	34	30	20	40
Awesome Autos									
16	28	24	26	36	34	30	28	26	24

A. Which dealer has the higher mean fuel efficiency?

_____

B. Which dealer has the higher median fuel efficiency?

_____

C. Based on these values, which do you think offers the better selection of fuel-efficient automobiles?

_____

7. Which of the following best summarizes the measure of center you can compare when you are comparing two histograms and two box plots?

(A) Histogram: mean; Box plot: median   (C) Histogram: mode; Box plot: mean

(B) Histogram: median; Box plot: mean   (D) Histogram: mean; Box plot: mode

8. Which data set is displayed by the box plot?

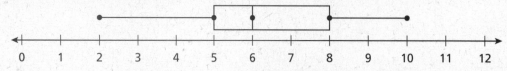

(A) {8, 10, 2, 6, 2, 5, 10, 8, 7, 6}   (C) {9, 10, 2, 6, 3, 5, 10, 8, 7, 6}

(B) {8, 9, 2, 6, 2, 4, 5, 8, 10, 6}   (D) {10, 10, 2, 6, 5, 6, 2, 7, 8, 6}

© Houghton Mifflin Harcourt Publishing Company